Struggle for Economic Freedom and Social Justice of Scheduled Caste in South India

Struggle for Economic Freedom and Social Justice of Scheduled Caste in South India

STRUGGLE FOR ECONOMIC FREEDOM AND SOCIAL JUSTICE OF SCHEDULED CASTE IN SOUTH INDIA

Y. Ashok Kumar

Publications

KALPAZ PUBLICATIONS
DELHI - 110 052

Struggle for Economic Freedom and Social Justice of Scheduled Caste in South India

Rs. 850

ISBN : 81-7835-316-4

Published in 2005 in India by
Kalpaz Publications
C-30, Satyawati Nagar,
Delhi-110 052
Email : kalpaz@hotmail.com

Laser Typesetting by: *Tact Computer Graphics*, Delhi
Printed at: Mehra Offset Press, Delhi

To My Father

Contents

Foreword

It gives me immense pleasure that Kalpaz Publishers are bringing out this volume "Struggle for Economic Freedom and social Justice for Castes in South India", authored by my colleague Dr. Veluri Ashok Kumar. This volume is the outcome of his Ph.D. this is for which he has further added relevant literature tracing the historical back ground of Land Reform Movements in Andhra and Telengana, and the practice of Untouchability in South India, the peasant, movements, struggles and revolts of the ryots and particularly the scheduled caste agricultural workers working on the farms, facing all sorts of humiliations and exploitations due to poverty and the prevalent practice of untouchability. He also reviewed the models and theories of Indian Untouchability, early image of Indian untouchability, out caste, images, models of diversity and unity throwing light on the theoretical perspectives relating to the practice of untouchability.

In the light of the theoretical background of untouchability the studies on untouchability and Paleru system were reviewed by the author. The Institution of Paleru has come into existence on account of agriculture need but in course of time the Paleru system became a part and parcel of land lord family activities. The Paleru system paved the way for the social, economic, political for ethical degradation of the scheduled caste people who served as contract Paleru from one generation to another. The present study is concerned with the identification of various circumstances, causes that led to the creation of tools of oppression that stood in the way of progress and development of paler us in the District of West Godavari under study.

The present study will focus on the various facets of untouchability in general and the problems of Paleru system in particular. The results of the study would help to throw light. On the practice of untouchability in rural areas, and the adverse conditions to which the scheduled castes and particularly the palerus are subjected.

I hope and with that this volume would reach all the concerned agencies and people incoluding policy makers so that needful action could intiiataed to ameliorate the adverse conditions and hardships, the Schedule Castes suffer from.

I congratulate the author for the strenuous efforts he has put in his research work and also for bringing out this volume.

Prof. M. Lakshmipathi Raju
Head Dept. of Sociology,
Social Work & TRPM.
Acharay Nagarjuna University
Guntur-522 510

Acknowledgements

I am thankful to Prof. R.G. Singh, M.A., M.Sc., M.Phil., Ph.D., D.Litt., Department of Social Development and Social Justice of B.R. Ambedkar National Institute of Social Science, Mhow for kindly guiding me of my present research work. I am immensely grateful to Dr. Ramphal, the then Director General of the Institute for giving admission into research.

My special thanks are to Sri I.S. Rao, I.A.S. (Retd.), the present Director General of the Institute for his kind and benevolent attitude towards my research work.

I am grateful to Prof. Y. Kumara Swamy, Prof. Y.G. Joshi and Dr. Deepak Varma of the Institute. My special thanks to Prof. M. Lakshmipathi Raju, Prof. D.Bhaskara Murthy of Nagarjuna University for going through final manuscript.

I am thankful to my mother for her love and affection towards me and also to my wife for her patience and co-operation during the period of research.

I am greatly indebted to the Paleru respondents of the West Godavari District for giving me information patiently when I disturbed them very often.

My thanks are due to help rendered by Mandal Revenue Officer of the West Godavari District and the Mandal Taluq Statistics Assistants, without whose timely help my work would not have been completed.

I thank Mr. K. Omkara Moorthy for typing the manuscript neatly and patiently on computer.

Y. ASHOK KUMAR

1
Introduction

Agrarian Structure in Andhra Pradesh : Historical Perspectives and Recent Developments

Agrarian structure[1] in India has largely been shaped by governmental policy, but the aims and objectives of such a policy before and after Independence have been entirely different. The main aim of the colonial government was to realize the maximum possible amount of net revenue and to ensure the supply of sufficient agricultural raw materials to their industries in England.[2] But the post-Independence policy aimed at the progress and development of the agrarian population[3] both in terms of the over-all increase in output and its equitable distribution.[4] Moreover in post-Independence India, there have been far-reaching developments in agriculture, and these also have come to shape agrarian relations in a significant measures.

The chief objective of the present paper is to analyse some of these developments in the Indian State of Andhra Pradesh between 1940 and 1987. This State has in fact been formed by integrating in stages the Telugu-speaking regions of the country. First in 1953, a smaller state of Andhra was carved out to comprise the Telugu-speaking districts of the erstwhile Madras Presidency. Later, in November 1956, the Telugu-speaking districts of the erstwhile Hyderabad State were added on to the initially formed Andhra State to form the present Andhra Pradesh. It is thus convenient to trace out the developments in three time periods. We first deal with the situation prior to Independence. This has to be done separately for the two Telugu regions of the erstwhile Hyderabad State and the erstwhile Madras Presidency, as they were administered differently and had evolved agrarian structures that were quite distinct from each other in several ways. For the Hyderabad State, the pre-Independence period may be dated upto 1949, for it was a couple of years after the Independence of the country that this State was integrated into India. The second period could have gone upto the integration of the State in its present form in 1956, but because of certain continuity of land reform measures initiated separately in the two regions, it is found analytically convenient to extend this period upto 1961. Till this year, then, the accounts remain separate for the two regions. Finally, we attempt an integrated analysis for the State as a whole for the period 1956 to 1987.

Agrarian Structure of the Erstwhile Hyderabad State (Pre-1949)

All the landholders in the Nizam's Territories of Hyderabad before 1949 fell into four main categories. The first and the largest group consisted of those who held their lands directly from the State. Their rights, in practice, were the nearest to those of the ryotwari land-holders of the neighbouring districts of the Madras Presidency. The second group included those who held their lands from the jagirdars, most of whom were the blood relations of the royal family. The third category was formed of the ryots who were under the *zamindars* of the native *samsthanams.* These cultivators enjoyed occupancy rights, even though they were treated in theory as tenants only. The last category covered all the cultivating tenants who leased in the lands from the numerous *inamdars* and other kinds of absentee owners of lands. There were no uniform rules governing their lease holdings, but they were largely governed by the type of relations between the tenants and the *inamdars.*

The Government of the Nizam maintained that in theory the State was the owner and overlord of all the land, and private rights were granted by the State. In actual practice, however, the claim of over lordship of the State did not affect the numerous landholders so long as they paid the land revenue and other charges levied by the State. The landholder was recognized as a legal occupant. He had the right to use, transfer, sell, mortgage, or otherwise dispose of his land legally.

Occupancy rights were subject only to the land revenue to which all land was generally liable. The land revenue assessment was a charge upon the crop but fixed for a period of 20 to 30 years and was periodically revised under a revision settlement. Every landholder was individually responsible for its payment. This was the common type of ryotwari settlement that prevailed in the Nizam's Territories.[5]

Large *Inams* in Telangana resembled ryotwari tenure except for the remission of a part or whole of the land revenue assessment and certain restrictions on the sale or transfer of the *inam land*. *Ijara* in Telangana was a special tenure governed by contracts made between the State and the *Ijaradars* on long term leases on very favourable terms in order to encourage reclamation of poor lands and habitation of deserted villages.[6] The rates of revenue collected from the Telangana districts under all the above tenures were very high when compared to the rates imposed on soils of similar fertility in the neighbouring districts of Madras, but a good portion of it never reached the State Treasury.

The ryotwari tenure in the beginning did not envisage the land-holder as a non-cultivating owner or a mere rent receiver. But because of the saleable or mortgageable rights, a separate class of non-cultivating owners and rent-receivers came into existence, in course of time, and this gave rise to evils of absentee landlordism and problems of tenancy.[7] The dissociation of ownership from the cultivators of land and the resultant growth of tenancy led to numerous problems, and in particular to an increasing number of poor tenants and the growing transfer of land and its concentration in the hands of economically powerful non-agricultural classes. Excessive competition among tenants for limited lands leading to the sky-rocketing of rents gradually created a situation in the ryotwari areas which had to be met by the tenancy legislation on lines similar to those adopted in the zamindari areas.[8]

Agrarian relations in the pre-1949 Hyderabad state were marked by the presence of a number of *pyravees*[9] and middlemen between the State and the actual cultivators that a large part of the revenue was swallowed by them. The State never inquired into the problems of the peasants except in case of local disturbances,[10] or else to enhance the rates of revenue.

Agrarian Structure of Pre-1947 Andhra Area of the Erstwhile Madras Presidency

The Andhra area, or the Telugu speaking districts of the erstwhile Madras Presidency, formed the northern and the north-western part of that Presidency upto 1953, when this area was separated out to constitute the then State of Andhra, which functioned for the next three years with Kurnool as its capital.

There were three main forms of land tenure in these Andhra districts ryotwari, zamindari and inamdari.[11] The condition of the cultivators under these three categories of tenure were broadly similar to those of their counterparts in Telangana (of the erstwhile Hyderabad State), but there were also important differences. There were no *jagirs* left in the Madras Presidency after 1857 and hence there were none in Andhra districts of this Presidency as well. Survey and settlement of land revenue had been carried out on scientific lines in the ryotwari areas. Many zamindaris were larger than the *Samsthanams* of Telangana both in area and revenue. The ryotwari tenure was the principal form of land-holding here.[12] The *pattadar* or the registered holder held the land direct from the government, subject to the payment of the land revenue. The ryot could alienate his land more freely than his counterpart in Telangana. The land revenue was fixed and generally remained so for a period of 30 years, at the end of which it could be decreased without limit or increased by a maximum of 18.7 per cent

Under the zamindari tenure, the zamindar held his estate under an agreement or *sanad* by paying to the provincial government a fixed sum of *peshkash.* The relations between the zamindar and his ryots were regulated by the Madras Estates Land Act of 1909.[13] Inams were numerous and had varied arrangements with the Government and with their tenant cultivators.[14] The common feature was that the land was held on relatively low rates of revenue. The Government. often enforced different conditions on these petty estate holders depending on the nature of the then existing problems. *Ijaras* also were there, but they were different from those of Telangana. The *ijaras* of Madras were large leases, involving one or more villages, granted to some middlemen by the recognized inamdars. Such middlemen leased them to small tenants at higher rates of rent.

The agrarian structure of the Madras Province, especially of the northern districts was seriously affected by the Great Depression of 1929-1935. A number of tenants, whose agreed terms of payment were mainly in cash, found it very difficult to satisfy the cash terms. A number of them were changed into produce terms and some were terminated in cases where the lessors insisted on cash payments. Seeing that the industries of the capitalist countries were falling prey to the depression, most of the investors in India turned towards the agricultural lands in the 1930s. W.R.S. Sathianathan observed in 1935 in his report:

Professional money-lenders, and traders and agriculturists who lend money are gradually turning out to be big absentee landlords. When their loans are not returned, they eventually take the land of their debtors in full or in part payment.[15] Almost all such lands were leased out and often to the same old owners who became tenants overnight. This kind of absentee landlordism was not healthy for agricultural growth, but activised the land market, and a number of rich urbanites were found visiting the villages to safeguard their investments. The prices of irrigated lands increased abnormally in the 1940s and tenancy too increased in number in the northern coastal districts of Madras. With the rising prices of foodgrains, tobacco and other agricultural products, commercial farming was increasing. There was no expansion of the public irrigation facilities and thus competition for limited land pushed up the rates of rent in this period, viz. 1920 to 1950.[16]

Post-Independence Developments in Telangana (1949-61)

The agrarian structure of Telangana (Telugu-speaking area of the erstwhile Hyderabad State) in 1956 was completely different from what it was before 1946.

The zamindari and jagirdari systems of Telangana were abolished in 1949 and consequently all their villages —3,598 jagirdaris and 497 zamindaris— were transferred to the government and were integrated into the surrounding ryotwari system.[17]

As a result, the proportion of the absentee owners declined to 2.24% in 1951 from about 11% in 1931, that of the tenants came down to 16.50% from about 27% while that of the cultivating owners increased from 31% to 53% (See Table 1).

Vinoba's Telangana Mission

Before the Telangana ryots could get settled after the economic and political upheavels of 1947-50, they had the benefit of a visit from the emissary of peace, Acharya Vinoba Bhave, who pleaded for voluntary surrender of lands from the bigger owners for distribution among the more needy small cultivators and the landless. Overwhelmed with the liberal donation of 100 acres of fertile land by Sri V.R. Reddy in Pochampalli village, Vinoba pursued other landlords in the districts of Nalgonda, Warangal, Karimnagar, Adilabad and Hyderabad and got liberal donations of lands from many others as well. It was estimated that during his tour of 51 days he passed through more than 200 villages of Telangana, received about 12,200 acres which he distributed among the poor cultivators. He

Table 1

Classification of Agricultural Population in Different Districts of Telangana, 1951

District	*Non-cultivating owners*		*Cultivating owners*		*Tenants*		*Agricultural labourers*		*Total agricultural population*	
	No.	*%*	*No.*	*%*	*No.*	*%*	*No.*	*%*	*No.*	*%*
Mahboobnagar	24.058	2.88	4.35.607	52.17	1.65.537	19.38	2.09.782	15.12	5.34.984	100
Hyderabad	7.913	3.07	1.07.739	41.85	72,670	28.23	69.139	26.85	2.57.461	100
Rangareddy Medak	21.676	2.76	5.51.823	70.50	86.798	11.07	1.22.799	15.66	7.84.096	100
Adilabad	9.913	1.55	3.06.059	47.81	1.25.842	19.66	1.98.336	30.98	6.40.150	100
Karimnagar	14.739	1.69	5.09.530	58.34	77.379	8.86	2.71.663	31.11	8.73.311	100
Warangal Khammam	17.241	1.67	5,56.471	53.89	1.78.931	17.33	2.80,056	27.12	10.32.699	100
Nalgonda	13.518	1.26	6.36.922	59.19	1.56.335	14.53	2.69.315	15.08	10.76.090	100
Total	**1,20,555**	**2.24**	**28,51,021**	**52.91**	**8,88,935**	**16.50**	**15,27,569**	**28.35**	**53,88,080**	**100**

Source : Census of Hyderabad State 1957. Table B I.

also settled a number of land disputes.[18] In fact, Bhave's mission was the greatest such event after the Communist movement of 'land to the tiller' in Telangana villages. It is not clear that what stopped him from visiting the rest of the villages in the State, nor did he arrange for the development of agriculture in these villages.

The nature of transfers between 1949 and 1956 in all the Telangana districts was in favour of the cultivating ryots.[19] The movements of the Communists against the Nizam and the *razakars,* helped the poor and downtrodden tenants to get hold of ownership rights of their tiny holdings which were being cultivated by them since generations. Vast tracts of lands held by the *zamindars, jagirdars, deshmuks* and other absentee landlords were thus transferred to their cultivators while a number of the owners of large estates sold their excess areas through the market process and realized whatever amount they could. The *razakars* often used to destroy the standing crops on the lands whose ownership was transferred to the poor tenants. Crops, haystocks, paddy and grain were stolen and burnt down in a number of cases, as is recorded by numerous eye-witnesses.[20]

The land hunger among the small cultivators of T ngana was so high around 1950s that it became impossible for the State to satisfy every aspirant with sufficient area of land. Consequently, there arose the question of distributing the limited acres among numerous aspirants. The tenants with long standing occupancy rights got preference and then came the chance of others who were traditional cultivators but got no leases. A number of applicants were from the artisan classes, especially from the weavers. The revival of handloom movement helped a lot to divert a number of such applicants to their ancestral and more profitable profession of weaving.[21]

It was a burning question before many of the Communist leaders as to whether to prefer distribution of lands to the poor peasants on the basis of individual ownership or to organise them into cultivating cooperatives or to follow collectivisation after the Russian model. Of course, they yielded to the idea of peasant farming at last.[22]

State Reforms in Telangana

To reform the agrarian structure through legislation, the measures adopted were mainly five-fold: (i) abolition of the feudal intermediaries, (ii) fixation of normal rates of rent and other tenancy reforms, (iii) imposition of ceiling on large holdings, (iv) consolidation of the fragments, and (v) distribution of the surplus lands among the poor.

Measure (i) was successfully carried out in Telangana between 1949 and 1956; measures (ii) and (iii) were regulated by legislation, but it took some time even beyond 1956 to complete the process. Measure (iv), viz, land consolidation, was abandoned after some initial efforts. The measure mentioned last, viz, the distribution of surplus lands, became so complicated a matter that it is alleged that there remain many cases of undistributed surplus lands even after 1980-81.[23]

All the declared *jagirs* in Telangana or the large landed estates, numbering 951 and covering an area of more than 12,000 square miles (or, 7,68,000 acres), were abolished by the Abolition of Jagirs Regulation of 1949 (Hyderabad);[24] involving a heavy compensation of Rs.1,078 lakhs in Telangana alone, which the government had to pay to the former *jagirdars* before March 1970. After carrying out elaborate census of landholdings, the Hyderabad State passed the Agricultural Lands Act of 1950, which imposed ceilings on the large holdings.[25] The Government of Hyderabad State proved its progressive outlook by other measures of land reforms including the Abolition of Inams Act 1955, whereby all the *inams* stood abolished. Prevention of Fragmentation and Consolidation of Holdings Act (of Hyderabad) was passed in 1956. After abolishing the feudal interests, the Hyderabad State was well placed on the path of agricultural progress by the time of the States' Reorganisation in 1956.

Tenancy Reforms in Telangana

The Tenancy and Agricultural Lands Act of Hyderabad 1950 was extended to Andhra Pradesh after 1956. This Act provided for a maximum rate of rent varying from 3 to 5 times of the land revenue, with the proviso that the total amount of rent should not exceed 1/4th, the produce in the case of irrigated lands and 1/5th in all other cases, including lands irrigated by wells.[26]

Tenants existing at the time of the commencement of the Act were divided into two classes: protected and ordinary. Protected tenants were those in continuous possession of land for the preceding six years while the rest were treated as ordinary tenants. Both classes of tenants were liable to ejectment on specified grounds, such as failure to pay rent, damage to land, subdivision or subleasing. In addition, ordinary tenants were liable to ejectment on the expiry of the period of lease. Protected tenants, on the other hand, were not liable to ejectment except in exercise of the right of the land owner to resume land for personal cultivation.

The resumption for self-cultivation was subject to many conditions. The land owner was entitled to resume his land upto 3 family holdings, of which the size varied from 4 to 60 acres depending on fertility of land. He was not entitled to resume more than one family holding unless income by the cultivation of such land was to be the main source of his income. Another condition of resumption was that the protected tenant be permitted to retain an area equal in size to a basic holding of 1/3rd the family holding or ½ of his leased holding, whichever was less. However, a resumor owning one basic holding or less was entitled to get back the entire area. By a subsequent amendment, all tenants holding land from the owners with a total area of more than 3 family holdings were declared protected tenants. Thus about 3.3 lakh lease holders were declared as protected tenants in Telangana districts by 1959.

The statistical data available from different official and unofficial sources about the extent of lands purchased by the ex-tenants, resumed by their owners or voluntarily surrendered by the tenants, are confusing and do not tally cross-sectional comparisons.[27] According to one source, 55.5% of the protected tenants of Telangana remained in that category in 1954-55 while 17.12% purchased the rights of ownership; out of the balance of 27.38%, 3.5% were evicted legally and 13.9% illegally evicted while 10.62% voluntarily surrendered their lands. The number of unprotected tenants in Telangana in 1963 was 1,34,350 and the area of land held by them was about 8,58,211 acres. 9,394 applications were filed for resumption of an area of 2.15 lakh acres and a majority of them were decided in favour of the original owners. Thus successes were more marked than failures under these Acts.

Maintenance of the permanent farm servants was one of the problems closely connected to the land transfers especially in Telangana districts. Many of such servants who had been working for the large landlords refused to leave their services abruptly with the transfer of the lands.[28] Finding it difficult to avoid their moral responsibility, many vendors made it a condition that the vendees should employ them until they found other alternative means of livelihood. As a consolation the vendees got such lands at some concessional rates. As an alternative arrangement, some of the liberal minded landlords gave away a few acres to their old farm servants and thus got relieved of their obligations.

Consolidation of Holdings

Preventation of Fragmentation and Consolidation of Holdings Act (Hyderabad) 1955 applied only to Telangana and no such legislation was there in the Andhra Area. About 8 lakh acres were reported to have been consolidated under this Act upto 1965.[29] The Telangana region surpassed the neighbouring Andhra by 1956 in the matter of land reforms by moving distinctly far from the feudal shackles in which it was held till the early 1940s, but even so lagged far behind the Andhra region in respect of productivity both per acre and per capita.[30]

Developments in Non-Telangana Parts of Andhra (upto 1961)

Agrarian reforms in Andhra, which too followed the All-India pattern, were slow and not so radically marked as in Telangana. The problems too were not as formidable as in Telangana. As most of the area in Andhra was operated under the ryotwari system since early 19th century, most of the land reform measures after Independence were aimed at the *Zamindaries* and the *Inams.* The main problem of the ryotwari areas was the growth of absentee landlordism and the exploitative terms of sub-tenancy. The details of these developments are not available from any authoritative sources published so far.[31]

Like the *Thebhaga* movement of Bengal, there had been an anti-*zamindari* movement in the Zamindari tracts of Andhra (Madras Province) in the 1920s and 1930s.[32] A weekly Telugu magazine *Zamin Ryotu* commenced - publication in Nellore in the early 1930s to highlight the problems of the *zamindari* tenants. Along with the zamindari tenants in the rest of the Madras Presidency, these tenants of the Andhra area fought for their three F's namely (i) fair rent, (ii) fixed tenure and (iii) free sale of tenancy right. Immediately after Independence, the Government of Madras tried through legislation to secure them the first two F's, but it could not immediately extend its reforms into the third F.[33]

Most of the rents in Madras Province were paid in produce at the beginning of the 20th century.[34] Cash began to replace the kind rents after the First World War and the proportion of cash rents increased in the 1920s.[35] The trend was reversed in the 1930s. The traditionally common rate of rent was one-half of the produce in addition to the land revenue, which was passed on to the tenants. However, scarcity of land and the consequent competition among the tenants pushed it up even further. This has been recorded by a Special Officer appointed for this purpose by the Government of Madras in 1947: "Under very good sources of irrigation and where the population is dense, the landlord's share is generally two-thirds of the gross produce of paddy. In some cases, it is even more than two-thirds".[36] Rental rates for different tracts and crops were recorded by this Officer, but no mention is made by him regarding the details of sharing of inputs and other non-market relations exogenous to the system. Thus, the net rates of rents that prevailed in the market cannot be estimated from his records.

Lack of security of tenure and tenancy were often cited as reasons for slow formation of capital assets in agriculture. Frequent changes in the occupation of the operational units or parts thereof were chiefly due to (i) sales of lands, (ii) short-term leases (iii) foreclosure of the long term leases, (iv) indebtedness and mortgages, and (v) the break up of the joint families.[37] The same factors also caused sub-division and fragmentation of holdings.

Some inquiries were made by V.V. Sayana in some of the South Indian districts regarding sales and other methods of land transfers[38] during 1940-50. The districts of Dharwad (Karnataka), Visakhapatnam, West Godavari, Guntur and Chittoor formed his sample. Except for Dharwad, the other four were from Andhra Pradesh. Incidentally, he made references to other districts like Nellore, Malabar, South Canara of the Madras Province and other Indian States as well. He came to the conclusion:

"Granted that the transfers of land, both permanent and temporary, have become very common in almost all States in India and that while a part of the lands lost have been in favour of the cultivating agriculturists themselves ... in the past few decades considerable and generally increasing area had fallen into the hands' of the big money lenders, big landlords, or big businessmen or trading communities."[39]

This statement was true in the first half of the 19th century, but not after 1950. A study of these aspects in the Nellore district[40] during 1860 to 1920 showed that most of the land transfers were in favour of the cultivating ryots. Most extensively, the transfers took place through outright sales, though cases of mortgage and redemption of past loans were also many. A few cases of gifts, made chiefly to temples, blood relations and faithful servants, are also reported. More than one-half of the latter category of transferees were not cultivators. The tenants were changed often in consideration of higher offers. Usually the rental rate was not increased so long as the same tenant cultivated a piece of land. This custom led to a change of tenants whenever the owner wanted to increase the rates of rent. There were many cases where the lands were leased back to the same old tenants after one or two years but now at a higher rate of rent.

About 11% to 14% of the total lands transferred passed into the hands of the non-cultivating owners during this period, i.e., 1860-1920. They were chiefly professionals like lawyers, businessmen like Komaties and Chetties, and big landlords who leased out their ownership holdings so acquired. There were further transfers, so that these three categories not only acquired land but also transferred lands among themselves and to others, chiefly through sales. In particular the business community raised funds through mortgages. Whenever they found the leasing uneconomic or difficult for smooth management, they used to sell away such lands. Most of the lands acquired by the lawyers were got either by outright purchases in the market, or else they were gifted to them by the parties that won the cases of land disputes.

Such transfers to the non-cultivating owners increased after 1920, and sharply during the early 1930s, the period of depression, and they declined sharply after 1950. As per the evidence available from the sample villages (only 15) 52% to 77% of the area of the land transferred passed into the hands of the non-cultivators during this period, i.e., 1920-50. A large proportion of them came from business community, moneylenders, lawyers and the salaried groups. The lessors of large tracts, like the ijaradars, inamdars, the Agraharikars, Khandrikadars, Jagirdars, i.e., who sold large chunks in an earlier period, viz., 1860-1920, slowed down or entirely stopped their sales and started in some cases, a type of self-cultivation in the late 1940s, aimed chiefly at legally retaining their large holdings.

The area of land and the number of sales increased sharply after

1948, in Nellore district, and this trend was evident in most of the south Indian districts.[41] In Nellore, the nature of transfers began to change once again in favour of the cultivating ryots. A number of the hitherto tenant cultivators got the lands for a nominal price or in some cases entirely free of cost. A number of *inamdars* left out the long pending and 'bad cases' and tried to make quick money from the 'amenable tracts'. Agricultural population as a whole continued to be the bulk, viz., 70% of the total population. But the internal proportions changed by considerable margins when compared to 1931. The proportion of owner cultivators and cultivating labourer increased while that of owner-lessors and tenants decreased. But these changes were not as extensive as in the Telangana region. However, one should, in this connection, use the occupational classifications of the censuses of 1931 and 1951 very carefully in view of their conceptual variations.[42]

The internal composition of different classes also varied widely from district to district. The peasants were 72% in Cuddapah while their proportion was only 38% in East Godavari. The tenants were 15% in West Godavari while they formed only 5% in Kurnool. The landlords were 43% in Kurnool district while they formed only 1% in Visakhapatnam (See Table 2).

It is found that in the districts where peasants were in large numbers, the combined strength of other classes, specially the tenants and labourers was low. In other words, peasants may employ some labourers, but not many tenants do. The landlords employ the tenants who again employ only a few labourers. Thus in the district of Cuddapah and Chittoor where peasants were more than 70%, the tenants were around 10% and the 'lords' were around 3%. In both the Godavaries where the peasants were less than 40%.

Thus in the districts of Cuddapah and Chittoor where peasants were more than 7%, the tenants were around 10% and the 'lords' were around 3%. In both the Godavaries, where the peasants were less than 40%, the labourers exceeded 40%. Thus there is a rough, correspondence between the peasants and the labourers and the tenants and 'lords'. Another feature that distinguishes these classes is that the dependency ratio is the highest in the case of 'lords' while it is the lowest in the case of the agricultural labourers. From this it may be inferred that the per capita income and dependency ratio are directly related.[43]

Table 2

Classification of Agricultural Population in Different Andhra Districts, 1951

District	*Peasants*	*%*	*Tenants*	*%*	*Labourers*	*%*	*Landlords*	*%*	*Total*	*% to the total population of the district*
Srikakulam	9,38,882	57.37	2,24,618	13.72	4,34,143	26.53	18,808	2.37	16,36,415	77.10
Visakhapatnam	9,57,595	65.27	2,07,077	14.11	2,83,355	10.31	19,093	1.30	14,67,120	70.80
East Godavari	6,37,780	38.43	2,30,302	13.88	7,17,814	43.25	73,834	4.45	16,59,730	68.70
West Godavari	4,96,717	39.90	1,91,082	15.35	5,00,931	40.24	56,146	4.51	12,44,876	73.33
Krishna	6,49,586	56.18	85,115	7.36	3,78,516	32.74	43,028	3.72	11,56,145	65.00
Guntur	10,47,822	59.07	1,02,393	5.77	5,58,649	31.49	63,969	3.61	17,73,833	69.50
Nellore	7,54,657	57.93	78,447	6.02	4,15,720	31.91	53,960	4.14	13,02,784	72.60
Kurnool	7,05,228	66.30	52,416	4.93	2,50,929	23.59	55,119	5.18	10,63,692	64.60
Anantapur	7,11,189	66.89	1,15,824	10.89	2,07,890	19.55	28,409	2.67	10,63,512	71.70
Cuddapah	5,39,659	7.169	43,914	5.80	1,42,239	8.89	26,983	3.85	7,52,795	64.80
Chittoor	9,56,796	70.27	1,48,384	10.90	2,21,412	16.26	35,089	2.65	13,61,681	75.20
Total	**83,96,111**	**57.98**	**14,79,552**	**10.22**	**41,11,688**	**28.39**	**4,94,438**	**3.41**	**1,44,82,719**	

Source Census of the Madras Province, 1951, Occupation Tables.

Most of the cultivating activities involved only human and animal labour. Machines were scarcely in use in 1951. There were about 34,12,795 bullocks and he-buffaloes in the 11 Andhra districts in 1951 used as draught animals for about 19,48,772 ploughs operating an area of 108,80,343 acres (See Table 3). The average number of draught animals for each plough works out to 1.75. If we assume that each holding was operated by a single plough, the average size of holdings would be about 5.58 acres. In actual practice the average size of the operated holding in 1950-51 would be more than this since more than one plough would be operated by many joint families. There are no other reliable sources that can provide us with the actual size of the operated holdings for this period.[44]

Table 3

Extent of Holdings, Ploughs and Bullocks in the State : 1950-51

Sl. No.	*District*	*Bullocks Nos.*	*He-buffaloes Nos.*	*Ploughs Nos.*	*Holdings in acres*
1	Srikakulam	2,42,971	1,59,922	2,15,957	1,90,188
2	Visakhapatnam	2,38,734	1,15,475	2,15,084	1,61,773
3	East Godavari	2,79,010	84,465	2,14,268	5,47,384
4	West Godavari	2,11,700	72,126	2,09,735	6,47,416
5	Krishna	1,84,433	61,652	1,11,817	6,09,989
6	Guntur	2,11,437	86,005	1,54,577	10,34,005
7	Nellore	2,17,161	83,407	1,67,467	9,35,955
8	Kurnool	2,49,635	14,527	1,29,863	21,02,685
9	Anantapur	2,98,977	24,344	1,72,941	21,48,862
10	Cuddapah	1,58,658	35,120	1,09,256	9,81,867
11	Chittoor	3,61,394	21,642	1,47,807	6,20,219
	Total Region	**26,54,110**	**7,58,685**	**19,48,772**	**108,80,343**

Note: The figures for Kurnool and Anantapur includes those taluks of Lur, Adoni and Rayadurg, which were a part of Bellary district upto 1953.

Source: *Statistical Atlas of Andhra, Hyderabad,* 1958.

The average land available per capita works out to about 198 cents, which indicates the density of population in the State. The average area of cultivated land per capita works out to only 74 cents. The average area of cultivated land per agriculturalist is estimated at 105 cents. The size of the holding, indicated by the number of pattas, both individual and joint, was about 4.6 acres. This decreases to about 2.4 acres when we take into account the number of shares in the joint holdings.[45] None of these figures provides an estimate of the average size of the operational holding, which is likely to be in between these two figures, considering the tenancy factor.[46]

After conducting some sample studies, the government proceeded in the matter of land reforms, rather hesitantly to begin with. The Andhra Land Reforms Committee (1955) defined the objective of the land reforms as follows:

The optimum utilization of all agricultural resources such as land, water, labour, animal power, capital, etc., so as to create the largest measure of continued contentment and prosperity among the population in general and the agricultural population in particular.[47] Obviously the objectives were defined in too general terms and indeed the Committee never emphasized any specific measures of land reform, nor analysed in depth the problems and needs of the times.

Andhra Land Reforms Legislation

Persuant to the Land Reforms Committee (Andhra State) 1955, the Andhra Tenancy Act was passed in 1956. Fair rents were higher than those in Telangana. These were put at 50% of the gross produce for lands under Govt. irrigation, 23.33% for lands partially irrigated from Government sources, and 45% of the gross produce in other cases and in the case of the commercial crops. The Report of the land Reforms Committee mentioned the advantages of tenancy. After listing some 10 benefits of tenancy, the Committee opined that tenancy as a pattern of farming should continue, subject to appropriate regulation.[48] The Committee did not search for alternatives to tenancy, nor did it discuss the merits and drawbacks of different forms of tenancy.

Abolition of Intermediaries

While in Telangana all the *jagirs* and *inams* had been abolished even before 1956, it took some further time to abolish them completely in the Andhra area. The process was completed there only by 1965, involving the abolition of 1,047 big and 6,769 small *zamindari* estates and 2,306 *inam* estates in all. The abolition of all these intermediaries involved a compensation of about Rs. 12 crores.[49]

The effects of the Zamindari abolition in Andhra were not as conspicuous and quickly felt as in Telangana, but emerged in quite positive terms in the later studies. Already in 1963, Prof. Sarveswara Rao observed "Statistical information relating to the sales and purchases of land by the villages, increase in the real value of their assets, and expenditure on land improvement and the sources of finance, indicates clearly that the economic position of the ryots has considerably improved after the zamindary system was abolished"[50]. However, Prof. Sarveswara Rao's study focused only on the immediate improvements in the material conditions of the cultivators and the growth of asset formation among them, and could not yet be well appreciative of the basic changes in the nature of agrarian relations, which were freeing the tenants from their age-old shackles and for once were placing the age-old traditional agriculture on to the path of progress and development.

State-wide Appraisal of Developments

Size of Holdings, 1956-1987

The present State of Andhra Pradesh was formed on 1st November, 1956, incorporating the former State of Andhra, comprising 11 districts (See Table 3) and the Telangana region, comprising 9 districts (See Table 1).

At the outset, in 1956, there were some differences between the regions of Andhra and Telangana in their land use patterns, as may be seen from Table 4.

Table 4

Proportion of different items of land used to the total area in Andhra and Telangana, 1956-57

Sl. No.	*Item of land use*	*Andhra*	*Telangana*	*Andhra Pradesh*
1	Net sown area	40.00	45.70	42.20
2	Forests	21.90	18.80	20.60
3	Barren and uncultivable land	10.70	8.00	9.60
4	Land put to non-agricultural uses	6.00	5.20	5.60
5	Culturable waste	8.80	3.40	6.70
6	Pastures and other grazing lands	3.00	6.80	4.50
7	Misc. trees, groves, etc.	0.80	1.00	0.80
8	Current fallows	5.50	8.20	7.00
9	Other fallows	3.10	2.90	3.00
10	Area sown more than once	5.50	1.60	3.90
	Total Geographical Area	**100**	**100**	**100**

Source: Season and Crop Report of Andhra Pradesh, Hyderabad, 1959.

These differences point to the relatively extensive use of land in the Telangana area. Also, the size of the operated holding in Telangana is found larger than in the Andhra region, implying that further spread of cultivation may not be possible except by shortening the period of fallows. With meagre irrigation facilities and inferior lands, even after thorough land reforms, the Telangana region lagged behind the Andhra region in the matter of productivity of all the major crops This drawback appeared in the form of reduction of the operational holdings in Telangana while it did not become a serious problem in the Andhra region.

Some changes are noticeable in the land use pattern of Andhra Pradesh between 1956-57 and 1979-80. Some of them can be attributed directly or indirectly to the land reform measures undertaken during this period. It may be seen from Table 5 that there was a small increase in area under forests in 1979-80 compared to 19,56-57. Barren and uncultivable land decreased by 1% while land put to non-agricultural uses, such as housing, erection of factories and so on increased by 2.2%. Culturable waste decreased by 3.5% and pastures by 1%, while both current and other fallows increased by 4.8%. These resulted chiefly in the decline of the net area sown, by about 3.8%, with most of the inferior soils left fallow.

Table 5

Land use in Andhra Pradesh, 1956-57 and 1979-80

Sl. No.	*Item of land use*	*1956-57 Area in acres*	*1956-57 % of total area*	*1979-80 % of total area*
1.	Total geographical area	6,74,84,246	100.00	100.00
2.	Forest	1,37,26,193	20.60	22.70
3.	Barren & uncultivable land	63,92,851	9.60	8.60
4.	Land put to non-agricultural uses	37,66,000	5.60	7.80
5.	Culturable waste	44,79,077	6.70	3.20
6.	Pastures & other grazing lands	30,54,004	4.50	3.50
7.	Land under misc. trees & crops but not included under net sown area	5,74,734	0.80	1.00
8.	Current fellows	44,11,209	7.00	9.80
9.	Other fallow lands	19,91,167	3.00	5.00
10.	Net area sown	2,81,06,325	42.20	38.40

Source: Season and Crop Report of Andhra Pradesh, 1956-57 & 1979-80.

Ceiling on Land Holdings, 1961

The Andhra Pradesh Ceiling on Agricultural Holdings Act, 1961, provided for ceilings on the existing holdings at 4 ¥ times the family holdings, varying in size from 27 to 324 acres depending on the class of land, and ceiling on future acquisition at three times the family holding, varying from 18 to 216 acres. In case of joint families, consisting of more than 5 members, an additional area of one family holding varying from 6 to 72 acres, was permitted to be retained by each member in excess of five.[51]

About 52,000 acres were estimated as surplus but no definite records are so far available regarding the implementation of the Act. A number of artificial divisions of the joint families and many benami transactions of lands are alleged to have occurred.[52] The ceilings anyway resulted in some reduction in the holding sizes, contributing to an intensive path of agricultural development. There were no drastic changes in the land use pattern of Andhra Pradesh between 1970-71 and 1982-83 (See Table 6).

This implies that the land ceiling legislation under which the distribution of surplus lands was actively pursued during this period did not bring about any conspicuous change in the land use pattern, except a slight increase in the fallows and the consequent decline in the net sown area. This strengthens the conclusion that re-distribution of ownership rights and intensification of cultivation were about the only major developments of this period. No ready data are available for the entire State regarding the changing size of the ownership holding between 1947 and 1987. Only the sizes of the 'operated holdings'[53] are recorded by the 'agricultural census', conducted quinquennially since 1970-71. The average size of the operated holding decreased from 2.5 hectares in 1970-71 to 1. 94 hectares in 1980-81.

The number of small holdings increased at the cost of the medium and big holdings in Andhra Pradesh between 1970-71 and 1980-81. All the six categories below 5 hectares increased by 20,75,358 while all other 6 categories above 5 hectares came down by 1,25,935, resulting in a net increase of 19,49,423. All the categories above 20 hectares were almost halved in numbers (See Table 7), while the number of those between 5 and 20 too were considerably reduced. This process shows the proliferation of small operated-holdings.

The proportion of wholly owned and self-operated holdings increased considerably, from 87.76% in 1970-71 to 97.9% in 1980-81. In 1970-71, only 10% were leased out in the category of under 0.5 hectare holdings while this proportion rose gradually to about 22% in the category of 40 to 50 hectare holdings (See Table 8). This shows that a large part of the tenancy was the result of differences in the size of the holding. In other words, the owners of large categories leadsed-out while the owners of small categories

Table 6

Classification of Land in Andhra Pradesh, 1970-71 to 1982-83

		1970-71	*Per cent*	*1975-76*	*Per cent*	*1980-81*	*Per cent*	*1982-83*	*Per cent*
1.	Forests	62,39,977	22.74	63,81,997	23.26	61,61,125	22.45	61.71495	22.50
2.	Barren and Uncultivable land	23,12,457	8.43	22,87,097	8.33	23,00,893	8.39	22,96,362	8.40
3.	Land put to non-agricultural uses	20,87,207	7.61	21,04,182	7.67	21,84,044	7.96	22.16.166	8.00
4.	Cultivable waste	10,42,238	3.80	9,55,955	3.48	8,88,913	3.24	9.01,265	3.30
5.	Permanent pastures & other grazing land	10,28,119	3.75	9,72,398	3.54	9,23,648	3.37	8,99,077	3.30
6.	Land under misc, tree crops	2,73,771	1.00	2,73,838	1.00	2,71,631	0.99	2,71,580	1.00
7.	Current fallows	23,32,338	5.50	26,47,107	6.65	20,66,535	7.53	14,69,480	5.40
8.	Other fallows	8,54,709	3.11	12,15,618	4.41	13,18,759	4.18	21,80,742	7.90
9.	Net area sown	1,12,69,233	41.07	1,06,01,757	38.64	1,13,24,501	41.27	1,10,33,882	40.20
10.	Total geographical area by village paper	2,74,40,099	100.00	2,74,40,049	100.00	2,74,40,049	100.00	2,74,40,049	100.00

Source :*Season and Crop Reports of Andhra Pradesh.*

leased-in. It could also be inferred that most of the large holders let out their holdings to more than one small holder.

Table 7

Size and Number of Operational Holdings in Andhra Pradesh 1970-71 and 1980-81

Sl. No.	Size in hectares	1970-71 No. of holdings	1970-71 % to total	1980-81 No. of holdings	1980-81 % to total	1970-71 to 1980-81 Diff (+/-)
1.	Below 0.5	15,40,462	28.42	23,05,240	31.28	+ 7,64,778
2.	0.5 to 1.0	9,51,091	17.55	14,99,151	20.34	+ 5,48,060
3.	1 to 2	10,64,840	19.54	15,90,689	21.58	+ 5,25,819
4.	2 to 3	6,13,876	11.33	7,93,095	10.76	+ 1,79,219
5.	3 to 4	3,27,865	6.05	3,81,089	5.17	+ 53,224
6.	4 to 5	2,33,039	4.30	2,37,267	3.22	+ 4,228
7.	5 to 10	4,55,700	8.41	4,08,567	5.54	- 47,123
8.	10 to 20	1,78,113	3.29	1,26,020	1.71	- 52,093
9.	20 to 30	34,986	0.65	18,844	0.26	- 16,142
10.	30 to 40	11,450	0.21	4,639	0.06	- 6,811
11.	40 to 50	4,254	0.08	2,322	0.33	- 1,932
12.	50 above	4,777	0.09	2,953	0.04	- 1,824
	Total	**54,20,453**	**100**	**73,69,576**	**100**	**+ 19,49,423**

Table 8

Number of Wholly Owned and Self-operated Holdings in Different Size Groups in Andhra Pradesh, 1970-71 and 1980-81

Sl. No.	Size in class	Number of holdings, owned & self-operated	per cent to the total of the class	Number of holdings, owned & self-operated	per cent to the total of the class
1.	Less than 0.5	13,93,131	90.44	22,47,255	97.48
2.	0.50 to 1.00	8,50,254	89.40	14,71,342	98.15
3.	1 to 2	9,35,273	87.83	15,62,548	98.23
4.	2 to 3	5,28,761	86.13	7,77,478	98.03
5.	3 to 4	2,80,863		3,74,458	98.26
6.	4 to 5	1,97,917	58.66	2,32,767	98.10
7.	5 to 10	3,81,049	83.62	4,00,208	97.95
8.	10 to 20	1,45,588	81.74	1,23,271	97.82
9.	20 to 30	28,033	80.13	18,489	98.12
10.	30 to 40	9,168	80.10	4,555	98.19
11.	40 to 50	3,339	78.40	2,283	98.32
12.	50 above	3,395	79.44	2,916	98.75
	Total	**47,54,171**	**87.76**	**72,17,570**	**97.94**

Source: Agricultural Census of Andhra Pradesh 1970-71 and 1980-81.

The picture was entirely different in 1980-81. Only 2% of the holdings were leased out. And the incidence of leasing was evenly felt in all the size groups. This shows that, it is not the inequality of size but some other reason that must account for the present day pattern of tenancy.

There is clear evidence that joint ownership of land is fast disappearing. It declined by about 62% in the decade 1970-71 to 1980-81. The rate of decline of joint ownership is inversely related to the size of holding. The last decline of 20% is found in the group of 0-5 to 1-00 hectare while the greatest decline of 91% is recorded in the category of 30 to 40 hectares group (See Table 9). Land ceilings, division of the joint families and improvements in the operational efficiency of small holdings may be some of the reasons for the disappearance of the joint ownership of land.[54]

Table 9

Number of Jointly Owned Holdings in Different Size groups in Andhra Pradesh 1970-71 and 1980-81

S.No.	Size in class	1970-71 No. of holdings	1980-81 No. of holdings	Difference	per cent of decreased
1.	Less than 0.5	2.799	1.961	838	29.94
2.	0.50 to 1.00	2.289	1.828	461	20.14
3.	1 to 2	3.377	1.913	1.464	43.35
4.	2 to 3	2.460	1.044	1.416	57.56
5.	3 to 4	2,039	806	1.433	70.28
6.	4 to .	1.686	426	1.260	7.73
7.	5 to 10	4,910	910	4,000	81.47
8.	10 to 20	3,058	451	2,607	85.25
9.	20 to 30	886	97	789	89.05
10.	30 to 40	342	31	311	90.94
11.	40 to 50	127	20	107	84.25
12.	50 above	224	29	195	87.05
	Total	**24,197**	**9,316**	**14,881**	**61.50**

Source: Agricultural Census of Andhra Pradesh 1970-71 and 1980-81.

These trends show that the land reforms did not result in any substantial extension of the area under the plough. On the other hand, some recent studies have found that in many cases most of the small and uneconomic holdings distributed to the poorer sections were allowed to remain fallow and used as grazing lands.[55] Two explanations can be provided for this state of affairs. In the first place, the technical innovations and improvements of cultivation did not make such strides as to render the cultivation of inferior land possible and economic. Secondly, the economic condition of the average ryot in this State did not improve materially so as to enable him to extend his cultivation into the inferior lands. Consequently, the entrepreneurial and perceptive cultivators could only follow the 'Intensive techniques of cultivation, involving the application of increased doses of inputs like fertilizers, water, pesticides, etc. to the same land, and multiple cropping based on HYV varieties of short duration. This trend explains well the recent cravings, demands and agitations for increased irrigational facilities in different regions of Andhra Pradesh. Environmental pollution is another but side effect of this type of intensive culture with chemical fertilizers and pesticides.[56]

Tenancy, 1970-71 to 1986-87

Some of the recent studies in several of the Indian States are indicative of the active functioning of the lease market in the form of concealed tenancy.[57] But, here we analyse only that selected data which has a bearing on the agrarian structure, specially the size of the holding, in Andhra Pradesh.

Some idea of tenancy can be had from the quinquennial agricultural census of Andhra Pradesh since 1970-71. It is the only macro-level source of data for the entire State. Even though tenancy declined in the agricultural census reports,[58] 4 from about 8% in 1970-71 to about 2% in 1980-81, the facts from other sources do not confirm this rate of decline, nor do they confirm the low incidence of tenancy in the State brought out by the census reports. An ICSSR-sponsored project conducted in about 534 villages of the districts of Nellore, Prakasam, Cuddapah and Chingleput revealed that the range of tenancy varied from 62% to 18% in 1970-74 while it was 32% to 14% in 1980-84 in the same villages.[59]

In addition to the ICSSR-sponsored project, under the auspices of the Dept. of Economics of the University of Hyderabad, a series of surveys were conducted on tenancy and related aspects of agrarian structure which together provide information on a more representative and wide ranging basis for the State as a whole. The findings of the surveys are summarised as follows.

The total of area under cultivation in any revenue village here refers to the area cultivated by all the farmers resident in that village; the same applies to the area under tenancy. Any area cultivated by farmers of other villages is excluded while any area in other villages cultivated by the farmers of the village in question is included. This makes the total figures of Table 10 somewhat different from those shown in the village records, which pertain to the geographic areas of the revenue villages. All the fallow lands, including the current fallows are excluded. The figures refer to the net area sown in the crop year of reference and the second crop is not taken into account. Pastures, grazing lands too are excluded.

The leased areas refer to the total areas leased irrespective of variations in terms and conditions of leases. Quite frequently, cultivators have mixed tenures, partly owning land and partly leasing-in land. Sometimes they may even be simultaneously leasing-in and leasing out lands. Here a tenant is defined as one whose operational holding consisted of 50% or more of leased-in land.

Whenever, the quality of land leased and owned differed widely, like wet and dry, the total produce was taken into account. Thus if more than ½ of the total gross produce expected/realised was from the leased-in lands, then he was included under tenants. The surveys of 12 villages from six districts during 1981-82 showed that at least 12% of the area was involved in the lease market and the proportion of tenants to total cultivators was about 11%. The average size of holding in these villages was about 5.24 acres. Not much difference is found between the sizes of holdings operated by the owner cultivators and tenants. (See Table 10).

A slightly different picture emerges from Table 11 for six districts during 1983-84. About 17% of the area was leased in by about 12% of the cultivators. The average size of the cultivators' operated holding was about 5.69 acres while that of the tenants was about 8.15 acres. The actual size of their operated holding should be more than this when the area owned by them is added to this leased in area. In the case of Karlapalem (Guntur district) 21.33% of area was leased in by only 7.41% of the operators (See Table 11). This situation implies leasing in by large and capitalist farmers from the owners of small holdings.

The latest survey undertaken for 1985-86 in 5 villages of 4 districts (see Table 12) shows almost the same trend as in Table 11, i.e., the size of holding operated by the tenant cultivators was more than that operated by the owner-cultivators. The average size of the holding works out to about 5.95 acres while that of the land leased in by tenants to about 9.61 acres. As already noted, the sizes of the actually operated holdings of

Table 10
Proportion of Leased Land and Tenants in Some Villages of Andhra Pradesh 1981-82

Districst	*Villages*	*Area culti-vated acres*	*Area leased acres*	*Per cent of area under lease*	*Culti-vators number*	*Tenants Number*	*Tenant as per cent culti-vators*
Cuddapah	Chennur	1,287	168	13.05	1,737	34	4.61
	Nandilapalle	720	116	16.11	81	22	27.16
Kurnool	Somthajutur	1,650	124	7.52	138	21	15.22
Medak	Kothur	1,260	87	6.90	158	26	16.46
Rangareddy	Keheda	2,150	320	14.88	216	17	7.87
	Bandlaguda	250	42	16.80	32	11	34.37
Warangal	Rampur	4,744	489	10.31	1,280	160	12.50
Nalgonda	Tripuravaram	3,850	416	10.81	460	38	8.26
	Narsingabhatla						
	Haripur	1,798	359	19.97	277	43	15.20

these tenants should be higher than this figure. The average size of the actually operated holdings of the owner-farmers suggests that the lease market in these villages involves villages involves leasing out of the small holdings to the 'capitalist tenants' who lease-in small areas to increase the size of their operated holdings to some 'optimum level' from their point of view.

Surveys of 9 villages between 1978-79 and 1986-87 show that there is no evidence of any decline in the lease market; rather there is a steady increase (See Table 13). Of course, this is not strictly confirmed since the villages surveyed differed from year to year. Data for successive years for the same villages may be more meaningful, but such data are not available at present. The main limitation of these studies is that they do not exhibit the time-series data. There is also the possibility of some underestimation of the total area leased-in and the number of tenants, since in cases where the areas leased-in formed minor proportions of operated holdings, these were not treated as tenancies.

Some general observation can be made on the basis of the data from all these 29 villages as summarised in the four tables above (Table 10 to 13). Land reforms were carried out in all these villages and large holdings were otherwise fragmented either by shares and gifts or by sales and transfers. None of the owners was found to have a holding above the ceiling limits. Peasant cultivators or the owner-operators dominated in numbers over 'other landed interests' in all the villages. Other landed interests refer to the absentee owners 'or non-cultivating owners and tenants, but not to agricultural labourers. Most of the leassors were found to belong to one of the following four categories (i) minors; (ii) widows; (iii) those engaged mainly in activities other than cultivation which were generally more remunerative; (iv) Govt. servants, teachers, lawyers. Not even a single able-bodied adult male owner was found living exclusively on rental income in any of these 29 villages.

There are some detailed recent studies conducted around 1980 but these cover few villages. One such study carried out in two villages of Godavari delta in 1979-80[60] found that the percentage of tenants to cultivators was 82 in Batlamaguturu village and 42 in Mori village and the land leased in by them constituted 71% of total operated land in the former village and 34% in the latter village. These two villages can not be taken as representative of the Godavari delta since the author selected them on the criterion that the institution of tenancy should occupy a prominent place

Table 11

Proportions of Leased Land and Tenants in Some Villages of Andhra Pradesh, 1983-84

Village	*District*	*Area culti-vated acres*	*Area leased acres*	*% of area under lease*	*Culti-vators number*	*Tenants Number*	*Tenant as % culti-vators*
Karlapalem	Guntur	4,046	863	21.33	1,566	116	7.41
Al	Rangareddy	7,220	2,200	31.16	597	215	36.01
Kothapalli	Medak	4,663	163	3.50	1,140	32	2.85
Rampur	Adilabad	430	160	37.21	12	5	41.67
Pendial	Warangal	10,600	1,190	11.23	994	149	15.00
Narsingabhatla	Nalgonda	4,750	840	17.68	1,260	154	12.22
Total		**31,709**	**5,466**	**17.24**	**5,569**	**671**	**12.05**

Table 12

Proportion of Land Leased and the Tenants in Some Villages of Andhra Pradesh, 1979-1987

Village	*District*	*Area culti-vated acres*	*Area leased acres*	*% of area under lease*	*Culti-vators number*	*Tenants Number*	*Tenant as % culti-vators*
Jagathi	Srikakulam	964	184	19.09	77	25	32.47
Kavvali	Godavari	4,870	1,620	33.26	910	106	11.65
Aruru	Medak	1.220	86	7.05	148	21	14.19
Konapur	Nalgonda	540	34	6.30	96	16	16.67
		3,220	420	13.04	588	76	12.93
Total		**10,814**	**2,344**	**21.68**	**1,819**	**244**	**13.41**

Table 13

Proportion of Land Leased and the Tenants in Some Villages of Andhra Pradesh, 1979-1987

District	*Year*	*Village*	*Area culti-vated acres*	*Area leased acres*	*Per cent of area under lease*	*Culti-vators number*	*Tenants number*	*Tenants as Per cent of cultivators*
Nellore	1978-79	Mypaud	1640	122	7.44	422	36	8.53
Medak	1979-80	Rudraram	1756	142	8.09	276	41	14.86
Prakasam	1980-81	Lakkavaram	1860	98	5.27	315	29	9.21
Rangareddy	1981-82	Aliabad	1120	141	12.59	272	30	11.03
Prakasam	1982-83	Bhattupalle	1105	38	3.44	92	14	15.22
Prakasam	1983-84	Tallur	2890	191	6.61	521	36	6.91
Medak	1984-85	Kandi	2217	136	6.13	392	47	11.98
Medak	1985-86	Donthi	1524	178	11.68	367	52	14.17
Rangareddy	1986-87	Agnoor	2440	321	13.16	252	21	8.33

in the economy of the sample villages.[61] Also the incidence of tenancy is likely to be on the high side in the fertile delta villages when compared to the dry villages of the State which constitute the majority. These changes in the lease market led to a major change in the agrarian structure of Andhra Pradesh. Most of the land that was leased in the pre-1947 period belonged (by ownership rights) to absentee landlords and large holders whose ownership holdings exceeded their operational holdings in size. The lease market changed slowly after Independence and in the 1980's much of the land leased out was (legally) owned by small holders who could not take up their own cultivation due to operational problems, such as smallness of size and lack of skills and capital, and/or due to availability of other opportunities of employment.

The latest legislation that helped increase the extent of concealed tenancy is the abolition of the posts of *Patel, Patwari, Karanam, Munsif* and other village level functionaries, by the Govt. of Andhra Pradesh. The recent visits of the author to a number of villages in the State showed surprising results of this abolition. Many of them have either already migrated to the urban areas or were shortly to move out after leasing out their lands.[62] Since these functionaries owned large tracts of land, this change added largely to the concealed lease market. An important effect of leasing by the old-time village functionaries is the creation of many small holdings. In a number of cases, especially in the Telangana villages, the tenants who leased-in such lands are not the capitalist farmers, but petty cultivators, some of whom happened to be the former farm servants of these functionaries. Thus some of the largest surviving operated holdings in many villages were divided into small pieces under concealed tenancy.

Conculsion

Some broad conclusions can be drawn from this limited study of the agrarian structure of Andhra Pradesh since Independence. Firstly, most of the feudal tenures were abolished and actually ceased to exist. Secondly, large sized ownership holdings got reduced and the number of small holdings increased. Thirdly, the area under cultivation did not increase appreciably and therefore, intensive practices of cultivation became common. Fourthly, the lease market showed a complete shift from the leases of surplus lands to those of uneconomic holdings. Consequently, there was a complete change in the class relations. Most of the lessors of the 1980's are no more large holders, or the feudal interests of the pre-1947 period, but numerous 'petty-holders'. Most of the lessees, on the other hand, are no more subsistence farmers. Consequent changes in the labour market and output and input markets need careful further appraisals.

Most of the post-1947 problems of the agrarian structure of Andhra Pradesh can be grouped under two main heads; (i) those involving the distribution of land as an asset, and (ii) those that are related to the distribution of its produce. In some ways, the first set of issues got settled during 1967-77, but, the second set of issues remains to be tackled more or less on an ongoing basis.

The second set of issues relate chiefly to the lease, labour and product markets, which cannot be abolished in a largely free enterprize economy like ours in India, but have to be regulated for the protection of the weak against the strong, if only to contain social tensions and to ensure a smooth path of socio-economic progress. Further research on all aspects of these problems is necessary for chalking out appropriate solutions.

Untouchability in South India : A Historical Review

There was in the prewar Indian Independence movement a fundamental dispute between Mahatma Gandhi and B.R. Ambedkar concerning the relation of caste to Untouchability. Gandhi felt that Untouchability was an "excresence" of Hinduism, an institution to be rooted out by reformist change "in the hearts" of high-caste Indians, so that the Untouchables might be integrated into the Sudras in a reformed, unranked, varna system. Ambedkar, himself of Untouchable Mahar origins, maintained that caste implied Untouchability and could not be thus "purified" of it. Varna, the great fourfold textual organization of classical Indian society classified into the categories of Brahmin (Priest), Kshatriya (Warrior), Vaishya (Merchant), and Sudra (Servant), likewise implied rank and caste, and could not be realistically recreated as a set of cooperative, egalitarian social groups. India's Untouchables, Ambedkar felt, would not win an improved position in Indian society by voluntary reform from above, but by a forced change in their economic and political subordination, and by internal India-wide political organization around initially separatist principles. They might then eventually become reintegrated as "citizens" into a modern secular Indian state.

Neither of the futures envisioned by Gandhi or Ambedkar has come to pass for Indian Untouchables in the 1970s. Ambedkar's legacy is the official government policy of protective discrimination—positions reserved for Untouchables in the civil service, in legislatures, and in higher education—and the constitutional illegality of Untouchability. Gandhi's legacy is a mostly verbal unease among educated Indians about the continued existence of Untouchability in Indian villages, and a relaxation of "Untouchability behavior" in the larger temples of India.

As for the past, Ambedkar's conception of the relation between varna, caste, Untouchability, and political action is far more realistic historically than is Gandhi's revitalistic vision. Both caste and Untouchability are deeply rooted in Indian history, in the agrarian social order that dominated the Indian economy until the advent of the British, and which remains today India's largest economic sector. Though the relation of India's rural Untouchables to this social order has shifted in subtle ways in the past two centuries, there remain pervasive continuities, especially of meaning and of cultural construction, with this deeply rooted past. Let us review this historical context, then, not only for cultural continuities, but for an understanding of the political and economic forces that have been acting on south Indian Untouchables both in pre-British and in modern times.

The earliest evidence for caste and Untouchability is textual, and dates back more than two thousand years. Varna is first mentioned in a late Vedic text (c. 1000 B.C.), and by the time of the law book of Manu (c. 200 B.C. to A.D. 200), varna and *jati* (or "caste") coexist as isomorphically ranked social orders. A vast number of extant castes of this period are explained and ranked by Manu according to a theory of mixture between the varna categories. According to Manu, marriage within a varna is best, and produces children of the same varna as their parents. Intervarna marriage is also recognized, and its offspring are generally lower than either parent. However, the offspring of parents who marry hypergamously or "with the hair" — a higher varna male marrying a lower varna female— are not so low as are the offspring of parents who marry hypogamously or "against the hair" -a lower varna male marrying a higher varna female (see Tambiah 1973 for a more systematic analysis of the logic of varnaic mixture in Manu).

According to Manu, the most extreme of these extravarnaic marriages produces the Candala, a being with many of the social attributes of Indian Untouchables two thousand years later. The Candala is the result of a hypogamous marriage of the most unequal type, between a Sudra male and a Brahmin female, and he is described as the "lowest of men": "The dwellings of the Candalas . . . shall be outside the village . . . and their wealth shall be dogs and donkeys. Their dress shall be the garments of the dead, they shall eat their food from broken dishes, black iron shall be their ornaments, and they must always wander from place to place. A man who fulfills a religious duty shall not seek intercourse with them; their transactions shall be among themselves, and their marriages with their equals" (Manu 10: 51-53). Thus, like contemporary Untouchables, the Candalas are excluded from the village and from the religious life of the high born. They are similarly recipients of low and inauspicious things (broken dishes and garments of the dead). They are not pictured as solitary outcasts, but as an endogamous community with "transactions . . . among themselves."

Thus in the law book of Manu, Untouchables are very much part of the logic of the system, and to be an Untouchable is not to be cut off from the operation of this logic. Untouchability is thus very old as an Indian social fact. For whatever the actual historical relation between varna and caste two thousand years ago, it is likely that low and excluded groups were part of Indian society at the time, in order for Manu's codification to have had a social referent.

The codifications of Manu applied to the great Hindu kingdoms of north India two millennia ago, and in north India today varna categories are still used indigenously to group castes into larger categories. Varna has apparently always been a less common way of conceiving of rank in South India, but textual sources from the south almost as old as Manu suggest the existence there of similarly ranked relations between humans, and of behavioral expressions of these relations reaching the extremes of Untouchability and of Unapproachability. The Sangam grammarian Tolkappiar (c. A.D. 300-600), for example, divides the south Indian society of his time into four varna like categories: Brahmin, Arasar or King, Vaniyar or Merchant, and Vellalar or Peasant. Unlike varnas, however, in this system the Brahmin has no clear precedence over the Arasar. Furthermore, the Vellalar category is divided into "superior Vellalars" and "inferior Vellalars." Superior Vellalars have the right to inter-marry with Arasars or kings, unlike inferior Vellalars, who are the "only class . . . considered *fit* to be employed as farm laborers" (Subrahmanian 1966: 280).

Many of the attributes of contemporary south Indian Untouchables were thus apparently present fifteen hundred years ago, in the Sangam period. We do not know how these features were structurally combined at the time, however. Society may have been pervasively ranked, its lowest members polluting by proximity those who were "higher born"; or it may have been simply segmented, without pervasive rank except with regard to certain groups, whose particular powers made their avoidance advisable by others. Whether the state of these avoided groups amounted to "pollution" in the modern Indian sense, or to more generalized "magical danger," we also do not know. It should be noted, however, that the proto-Untouchable groups were explicitly said to be "low." In particular, lowness was associated with leather, with drumming, and (in the case of the two types of Vellalars) with agricultural labor. *Paraiyans* existed, though we might assume that they were only one small group among others.

From the Sangam period to the Chola period of South Indian history (c. A.D. 600 to 1200), political consolidation proceeded in the south Indian "nuclear areas," zones ecologically adapted to irrigation or to tank-fed agriculture. In these regions, state-level political authority was in the hands of relatively low, Vellalar chieftains, who endowed local and legitimized by them (see Stein 1967). It is probable that during this period the ideological lineaments of caste were more formally established, along more all-India lines. There is a little mention in the written sources of this period (most of which are temple inscriptions) of non-dominant groups, but one clear reference to Paraiyans and to the spatial distancing of the very low is found in the period of Rajarajachola (c. A.D. 1000). This is a temple inscription that specifies the tax-exempt status of certain sections of a village *(uur)* under the Chola rulers, and mentions the *uur-nattam* (the main village), the *kammaancceeri* (the hamlet of the Kammalars or Artisans), and the *paraiceeri-the* hamlet of the Paraiyans (Sastri 1955: 535). There is also mention of "Paraiya chieftainships" in the eighth and tenth centuries, however, though what these were, and how they were integrated into the diffuse overarching Chola political integration, is not known (Ludden, personal communication).

Another type of evidence for the nature of caste and of Untouchability in medieval south India is found in the literature of the bhakti movement, which swept the region between the seventh and ninth centuries A.D. Bhakti devotionalism postulates that one's personal devotion to god is more important than one's birth or one's use of Brahmanic ritualism, and apparently constitutes a challenge to a caste order founded on worship mediated by a hierarchy of human specialists. The "saints" of both the Saivite and the Vaishnavite bhakti movements (the sixty-three *Naayanaars* and the twelve *Aalvaars*, respectively) include one (and only one) Untouchable figure—Nandan in the case. of the *Naayanaars* and Tiruppan in the case of the *Aalvaars*. The stories of Nandan and of Tiruppan are similar. Each is a character who, for reason of his low birth, cannot enter the temple of the god to whom he is devoted. And each is, after years of intense devotion to the god, miraculously absorbed by his deity, by Siva or Vishnu (see Sastri 1963).

In a text from the twelfth century, there is a description of the Untouchable *ceeri* into which the saint Nandan was born. In its high-caste stereotyping, the text is consonant with modern high-caste views of the Untouchable milieu:

> In the threshold of the huts covered with the strips of leather, little chickens were seen moving about in groups; dark children who wore bracelets of black iron were prancing about... there were mango trees from whose branches drums were hanging. ... The music of many instruments accompanies the drinking *fetes* of Pulaiya women . . . who staggered in their dance as the result of increasing intoxication. In this abode of the people of the lowest caste *(kadainar)*, there arose a man with a feeling of true devotion to the feet of Siva *(Seekkilaar Periya Puraanam*, in Sastri 1955: 568-569).

Nandan is further described as a temple servant, a leatherworker who supplies straps for drums and gut-string for stringed instruments to the Saivite temple at Śrirangam which he himself is not allowed to enter.

Thus around A.D. 1000, some groups or possibly castes in the Chola integration were very low, particularly those whose occupation associated them with leather and with other polluting substances. Though south Indian society underwent major transformations between this time and the advent of the British, those at the bottom did not change their position in any fundamental way. A social category and a set of functional groups that did begin a slow upward climb at this time, however, was the Kammalars or Artisans, who like other proto-Untouchables were relegated to their own *ceeris* in earlier times. Sometime after the thirteenth century, the Artisans began to pursue a strategy of collective upward mobility, supported by an urbanizing trend and by new warrior-kings to whose wealth their "contribution. . . was important and whose protection they enjoyed" (Stein 1969: 195). At present in south India, Artisans usually hold middle-range ranks in local caste hierarchies, following "minimizing strategies" transactionally (see Marriott 1968, 1974) and claiming Brahmin like identities.

For the bulk of South India's Untouchables, however, the only significant change in the next five hundred years was one of numbers. We can speculate that in the Sangam period, Untouchable "communities" were small, specialized groups, most of whose members actually made their living from performing their low function,for instance, from drumming. In contemporary Tamil Nadu, on the other hand, Untouchables compose eighteen per cent of the state-wide population, and a much greater proportion of the population in the old lowland nuclear areas. Though these contemporary Untouchables have a "right" to perform their caste-definitional occupation, most of them survive by working as agricultural labourers. How do we account for this tremendous demographic change?

Two other demographic factors may have played a role in the growth of the major south Indian Untouchable castes in the last thousand years: the slow addition to them of outcasts from the higher castes, and higher birth rates than the higher castes. Neither factor seems particularly important in the last hundred years, however. The rate of permanent out casting is impossible to estimate, though it appears to be very low. The current fertility ratio for Paraiyan women (measured by the ratio of women to children ages 0 to 4) is slightly higher than that of the general population—0.64 versus 0.60 but the unmeasured mortality figures are undoubtedly also higher. And the overall growth rate for the two major Tamil Untouchable castes between 1921 and 1961 is in fact lower than the growth rate of the general population (45 per cent for the Paraiyans and 47 per cent for the Pallans, compared to 51 per cent for the general population) (see Census of India 1961: 22-29).

An account from Tamil Nadu in the late eighteenth century is similarly graphic about Paraiyans and their ability to pollute higher caste persons by sight, sound, and proximity, as well as by touch:

[Paraiyans] are prohibited from drawing water from the wells of other castes; but have particular wells of their own near their inhabitations, round which they place the bones of animals, that they may be known and avoided. When an Indian of any other caste permits a Paraiya to speak to him, this unfortunate being is obliged to hold his hand before his mouth, lest the Indian may be contaminated with his breath. . . the Brahmins cannot behold them, and they are obliged to fly when they appear. . . if they are employed in any work [inside a high-caste household] a door is purposely made for them, but they must work with their eyes on the ground; for, if it is perceived they have glanced at the kitchen, all the utensils must be broken (Thurston 1909, 6: 78-79, quoting Sonnerat's *Voyage to the East Indies,* 1774 and 1781).

There were also in the immediately pre-British period formal and informal sanctions limiting the power of the higher castes over the lower castes. Culturally, the high castes were to some degree restrained by fear of the powers of sorcery of the very low. Economically, the non-cultivating high castes were exceedingly dependent on low-caste agricultural labourers, giving the low castes a degree of bargaining power. Politically, the high castes needed the support of low-caste retainers in factional disputes; and low castes could appeal to extra village royal authority if the local dominant castes were unduly oppressing them. The low castes also had the right to boycott a high-caste patron who mistreated one of their members. Cohn describes the operation of this sanction in contemporary north India, where if a dominant Thakur patron wishes to change the Untouchable Camar leatherworker who serves his particular family, he must have the consent of the local Camar caste council. Any new Camar who accepts service from the Thakur without this council's approval can be outcaste from the Camar caste for his strike breaking (Cohn 1954: 29).

The British worked largely unplanned changes in the older village system after the beginning of the nineteenth century. In the south, they were concerned with consolidating the enormous areas that they had won in the lengthy Carnatic wars of the eighteenth century, and they needed to generate maximum revenues through land tax to pay the costs of this consolidation. In their search for the originally nonexistent ultimate proprietor of the land, the British eventually created a new economic being, the private landowner (cf. Stein 1969: 196-212). By the end of the nineteenth century, the British had begun to convert ranked economic rights into absolute economic rights, had monetized the rural economy, and had usurped the position of royal overlord to the village dominant castes. The effects on south Indian Untouchables of this British transformation of the village system can be determined only by a far more thorough historical analysis than we are undertaking here, but we can note a few of the trends.

To begin with the most predictable trend, the new private landowners were in most cases the old dominant castes. In some areas, the older relationship between dominant-caste landowners and low-caste labourers then became monetized and more contractual in ways detrimental to the lower castes. For the Untouchables lost their rights under the old system, and they were not always able to benefit from the opportunities of the new rural capitalism.

Kathleen Gough describes the effects of this process on the Untouchable Pallans of Tanjore district, Tamil Nadu. In 1843, the British abolished "serfdom" in south India, the *adimai* or "slave" relationship of a field labourer to his high-caste patron. Although *adimai* does in fact mean something like "slave," a field labourer in the old system also had "rights" *(urumai)* with respect to his patron and these the British were also unwittingly abolishing (a point not noted by Gough). High-caste employers of the period then proceeded to tie the same Untouchable labourers to them monetarily, by making them the cash loans they needed to function in the changing economy. What resulted was a new form of tie between landowner and low-caste labourer that worked more to the advantage of the landowner. The Untouchable could not break the tie because of exorbitant interest rates on the loan. The high-caste landowner could dismiss the Untouchable more easily, however, and could legally evict him from any land but the *ceeri,* by foregoing the (to him) small loan.

A second countervailing political and economic trend for Untouchables in the last hundred years has had two facets: protection and remedial action on behalf of Untouchables by the British government and later by the Indian government, and land acquisition by Untouchables under the umbrella of this protection. The result of these economic actions has been to lock many rural Untouchables into a modern peasant adaptation, tending to foster political conservatism among the very low.

For a description of early events in this trend, consider the report of the administrator Charies Crole, writing from the vantage point of 1879, of nineteenth-century British experiments at land settlement in Chingleput district, Tamil Nadu. Crole's account describes a flirtation with each of the major landownership hypotheses employed by the British in India in the nineteenth century, followed in each case by remedial action designed both to protect the suspended rights of the lower castes and to serve the economic interests of the British—to extract maximum land revenue from the villages.

After the surrender of the district to the British in 1760, Crole writes, the government was "impregnated with the germs of the zemindari heresy" until 1796. This attempt at informal tax farming then required the "reforms" of the Collector Mr. Place in 1796, in which the village level offices of *karanam* (accountant), *munsif* (policeman), and *talaiyari* (policeman's assistant) were restored, as was the *maniyam* land attached to each service-which "had often excited the cupidity of the villagers." *Talaiyari* duty and its *maniyam* land belong to Untouchables in contemporary Chingleput; both presumably had become negotiable in the late eighteenth century, and had to be returned to those to whom they belonged. Between 1800 and 1807, Crole continues, the British experimented with a better organized zamindari settlement, which was as disastrous as the previous one, although the few tax farmers who succeeded were made permanent.

In the next experiment, the British instituted ryotwari settlement, a settlement with the individual cultivator, between 1807 and 1822. Here, however, it was often difficult to identify the actual cultivator, and a mixed system of joint-village responsibility *(mirassi)* coexisted with ryotwari. By 1859, however, the private landowners in most Tamil villages had been better defined. In effect, those with dominant rights over the land had converted these rights to "private property." The joint-village system was then abolished.

A second-round of reforms on behalf of the lower village servants was again necessary, however. Between 1859 and 1863, the village-level offices of *karanam, talaiyari,* and *vettiyan* (scavenger) were again reestablished, and regular salaries were attached to each. Vettiyan work, like Talaiyari work, is presently an Untouchable prerogative. Though it is doubtful that anyone but an Untouchable would try to be a cattle scavenger, the attachment of a salary to this position and to the other positions reflected the needs of the service castes for payments in a medium other than grain. At the same time, the British introduced new land rules in Chingleput district and elsewhere that provided the lower castes with an opportunity for land acquisition. Under the *darkhast* ("petition") rules, a person who cultivated a piece of waste land for five years could make a legal claim to ownership of it (Crole 1879: 238-303).

Tamil Untouchables proceeded to acquire land during the next eighty years under British protection. Some earned directly under the *darkhast* system and under other systems devised by the British in order to define the individual cultivator. Other land the Untouchables purchased with capital from a variety of sources. A local source was wage labour and salary payments for village services; more concentrated sources were found in the cities, in the army, and in plantation labour overseas. Since 1930 or so, and increasingly since 1947, the government-level policy of protective discrimination has meant a higher incidence of government jobs for Untouchables, the salaries from which are often fedback into rural land purchase.

At present, Tamil Untouchables own land in proportions not adequately suggested by case studies from Tanjore. Figure 2-2, constructed from data in the 1961 Census of India, compares landownership in the general population for the ten districts of Tamilnadu. It further shows within each district the percentage of higher-caste families who own land, versus the percentage of Untouchable families who own land. We can note initially that Tanjore ranks last in its proportion of general landowning families, and second to last in its proportion of Untouchable landholding families. One reason for this, in all probability, is that in Tanjore there was very little waste land available for new cultivation in the late nineteenth century; there was nothing available for the Untouchables to buy under the newly relaxed British policies. Ramnathapuram, on the other hand, was much less densely populated, and its caste hierarchy was far less complex and involuted than that in Tanjore. For these and other reasons, Ramnathapuram is the district with the highest percentage of Untouchable land-ownership.

In other districts, the percentage of Untouchable families owning land roughly follows the trend in the general population. Although the land the Untouchables own is usually poorer and drier than that of the higher castes, and though the average size of an Untouchable family's holding is smaller than a higher-caste family's holding, the Tamil Untouchables have done reasonably well in the last hundred years, considering the zero baseline from which they have started, and the continuous economic discrimination to which they have been subjected.

With their developing land base, Untouchables in south India began in the early twentieth century to make new status claims, mostly by Sanskritizing. An extraordinary document from Ramnathapuram in the early

1930s reflects a dominant caste's reaction to an Untouchable caste's attempt to upgrade its caste code for conduct, on the basis of an improved landownership base. In this document (reported by Hutton 1963: 205-206), the dominant Kallars began by forbidding behavior on the part of the local Untouchables (probably Pallans) that was associated with their own dominant caste's code for conduct. Prestigious behaviors forbidden by the Kallar included, for example, males and females wearing anything above the waist, or wearing flowers or saffron paste. No Untouchable was to use umbrellas or sandals, music and mounted bridegrooms were prohibited in the Untouchable marriage ceremony, and nothing but earthen-ware vessels were to be used in the home. When the local Untouchables did not obey these demands, the Kallars attacked them, beat them, destroyed their crops-and presumably attracted the attention of the British.

The British were a possibly more liberal court; though they tried not to interfere with the general workings of the caste system, Untouchability struck them as an extreme custom, one that—like widow—burning and *thugee-could* not be treated entirely dispassionately.[63] They were only the court of last resort, for the local dominant caste retained the most immediate local Untouchables in most cases. The local dominant caste's awareness of the British, however, may have made them less able or willing to control all behavior of the Untouchables. Though this can in no way be proved on present evidence, it appears that in the early twentieth century, rigorous local control of Untouchables (along the lines suggested by Barbosa and Sonneret above) relaxed somewhat, and Untouchables were permitted to add auspicious, "Sanskritic" behavior to their caste codes.

The best-known attempt of a low south Indian caste systematically to raise its status in the last hundred years is that of the Nadars. The Nadars, the "toddy-tappers" of Tamilnadu, have a history quite unlike that of the main body of Tamil Untouchable castes. Their movement is therefore instructive for its suggestions of what the main Untouchable castes might require to build a more successful collective challenge to their low status. The Nadar movement also suggests the severe limits of such collective action.

To begin with some differences with the main Untouchable castes; the Nadars, who in most of Tamilnadu are ranked between the main village castes and other Untouchables, due to their occupational association with country liquor, had at the beginning of the nineteenth century a unique resource for a very low caste: a territorial homeland. In this homeland, south of the Tambraparni river in Tinnevelly, the Nadars formed the vast majority of the population; thus they were not accustomed to being treated collectively as near-Untouchables by a set of powerful higher castes. And in this homeland, the Nadars were internally differentiated into a replicatory, caste like order. The two most important internal divisions were between the higher ranking Nadanrs, an endogamous division of landowners and tax officials for royal overlords outside the territory, and the lower-ranking Shanars or toddy-tappers. Other specialized subdivisions may have included high-ranking Priests and low-ranking Barbers. Finally, there was in the main body of the Shanars a group of mobile traders, who moved around the home territory trading the Shanar's products (country liquor and jaggery sugar) for salt, fish, and garden produce (see Hardgrave 1969: 21-35; 95).

With the advent of the *Pax Britannica* in the early nineteenth century, both the trading and toddy-tapping Shanars moved north in large numbers, into a region where for the first time they were faced with a fully developed non-Nadar caste hierarchy. The toddy-tappers were relegated to village hamlets halfway between the main caste habitation sites and the Untouchables' *ceeris,* while the traders retreated into fortified enclosures, *pettais,* which became the "Six Nadar Towns of Ramnad." In these towns the traders prospered enormously and built well-financed caste associations. But the local dominant castes of the region, the militant Maravars, Tevars, and Kallars, attempted to assimilate them in status with the still-polluted toddy-tapping Shanars.

No uplift movement among the other Untouchable castes of Tamilnadu has been so thoroughly organized from within as the Nadar movement. No other Untouchable caste has had wealthy members so willing and able to build caste solidarity. And no other Untouchable caste has had the equivalent of the wide horizontal ties that the Nadars' history of migration and trade provided.

For the toddy-tapping Nadars of the villages, however, the Nadar movement has not been an unqualified success. Although the caste association continues to be active at the village level, the richer urban traders who have always directed the movement seem in recent years to have won a type of class-based respect in the cities-based on their economic and political success and to have lost interest in the solidarity of their caste. And in the villages, Nadars who engage in toddy-tapping still rank where they did a century ago—just above the other Untouchables

(Hardgrave 1969: 159). Despite strong outside political pressure, the higher village castes simply have not conceded rank to the Nadars.

The main Untouchable castes of Tamilnadu have been far less active politically than have the Nadars in the twentieth century. A tiny Untouchable elite, which calls itself *Adi Draavida* ("original Dravidian"), formed in Madras in the late nineteenth century, and it has experimented with a range of ideologies and political tactics in the last eighty years but it has no mass following. Untouchables have been involved in numbers far below their proportion of the population in twentieth-century south Indian political movements: the Justice Party, the Self-Respect Movement, the Congress, and the *Draavida Munnetra Kazagam* (the DMK). The Depressed Class League and other non-Untouchable directed organizations have won temple entry cases for Tamil Untouchables in the past thirty years, and certain types of village level discrimination have diminished, though intervillage variation on this point is tremendous. No figure remotely comparable to Ambedkar has risen from the ranks of the Tamil Untouchable castes, and though Ambedkar's ideas are known diffusely among Tamil Untouchables, his movement has had little success in the south, where there has been virtually no conversion to Buddhism, and the Ambedkar-inspired Republican party has remained at a state-wide membership level of about 2,000 (1972 estimate). In 1968, the General Council of the ruling party of Tamilnadu, theDMK, contained 2 Untouchables out of 150 members, and Untouchable representation in local-level DMK leadership was estimated at 6.7 per cent, as against 18 per cent of the general population which is Untouchable (Barnett and Barnett 1973).

A legion of factors can be cited for the low participation of Tamil Untouchables in contemporary politics. First of all, Tamil Untouchables are still disproportionately located in the villages, and the cities are the locus of modern politics. Second, members of the small urban Untouchable middle class that has resulted from the educational benefits of protective discrimination often elect to "pass" as non-Untouchables and thus to break contact with the rural masses (see Isaacs 1965). The few highly visible Untouchables in state and national-level politics have generally been in token positions, in parties or movements that have had no real interest in further Untouchable participation. Thus, unlike the Nadar elite in the late nineteenth century, the Untouchable elite has not put its resources behind mass mobilization of its other caste members.

At the village level, many landowning Untouchables have relatively conservative economic interests in common with rural peasants of other castes, and few interests in common with the landless members of their own castes. Other Untouchables remain in tied-labour relationships of vertical solidarity, in client groups that cut across even the localized segments of a given Untouchable caste. These Untouchables thus remain very much in the power of the local dominant castes, and often serve the political interests of the latter. Also working against low-caste solidarity is the fact that territorial segmentation is particularly strong among the lowest castes. The social relations and communications networks of these castes are extremely localized; there exists among Untouchables nothing like the wide regional ties of the trading Nadars. The three major Untouchable castes of Tamil Nadu are each clustered in different parts of the state. Caste consciousness is particularly strong between them, and they have rarely shown the ability to join together for common political purposes.

Finally and perhaps most fundamentally, the consciousness of rural Untouchables in Tamil Nadu is basically in consensus with the system that has placed them lowermost. Given their position at the bottom of the system, and given the small stage on which they operate territorially, their arena in the "game" of caste interactions is doubly sequeezed. An Untouchable can score in status terms over only a small number of people. The result is status differentiation at the bottom of local caste hierarchies at least as elaborate and as culturally orthodox as that found higher in the system. Such differentiation is clearly counterproductive to large-scale caste solidarity, and to any political action at an "all-Untouchable" level. It is the contours of this internal differentiation that we will be analyzing most closely in what follows.

Peasant Movement in India

A proper appraisal of the peasant movement in India becomes difficult on account of the paucity of comprehensive data on the subject. With this basic limitation, an attempt is made here to analyse it in terms of its historical evolution in India.

Evolution

Historically the peasant movements in India can broadly be grouped in the following three distinct phases:

1. *The Initial Phase (1857-1921):* This phase was characterized by the sporadic growth of peasant movements in the absence of proper leadership.
2. *The Second Phase (1923-1946):* This phase was marked by the emergence of the class conscious peasant organisations. Its distinct feature was that during this period peasant movements were led by people who gave priority to kisan problems in the struggle for national liberation.
3. *Post-Independence Phase:* This era witnessed the uninterrupted continuity of the agrarian movements due to the failure of the ruling party to resolve any of the basic problems of the toiling masses in rural India. The peasant struggles in this period were led predominantly by left political parties like the CPI, the PSP and the SP through their kisan organizations.

The Initial Phase

The tyranny of zamindars along with the exorbitant rates of British land revenue led to a series of spontaneous peasant uprisings in different parts of the country during this period. The periodic recurrence of famines coupled with the economic depression during the last decades of the 19th century further aggravated the situation in the rural areas and consequently led to numerous peasant revolts. The following were the notable agrarian movements of this phase: 1. The Santal Rebellion of 1855 against the oppression by the British Government; 2. The Deccan riots of 1875 against the moneylenders; 3. The Bengal tenants struggles against zamindari tyranny during 1870-85; 4. The Oudh Insurrection; and 5. The Punjab kisan struggles against the moneylenders in the last decade of the nineteenth century.

In 1917-18, under the leadership of Mahatma Gandhi, the Indian National Congress led two significant peasant struggles. It organized the struggle of the peasants of Champa ran in Bihar against the indigo planters, most of whom were Europeans. Thereafter, it launched the satyagraha movement of peasants in Kaira against the collection of land revenue which they were unable to pay due to failure of crops.

The Role of the Indian National Congress in Peasant Movements

Despite the fact that the Indian National Congress came into existence in the late 19th century, it took cognizance of the peasant problems only in the second decade of the 20th century. In the initial years, the Congress laid exclusive stress on the needs of the Indian industrialist class, ignoring the urgency of agrarian problems. Its manifesto just reiterated some of the superflous demands such as permanent settlement of land revenue and the abolition of salt tax etc. But the Congress leaders remained scrupulously silent about the problems of the vast bulk of tenants in zamindari areas during the earlier phase of the movement. With the appearance of Mahatma Gandhi on the Indian political scene, the Indian National Congress experienced a metamorphosis. Its sphere of influence was extended and it assumed a mass character. The Congress formed peasant committees in rural areas and took note of peasants' grievances. However, the peasant movements initiated by the Congress were invariably restricted to seeking relief against the excessive rates of land revenue, and were in no case directed against the zamindars.

The Second Phase: Emergence of Class Conscious Organizations

The Congress policy of safeguarding the interests of zamindars and landlords led to the emergence of independent class organizations of kisans in rural India. Radical sections in the peasant movements increasingly realised that the Congress was solicitous of the interest of the capitalists and land magnates. They felt that to protect the interests of the kisans, their own class organizations and leadership must be evolved. Consequently, the kisan organizations came into existence in different parts of the country.

The first Kisan Congress held at Lucknow in 1935 led to the formation of the All India Kisan Sabha. The programme of the Sabha reflected the aspirations and needs of the entire peasantry in agrarian India. The All India Kisan Sabha was composed of radical petty bourgeois individuals, within and outside the Indian National Congress. It was also supported and strengthened by the Congress Socialist Party and later on by the Communist Party of India. We shall now refer to some of the significant struggles launched by the Kisan Sabha in different parts of the country during the initial period of their inception.

In Andhra Pradesh it launched an anti-settlement agitation against zamindari 'zulum' in 1927. Swami Sahajanand, one of the eminent leaders and pioneers of the All India Kisan Sabha led a heroic movement for the abolition of zamindari in Bihar. A powerful struggle was initiated against the oppressive forest laws in South India in 1927. Similarly, in UP and other parts of India agitations were launched against the tyranny of zamindars.

The Provincial Ministries and Peasant Struggles

In Bihar, the Congress-zamindar agreement prevented the Ministry from adopting any radical measures in the interest of the peasants. Similarly, in Central Provinces and Bombay, the Congress Ministries refused to entertain any such proposals. The enactment of the ambiguous land legislations by the Bengal Ministry resulted in widespread eviction of the tenants. Thus the miserable performance of the Congress Ministries worsened the plight of the peasants and the resultant growing unrest led to a series of uprisings in different parts of the country. The massive agitation launched by Bihar kisans against the betrayal by the Congress Ministry, anti-settlement campaign in UP, debt relief struggle in Bengal, the Koya revolt, the Bhil disturbances in Mayurbhanj are instances of heroic peasant struggles. This in turn led to a chain of Kisan revolts in Indian States against feudal brutalities during 1937-46. The Mysore and Travancore struggles for responsible government, the Orissa agitation against princes, the Jaipur, Udaipur, and Gwalior revolts against local Thakurs are some of the glorious events in the history of the Indian peasant movement. However, it should be noted that during this phase too the All India Kisan Sabha with its roots in the upper section of the peasantry could not develop any effective struggle for the problems of the sub-marginal farmers and agricultural labourers. Secondly, in the absence of a clear Marxist perspective the Kisan Sabha movements at times took even communal turns.

In 1942, Indian kisans responded to the Congress call of Civil Disobedience movement most heroically. In Uttar Pradesh, Bihar, Bengal, Maharashtra and Tamil Nadu, they formed parallel governments. Nevertheless, the outstanding achievement was in Midnapore in Bengal where for years the British rulers were unable to regain their control. It may not be an exaggeration to say that if the peasant movements had received proper guidance from a mature Marxist leadership, Indian history would perhaps have taken a different course.

Post-Independence Era

The failure of governmental measures in resolving agrarian problems has been widely recognized and admitted today. The land reforms and community programmes meant for promoting capitalist farming in India have only succeeded in intensifying the agrarian crisis. The Congress Government has not only failed in providing relief to the vast bulk of deficit farmers and agricultural proletariat, but its agrarian policy has aggravated their miseries. This fact has been sufficiently demonstrated by the various Government Evaluation Reports and non-official enquiries on the impact of welfare measures on rural society. Consequently, Indian agrarian society is seething with discontent even after independence. This has led to a series of peasant struggles in different parts of the country. We shall briefly refer to the principal movements organized by major left parties through their kisan organizations in recent years.

Agrarian Movement of Kisan Sabha

The All India Kisan Sabha under the influence of the CPI led numerous struggles. The following are some of the more significant amongst them.

On the eve of independence, the All India Kisan Sabha led a very heroic battle of the peasants in the Telangana district of the erstwhile Hyderabad State. Over 2,000 villages set up their own people's committees, took over the land and maintained their own administration and armed defence over an area of 15,000 sq. miles and resisted the onslaughts of the notorious bands of Nizam for a considerable period. It is hardly necessary to point out that in the absence of preparation on All India basis and poor response of the toiling masses, this isolated and adventurous action resulted in massive massacre of innocent tillers who responded to the call of the Kisan Sabha. Tebhaga movement of crop-shares for reduction of landlord's share in Bengal, Warli revolt against forest contractors and moneylenders in Maharashtra, anti-betterment levy against excessive rates of irrigation in Punjab, agitation against food-hoarders and rise in food-grain prices in Bihar, struggles for proper implementation of land ceilings in Bengal, and agitation for fixing higher prices of sugarcane are some of the instances of significant movements initiated by the Kisan Sabha since independence. Besides this, the Sabha led an agitation for higher wages for agricultural labourers in Tamil Nadu and Maharashtra. In Kerala, it led numerous struggles for land reforms. In Andhra, it launched a movement for rehabilitation of landless labourers on waste lands in recent years

Peasant Struggles under the PSP and the SP

Now we shall briefly enumerate the principal struggles under the leadership of the Praja Socialist Party in rural India.

In 1958, the PSP launched a satyagraha for relief measures in the famine-stricken areas of UP and further organized protest movements against irrigation cess levies from UP peasants. A struggle for proper implementation of land ceilings in Bihar, an agitation against heavy water tax in Rajasthan, a movement against food scarcity and for rehabilitation of landless labourers in Madhya Pradesh, and the Bhil agitation against oppressive forest lands in Rajasthan are some of the significant peasant movements organized by the PSP in recent years. Besides this, the PSP organised a massive satyagraha for the settlement of the landless labourers on grassland in the Paradi taluka of Gujarat State.

In contrast to the CPI and the PSP the Socialist Party prepared a comprehensive plan for launching civil disobedience movements simultaneously in different parts of the country. 'Ghera Dalo' movement, started in Uttar Pradesh during 1956 was a part of this broad programme. These struggles were mainly directed against high prices of foodgrains and for relief measures in the famine-stricken areas in Uttar Pradesh. The demands of the SP included (a) free kitchen and cheap foodgrain, (b) fixation of reasonable prices by the Government and legal action against the hoarders and profiteers, (c) remission of taxes, levies, rents etc., in famine-stricken areas, (d) fixation of ceiling and completion of land redistribution programme within the prescribed time, and scaling down of irrigation rates, and (e) abolition of taxes on profitless agriculture, etc.

According to the Socialist Party, the movements led by the CPI and the PSP are mere symbolic protests against the government's agrarian policy while the 'Ghera Dalo' and other struggles launched by the SP involved direct action by hungry peasants themselves.

The Supra-class Approach of the CPI and the PSP

It can be seen from the peasant movements led by the CPI and PSP that there is no basic difference between them. Not only are the forms and demands of the struggles the same but even the approaches of both remain essentially identical. Both the parties suffer from illusions of 'progressive aspects' of the Congress Government. Both have betrayed their faith in the consolidation or strengthening of the national economy as a result of the state policy of the public sector. This illusion restricts the scope of the movements initiated by them. It also explains their arbitrary suspension and sudden withdrawal of the movements for appeasing the so-called progressive bourgeoisie in the Congress government. It can alsobe observed that most of the struggles initiated by these parties were limited to the effective and speedy implementation of agricultural legislations. The supra-class approach of the CPI at the national level also prevents it from organizing any genuine tillers' movement which would jeopardise the interests of the rich peasantry. Its sole object seems to be the preservation of a mythological village unity even if it involves the persistence of the sufferings of the vast bulk of deficit farmers and agricultural labourers. In consonance with its policy to woo the rich peasantry none of the Communist-led agrarian movements was launched for the specific problems of the large bulk of the submarginal farmers, like abolition of taxes in uneconomic farms. Even the CPI enthusiasm for land ceilings seems to be motivated from its desire to assist or accelerate the development of small-scale capitalist farming in rural India. From the point of view of the CPI, the only obstacle to development of productive forces in Indian agriculture is survival of feudal mode of cultivation, as if the elimination of feudal remnants from Indian agriculture would usher in a new era of progressive peasant proprietorship as in European countries in the 17th and 18th centuries during the hey-day of capitalism. Nothing seems to be more unhistorical and arbitrary than this borrowed belief in the possibility of a healthy growth of small-scale capitalist farming within the matrix of underdeveloped Indian economy. It is no wonder that with its reformist approach the peasant movements led by the CPI today remain ill-organized and sporadic in nature without even assuming a national level.

In this connection, it is interesting to note that even a non-Marxist American scholar, Myron Weiner has distinctly pointed out the supra-class approach of the Communist kisan organisations in his recent work, *Politics of Scarcity.* He observes: "The Fifteenth Provincial Conference, meeting in 1957, announced that the Kisan Sabha favoured compensation for those small intermediaries whose holdings were confiscated by the Government. It further declared that the organization would launch agitation for agricultural loans, improved irrigation facilities, manure, education, health and drinking water, and would continue agitation against excessive irrigation taxes and other taxes, including a proposed development tax. The Sabha also announced that it would work within the existing legislative framework, would take the initiative in forming panchayats (local govt. councils) under the new Panchayat Act, and would support credit co-operatives, marketing societies, handicraft co-operatives, and even the government's community development programme and National Extension Service. In short, the Kisan Sabha proposed to minimise agitations and maximise the benefits, peasant (and the Kisan Sabha) might receive by working within existing legislation, while at the same time putting pressure on the State government for greater rural expenditures. Rural harmony rather than class conflicts was the new theme of the West Bengal Kisan Sabha" (p. 159). Further, 'a similar position now guides the national All India Kisan Sabha. The groups in Kerala, Bihar, Assam and Tripura all want a moderate Kisan position.'

It must be said to the credit of the Socialist Party that its approach towards peasant movement appears to be more dynamic than that of the CPI and the PSP. Nevertheless, the absence of a clear perspective and resultant inconsistent and contradictory policy prevents its leadership from developing any effective agrarian movement on a national plane.

The paradox of the Indian situation is that non-Marxist organizations like the Republican Party today champion the cause of the agrarian proletariat and even lead their struggle at an all-India level, while the so-called vanguards of the toiling strata in the rural society vie with each other in sub-serving the interest of richer peasantry.

Under the circumstance it becomes all the more imperative for the Revolutionary Socialist Party to build up class organizations of the rural poor and agricultural labourers and champion their cause.

Peasant Struggles

In the second half of the nineteenth century there was the beginning of a new kind of peasant struggle in India, which centred mostly on the rent question. Broadly speaking, the peasants rose in struggles against enhancement of rent, evictions and exactions of landlords who were often moneylenders. Apparently, the peasants wanted to loosen the bonds of feudal exploitation. Evidence that has accumulated in recent years makes it clear that all categories of peasants were involved in these agrarian struggles. Particularly conscious of feudal exploitation were the rich peasants which had developed as a distinct category in both zamindari and ryotwari areas. What is noteworthy is that the rich peasant was a cultivator who wanted to improve farming and sell foodgrains and cash crops in the market. Resourceful and ambitious, he was eager to add field to field so that he could sell a large proportion of the produce in the market. What is sometimes overlooked is that commercial agriculture had been extended in some regions and the rich peasant often became linked with merchant and moneylending capital. It was not fortuitous that the rich peasants frequently emerged as the leaders of peasant struggles. So long as the abolition of the feudal system was the main point at stake, the interests of both rich peasants and poor peasants were the same. As the process of social differentiation (which was marked by the growth of a stratum of rich peasants on the one hand and a class of landless agricultural labourers on the other) became accelerated, different categories of peasants were likely to be swayed by different aims and ambitions.

The peasant movements in mid-nineteenth century were intermittent and remained confined to a few regions. What is remarkable is that these movements were becoming secular, cutting across caste and communal barriers. It is noteworthy that the Farazi movement which grew in early nineteenth century in Barasat, Faridpur, Dacca and Barisal was essentially a movement of the Farazi sect and hardly spread among Hindu and tribal peasants; the *Pagalponthis* of Sherpur represented a puritanical sect of the Muslims. Between 1765 and 1850 "civil disturbances" flared up in different parts of India. Although peasant masses were involved in these struggles, which were often protracted, they were often led by Hindu or Muslim petty rulers, revenue agents who served the Moghuls, tribal chiefs and *poligars* (military officers) of South India.[64] These struggles revealed peasant discontent but hardly brought to the fore the rent question that exacerbated the relations between landlords and their tenants. One may say that the alliance between the feudal nobility and the peasants which was useful up to a point ultimately proved to be fragile. As we shall see, the rent question came increasingly to the forefront in midnineteenth century. It was during this period that the ruling class undertook tenancy legislation in the face of the opposition of the landlords.

The nineteenth century witnessed the long series of tribal rebellions, which could be related to the disintegration of the tribal system. The tribal peasants were losing their land and forests. In Chotanagpur the old communal system disintegrated towards the close of the nineteenth century. In villages by the new non-tribal landlords. There was large scale land alienation among the tribal peasants; their best land often passed into the hands of outsiders. The Settlement Report of 1920 indicated how the Oraons and Mundas lost their land and swelled the ranks of non-occupancy tenants and agricultural labourers. The Settlement Reports of the Bengal districts tell the same story. In Midnapore, Bankura, Birbhum, Malda and Dinajpur, the Santal who cleared the jungle, was for the first few years, exempted from rent, and thereafter was reduced to a bargadar. When the work of reclamation was done, the Santal was ousted and his land was leased to those who could pay high cash rent. When money rent proved to be less profitable than produce rent, the land-owner thought it wise to swing over to sharecropping. Tribal rebellions, by and large, broke out in this background. As we shall see, some of the tribal rebellions had millenarian overtones and revealed the passionate longing of the tribal peasants for another and better world; they remained devoted to the leaders who invariably came from the same community and predicted the advent of a new social order.[65] Although they often rose in violent struggles, the oppression of non-tribal landlords and moneylenders continued unabated. The Christian missionaries never ceased to work among them and achieved a large measure of success in bringing the tribal communities under their control. For years the missionaries remained sunk among them in different parts of India.

Tribal Rebellions

The Santal rebellion of 1855-56, which spread to Birbhum, Bankura, Singbhum, Hazaribagh, Bhagalpur and Monghyr was mainly directed against the moneylenders, although the rent question also stirred the Santals. Sidu, the Santal leader, declared that the moneylenders committed "*heramis* (treachery), *pap* (sin) and all have acted unjustly". The Santals objected to the idea of paying rent on the basis of a defined area. As Sidu argued, rent should be determined on the basis of the number of bullock ploughs or buffalo ploughs. What frequently happened was that the amount of rent increased with each phase of reclamation.[66] As a contemporary newspaper noted, the "zamindars, the police, the revenue and court *amlas* have exercised a combined system of extortions, oppressive exactions, forcible dispossession of property. . . ."[67] The Santal "saw his crops, his cattle, even himself and family appropriated for a debt which ten times repaid remained an incubus upon him still."[36]

On 30 June 1855, about 10,000 Santals met at Bhagnadihi and decided to address letters to the Officers, darogas and zamindars, in which they expressed their determination to fight the Bengali and bania moneylenders, and to "take possession of the country and set up a government of their own." Sidu and Kanhu, two brothers of a poor peasant family, claimed that they had received divine message and were accepted by the Santals as their leaders. One of the first casualties of the Santal rebellion was Mahesh Datta, who worked as a suzawal (collector of rent) for twenty one years. As the revolt spread, a few moneylenders were killed and the Barhait market place, which was the residence of the moneylenders, was raided. Railway communications between Bhagalpur and Rajmahal were suspended. The Santals proceeded to Pakur in Murshidabad district; the house of Rahamdi Mandal, a Muslim land-owner, was burnt, and as Dindayal Roy, the richest moneylender, was killed the Santals exclaimed: "with those fingers you counted your interest." On 14 July the Santals plundered the house of the Raja of Maheshpur. On 28 July the Commissioner of Bhagalpur reported that "the Santals are let on and incited to acts of oppression" by milkmen, oilmen and other castes who "supply them with intelligence, beat their drums, direct their proceedings and act as spies."

On 11 August 1855, the Commissioner of Bhagalpur wrote to the Magistrate of Monghyr that the Santals were "openly at war with our troops in this district and in those of Murshidabad and Birbhum." On 24th September, the Magistrate of Birbhum reported that "the whole of the country from Lorajore, four miles west of Nagore, to within a short distance of Deoghar, is in their hands. The lats (mails) are stopped, and the inhabitants deserted their villages and fled."[69]

It seems that the urban middleclass had little sympathy for the Santal rebellion. The *Somprakash,* a liberal newspaper, asked the authorities to garrison the small towns so that the insurgents were contained in the forest. The *Sam bad Bhaskar* reported that "the Muslim infidels of Bihar were spreading a rum our to the effect that the Santal insurrection would soon force the British government out of power." The *Friend of India* wrote in December 1855 : "It is only by striking terror into these blood-thirsty savage's. . . that we can hope to quell the insurrection. . . . the retribution must be complete, leaving no calculation of chances for future rioters... ."[70]

The Government employed the army to suppress the Santal rebellion. Although the Santals showed reckless courage in resisting the army, the revolt was suppressed. The operation of Martial Law was suspended in January 1856; Kanhu, the Santal leader, was arrested in February and executed within a few days. Hundreds of Santals were tried and sentenced to long-term imprisonment varying from seven to fourteen years. The district of the Santal Parganas was created, which was to be administered as a non-regulation district; Ashley Eden was appointed the first Deputy Commissioner. On the morrow of the rebellion the Christian missionaries spread out in Chotanagpur and the hill districts.

With the loss of their land and forests the tribal peasants in other parts of India were also restive. In Chotanagpur, for instance, a series of revolts occurred in the nineteenth century. The Hos, Oraons and Mundas joined hands in the Kol Insurrection of 1832-33. As the Maharaja of Chotanagpur leased his land to the Muslims and Sikhs, the Mundas felt that they had been dispossessed of their land. In fact, the new landlords often resorted to *begari* (forced labour), *jarimana* (fines), and often took away their cattle. The Kol Insurrection started in the winter of 1831 when the farm of two Sikh *thikadars* was plundered and burnt; the villages leased to Muslim *thikadars* were also burnt. By January 1832, the Kols in Chotanagpur and the five parganas of Tamor, Bundu, Barenda, Rai and Silli had "taken up arms", as Cuthbert reported, against "the respectable portion of the inhabitants"; the Oraons had joined the Hos and Mundas. There were clashes between the armed forces and the tribal peasants; in a memorable resistance Bhundu Bagat and his followers fought with bows and arrows until they perished to the last man. By the summer of 1832 the revolt was suppressed.

The Kol insurrection was followed by the Sardari agitation in the 1880s, which was directed against *beth begari* and enhancement of rent. The Sardars held meetings, collected money from the peasants, contacted Calcutta lawyers, and sent numerous petitions to the government. It seems that they wanted to form village communities untrammelled by rent collections and administered by the government. By 1887 the Mundas and Oraons refused to pay rent to the landlords, who were mostly non-tribals, and agreed to pay rent only to the *Sarkar.* Although the agitation petered out, the Sardars remained restive. In the 1890s they joined hands with Birsa who led the Munda revolt. Birsa, a young handsome Munda peasant who received education in a missionary school in Chaibasa, came under the influence of the Sardars, broke with the missionaries and called himself the messenger of God. Within a few years the popularity of Birsa as a healer, miracle-worker and preacher spread among the Mundas and Oraons. A new turning-point came in Birsa's life as he chose to embark on a popular movement. Birsa's declared object was to establish Munda raj; the peasants were asked "to rise, drive out or slay all foreigners."[71] As it happens in millenarian movements, Birsa, the leader, predicted the coming of the great day when the land was to be held rent-free. Apparently, Birsa had come under the influence of the Sardars.

Since its inception, the movement was faced with repression. In the summer of 1895 Birsa was arrested along with some of his followers. There was considerable tension; an immense crowd, about 7000 people, collected at Chalkad and waited in vain for the return of the master. The Munda Sardars took advantage of the general excitement to "revive their revolutionary propaganda." After spending two years in Hazaribagh jail Birsa got his release and received warm welcome in his village. It seems that the Sardars who had joined Birsa's movement favoured armed resistance. The official reports refer to the preparations of an attack on the Christian missions during 1898-99 when numerous meetings were held in the night in the forest; messengers went to distant villages, and a fighting force was formed.[72] Telis Munda, a witness in the trial of Munda prisoners, described how Birsa recruited followers:

"..... Birsa was seated on a mat. He had a white *chadar* on his body Birsa said 'I will tell you something to which I invite your attention. The Hakims give decrees to zamindars and *thicadars* and lend deaf ear to what we urge. You must all prepare bows and arrows and on the day of the Christmas festival in Pous, aim your arrows against each mandali. When this is done, the Sarkar's people will certainly come and we will all cut and kill them. The Raj is mine and not of the Hakim. We will kill zamindars and *thicadars*, and then we will go to Ranchi and then kill the Hakims'. Tokey and Chadra said — 'Sarkar has guns'. Birsa replied, 'The guns will turn to water'. At the end nobody objected."[73]

It seems that the movement was confined to a small area comprising Chakradharpur in Singhbhum district and Khunti, Karra, Torpa, Tomar and Basia in Ranchi district. On 24 December 1899, arrows were shot at a few missions, but zamindars and *thicadars* were nowhere attacked. There was a general rising of the Mundas in early 1900. On 6 January two constables were killed at Etkedih. On 7 January about 300 Munda peasants attacked the Khunti police station, killed one of the constables and set fire to a few houses of the *banias.* Armed forces were put on guard on roads leading to Ranchi. The rebel peasants did not attack Ranchi, but took shelter on Dombari hill, fortified their position by erecting stockades at intervals and collected stones, axes, bows and arrows. Apparently, they knew that a fight with the *Sarkar's* forces was in the offing. On 9 January the memorable fight took place on Sail Rakab hill, a little away from Dombari. Birsa's prophecy failed. Guns or bullets did not turn into water. With stones, bows and arrows the Mundas, who refused to surrender, tried to resist the army. As volleys were fired about 200 Mundas including women were killed, while the majority managed to take shelter in the jungles.[74]

The movement quickly collapsed. Hundreds of Mundas were rounded up. There was hardly any resistance. Two leading Sardars, Donka and Majhia, surrendered to the police when their property was attached, and they were punished with transportation for life. Hunted by the police, Birsa moved about in the forests evading arrest for two years. But he was betrayed by the Mundas who received a cash reward of Rs. 500 for his arrest. Birsa ultimately died of cholera in Ranchi jail. Birsa, a poor peasant, became a charismatic leader as he predicted the coming of Munda raj and the Munda peasants followed him with unquestioned obedience. It seems that the movement had a peasant base but the agrarian programme receded in the background. As Eyre Chatterton, a missionary who spent fifty years in Chotanagpur, tells us, the attack on the missions on the Christmas Eve of 1899 was intended to frighten "the native Christian Kols", so that they could be led to join the movement.[75] The Khunti police station was raided, but it was not followed by an agrarian movement. Within a few months the movement was crushed, while the leader whose predictions had failed searched for shelter in the forests and was betrayed by his followers. The Chotanagpur Tenancy Act, 1908, which came in the wake of the Munda revolt, hardly improved the condition of the Munda peasants. Although *beth begari* was abolished, land alienation and moneylender's oppression continued as before. Yet there was no recrudescence of Munda revolt in Chotanagpur.

The Birsaites lived as a distinct sect that worshipped "Birsa Bhagwan", while the Munda peasants remembered Birsa as the leader of the fight on Dombari hill: "Birsa is beating the drum on Dombari hill, they dance." It seems that the influence of Birsa's movement fell on the Oraons of Chotanagpur who organized the Tana Bhagat movement. The Tana Bhagats started a: no-rent campaign, declaring that the land, reclaimed by their forefathers, belonged to them. In the 1920s, the Birsaites and Tana Bhagats were drawn into the nationalist movement.[76] Over the years the tribal community of Chotanagpur became a volcano whose rumblings the zamindars and missionaries dreaded.

We shall now briefly review the tribal unrest in Tripura in the second half of the nineteenth century, which revealed the discontent of the tribal peasants against the moneylenders and the feudal exactions of the king of Tripura and his officials. The tribal peasants who lived in the hills were used to *jhum* cultivation in which the yield per acre was low. They had to pay taxes on their forest products. As the king of Tripura leased his land to his officers who again sublet it to the farmers, the rent of the tenants increased, and there was a great deal of migration of the tribal peasants to the Chittagong Hill Tracts. With the introduction of money economy the tribal system was shattered to its foundations. The tribal peasants who produced cotton and sesamum, the principal cash crops, had to turn to the moneylenders, mostly Bengalees, to raise capital, and the system of *dadan* (advance) became pervasive. Under this system they had to pay a portion of their produce to the moneylender at much below the market price. As soon as the crop was harvested the peasants had to repay the *dadan,* with the result that they had to borrow again at the closing months of a *jhum* year.[77]

The tribal problem in Tripura, however, remained explosive. With the influx of peasant immigrants from Bengal, the area under *jhum* cultivation diminished, while the Bengali peasants were settled on reclaimed lands. Since most of the moneylenders and petty shopkeepers who dealt in *dadan* were not licensed moneylenders, the system of *dadan* could not be restricted. The low rate of yield under *jhum* cultivation and loss of rights in the forest seemed to be intractable problems, and very little was done to protect the forest wealth and settle the *jhumia* peasants on new lands. With the extension of commercial agriculture the problem of rural credit became acute, while the peasants clamoured in vain for remunerative prices for cotton, sesamum and jute.[78]

Indigo Revolt

Meanwhile, the Indigo growers' revolt had flared up in Bengal in the autumn of 1859. On the one hand, this revolt was directed against the indigo planters; on the other, it grew into a rent strike against the planter-zamindars. We shall refer briefly to the system of indigo cultivation in order to comprehend the issues involved in this peasant uprising, which was a landmark in the history of peasant movement in Bengal.

The British merchants embarked upon indigo cultivation in Bengal and built factories in Malda, Pabna, Nadia, Jessore, Midnapore, Rangpore, Rajsahi and Purnea. There is a great deal of evidence to show that the planters had to pay high rent to the Bengal zamindars to get land for indigo cultivation. Some of them, notably Dwarkanath Tagore, chose to be planters. The value of land increased in the villages where indigo cultivation had extended. Apparently, the Bengal zamindars had a stake in indigo cultivation.

"A regular league was formed against indigo cultivation, oaths were subscribed to by both Indus and Musalmans. Ryots of one village were called upon by beat of drums to assist those of another, and if pressed by planters they were to resist; signals were made and given, subscriptions raised; villagers turned out by beat of drums and proceeded in large bodies armed to any alleged threatened spot … ."[79]

The rising urban middle class showed for the first time considerable interest in the peasant movement. The *Hindu Patriot* took up the cause of the ryots, and its editor Harish Mukherjee, who came of a middle class family and worked as a government employee, was virtually driven to financial ruin as he offered help to the peasants who often thronged at his Calcutta residence. Sisir Kumar Ghosh, a talukdar of Jessore, threw himself in the movement and sent eyewitness accounts of popular struggles for publication in the *Hindu Patriot.* The horrors of indigo cultivation were depicted by Dinabandhu Mitra, a government employee, in his famous play *Nil Darpan*, which, as Sivnath Shastri has noted, "engrossed us all". A few muktears, mostly employed by Harish Mukherjee, pleaded for the ryots in the mufassil courts.

In the autumn of 1860, the indigo growers' revolt merged with rent disturbances that came in the wake of the Rent Act of 1859. As Hunter tells us, the operation of the Act "has resulted in enhancement of rents and this increase has been most marked in those parts where the indigo planters are landlords." A new phase of the revolt started as the ryots resisted the payment of rent charged by the planter-zamindars. The peasants of Jessore launched a rent-strike against the planter-zamindars of Poradah concern; within three months the movement spread to Pabna,

Nadia and Faridpur. The Bengal zamindars did not fail to read the signs and "started immediately to decelerate on their collision course."[80] It seems that rent disturbances hardly developed into a mass movement partly because the rent-paying tenants were unorganized in the 1860s. Kling writes that the indigo disturbances "mark the transfer of power from the planter to the moneylender in Lower Bengal." This seems to be a sweeping statement.

Peasant Revolt in Pabna

We turn now to the rent disturbances which were directed against the Bengal zamindars. The Tenancy Act of 1859 was primarily designed to safeguard the interests of the rising class of jotedars and rich peasants. Tenants were not given the occupancy right. As Glazier, the Collector of Rangpur, noted: "the protection of only occupancy ryots would leave more than half of the tenantry unprotected."[81] The zamindars were allowed to enhance rent. In fact, they tried to evade the act and resorted to enhancement of rent and eviction of the tenants. The familiar methods were to consolidate abwabs with the original rent and increase rent by false measurement to show the excess land of the ryots. All the evidence confirms that enhancement of rent proceeded after 1859. Hunter refers to the high increase in rent in Hooghly, Mymensingh and Dacca. The Pabna zamindars, as Campbell noted in 1873, "served no notices of enhancement", and "attempted in the present year to make both further enhancement and a consolidation of the irregular cesses with the rent by illegal and improper means."[82] In Rangpur, the usual device was to give short leases to ryots. In many districts rent receipts were refused and kabuliyats were taken from tenants to destroy evidence of occupancy. Meanwhile, jute cultivation had extended to East Bengal districts and also to Murshidabad, Nadia and 24 Parganas in West Bengal; the area under jute cultivation was about 850,000 acres in 1874. Rich peasants benefited from jute cultivation and appeared to be "sufficiently well-to-do to offer an effectual resistance to the zamindars."[83]

In May, 1873 an agrarian league was formed in Esafshahi in the Pabna district; by June the struggle spread to the Sadar Subdivision. Romesh Dutt, a contemporary witness, traces the origins of the uprising in the enhancement of rent and quotes the following statement of Taylor, the then Magistrate of Pabna: "There can be no doubt that at the time of the Nattore raj the rates were very low. . . . The zamindars have collected abwabs, and this has been going on for so many years that it is now scarcely clear what portion of the collection is rent, and what illegal cesses . . . . The Banerjees did manage to persuade many of the ryots to grant kabuliyats, the terms of which were most unfavourable to the ryots, as they appear subsequently to have discovered. . . . The ryots seeing or rather being shown their danger by others, commenced about. May last to form themselves into a league to resist the demands of the zamindars."[84] The movement in Esafshahi quickly spread to other parts of the district. As the Pabna Magistrate noted: "There is hardly a portion of the district from which ryots have not come in and filed petitions praying for protection against zamindars."[85] The agrarian league raised subscriptions to meet the expenses of litigation; peasants were asked by beat of drums or by sounding buffalo horns to assemble in a particular place; messengers were sent to the villages which had kept aloof; circulars were issued asking peasants to join the struggle. In Pabna, a Muslim majority province, the Muslim peasants fought hand in hand with the Hindus; more than two-thirds of the ryots convicted by the courts came from the Muslims.[86]

It is noteworthy that rent disturbances occurred in Bogra and other East Bengal districts. the main centres of jute cultivation, between 1870 and 1885. In Dacca the peasants formed agrarian leagues and resisted the landlords' demands. The Joint Magistrate of Dacca reported in September 1873: "There are signs . . . that they (the ryots) are fast learning the irresistible power that they acquire by combination . . . I have no hesitation in saying that the future of the movement is the great social question of the day in Bengal."[87]

In the wake of the peasant struggles in Pabna, Bogra and other East Bengal districts, the rent question came to the forefront. The contemporary newspapers generally adopted an equivocal position with regard to the rent disturbances. While pleading for a permanent settlement between the landlords and the tenants, the *Som Prakash* deprecated violent methods. The *Sadharani* described the peasant revolt in Pabna as an explosion of the tenants against traditional oppression, although the zamindary system was not condemned. *The Bengalee* wrote on the Pabna peasants: "If they were oppressed by their Zamindars they had the courts of justice open to them. Nothing can palliate, much less excuse the outrages which are committed by them."[88] In "An Apology for the Pubna Rioters" Romesh Dutt emphatically asserted that the ryots' demands were just. Dutt's article reads:

"Fugitive zamindars crowding in Calcutta or suffering zamindars writing from Pabna, did not fail to influence the press ... the ryots were guilty of ... some acts of violence... yet those who condemn too severely such acts should remember that a rising like that of Pabna seldom concludes without some acts of violence .. .. When the zamindar wants to increase his share of the produce of that land, the ryot will bear no more—the last straw breaks the camel's back."[89]

During 1880-85, *ryot sabhas,* the earliest form of peasant association, sprang up in the Bengal districts. The Indian Association in which Surendranath Banerjee, Ananda Mohan Bose, Dwarkanath Ganguly, Krishna Kumar Mitra played the leading role, organized ryots' meetings in Nadia, Hooghly, 24 Parganas, Midnapore and Birbhum; in 1881 the Association held a meeting in Wellington Square in Calcutta, at which ryots from remote villages thronged.[90]

Maratha Peasants' Uprising

We turn now to the peasant uprising in Maharashtra which was mainly directed against the Marwari and Gujarati moneylenders. In Maharashtra moneylending was mostly in the hands of the Marwari and Gujarati moneylenders. Usurious rates of interest were common. For crop loans, one and a half maunds had to be repaid for every maund borrowed. Loans were advanced on mortgage of land and the common practice was to resettle the debtor on the land on condition that he would pay half of gross produce as rent. Over the years there had grown a category of tenants who had no occupancy right. In Poona and Ahmadnagar there was a considerable increase in sales and mortgages between 1869 and 1874. In 1873 the Bombay courts disposed of about 4 lakh suits; peasants seldom opposed a suit, since they did not want to alienate the sowcars. In Ahmadnagar about an eighth of the occupancies had "on an average been transferred to sowcars."[91]

In the village peasant unrest had been growing for a variety of reasons. The Kunbis that constituted the agricultural community were being dispossessed of their land; they had little hope of getting redress, as "subjudges and judges of subdivisional courts are tools in the hands of the Marwaris." There was a drought in 1866-67, and a partial failure of crops next year; as prices fell after 1870-71, the ryots' capacity to pay revenue was reduced, and the moneylenders showed a tendency to convert personal debt into mortgage debt. Since public works slowed down after

1871, wages suddenly contracted.[92] But the main cause behind the agrarian disturbances seems to be the increasing tension between the moneylender and the Kunbi. In 1852, Wingate reported that two moneylenders had been killed. Between 1871 and 1875, nine moneylenders were killed in Kaira, two in Ahmadnagar and one in Poona. Few looked upon these incidents as pre-storm signals.

The Deccan disturbances seemed to be spontaneous. On 12 May, 1875, the sowcars' houses and shops at Supa, a small market town in Poona, were attacked and burnt. Within twenty-four hours the house of the leading Marwari moneylender of Khoirgaon village was burnt down. The disturbances spread to four villages. In Sirur taluk the Marwari moneylenders were the main targets of attack. Almost simultaneously similar outbreaks occurred in Ahmadnagar, where twenty-two villages were affected. For a few weeks the revolt was in full swing. It seems that the main object of the peasants was "to disarm the enemy" by destroying the bonds, decrees and accounts. The Deccan Riots Commission referred to "wholesale plunder of property," "murderous assault on the moneylenders," "burning of stacks of produce belonging to moneylenders." The Marwari moneylenders mostly left the village and moved to the towns. There was a great deal of repression; in Poona and Ahmadnagar 951 persons were arrested, of which 501 were convicted. The last incident occurred on 22 July when the nose of a moneylender at Nimbal was cut off.[93]

Punjab Disturbances

Towards the close of the nineteenth century agrarian discontent had been growing in Punjab, *albeit* slowly, as land passed to "capitalists and moneylenders" and "the homogeneous character of the community" was disappearing. With the extension of irrigation land increased in value and land transfer was accelerated. Darling has noted that mortgage which was rare in the days of the Sikh rule became a prominent feature in rural economy in the 1870s.[94] To the ruling class the expropriation of owner cultivators posed a "political danger", and the Land Alienation Act, 1900 was passed, which was intended to restrict the sale of agricultural land and also its sale by agricultural tribes to non-members. It was assumed that mortgages would increase, and "the moneyed classes... will still have their opportunity of obtaining land."[95] What was a growing feature was the passing of land from Rajputs and Gurjars to the Jats, "the most thriving community," in Ferozepur, Ludhiana, Hissar and Lahore.[96]

Agrarian disturbances broke out in the Punjab in 1906-7. The scene of the disturbances was the Chenab canal colony where vast tracts of desert land had been brought under cultivation with the help of canals. Cotton, a commercial crop, was grown on irrigated land. All the evidence points to the growth of a stratum of rich peasants that benefited from the extension of irrigation and the consequent development of commercial agriculture. It seems that the rich peasants embarked upon a movement when the Punjab Government brought a Bill on 25 October 1906; the Bill stipulated that land could only be transferred to a son or widow, tenants would have to fulfil the conditions concerning sanitation, tree planting, construction, etc., and that fines would be collected as before "in the same fashion as revenue" in case of breach of the conditions. Over the years discontent had been growing against the fine system which was often used by the local officers to extort bribes. In fact, corruption was rampant among the Punjabi officers. It seems that the Government wanted to tighten its control of the canal colony from which it received over seven lakhs of rupees annually as net profit from water charges and land revenue. Meanwhile, water rate in the Bari Doab canal area had been increased.[97]

From 1903 onwards the *Zamindar,* a local newspaper, had been focussing attention on the condition of the colonists; the "Yeomen farmers" had been organized in an association. Meetings were held and memorials were signed denouncing the bill; ex-government servants and the educated middleclass were in the forefront of the movement. Hindus and Muslims, who were equally affected by the Bill, joined the movement, which spread to the central districts. In a mammoth meeting held at Layalpur, capital of the colony, on 3 February 1907, Hindus and Muslims were urged to unite against British *zuloom*; Lajpat Rai, the nationalist leader, and Ajit Singh, the revolutionary leader, called upon the colonists to stop payment of revenue. Or 4 April Ajit Singh held a mass meeting of 12,000 zamindars (in Punjab peasants were called zamindars). As the movement gained momentum the zamindars raised the cry of non-payment of the new water rate. The agrarian unrest became serious with riots in Amritsar, Lahore. and Rawalpindi. At this point Minto decided to veto the Act which had affected "a warlike and loyal section of the Indian community." When Popham Young, the Settlement Commissioner, visited the canal colony ten days after the veto, he was greeted with garlands, and the local lawyers did not forget to apologize for their action.

The colonists were allowed to buy land rights. Apparently, the rich peasants had won the battle, Irrigation made further advance. During the decade 1911-20, the Triple Canal Project was completed, and the canal-irrigated area was 10 million acres. Then came the Sutlej Valley Project, and the canal-irrigated area rose to 12.4 million acres in 1929-30. With the extension of irrigation commercial agriculture made considerable progress. The area under desi cotton increased from 6.2 lakh acres in 1866-67 to 1.1 million acres in 1901-02, and to 2.1 million acres in 1919-20; the rich peasants had started producing American cotton, which required a high level of paid-out costs per acre. The peasants also grew sugarcane on irrigated land.[98] As Blyn has shown, foodgrain yield per acre showed an upward trend in the Punjab between the two world wars.[99] Surely the peasants received an impetus from high prices during and after the First World War. From 1921 onwards, new implements were being used. There is no doubt that only large landowners and rich peasants could use new implements. Although the number of rent-paying tenants and agricultural tenants and agricultural labourers increased over the years, rural Punjab generally remained quiet, while peasants were drawn in the nationalist movement in other regions from 1920 onwards.

Agrarian Revolts

The Kisan Movement has had a history of at least 120 years since the British regime came to be established in India. To those of us who are used to peasant agitations organized and led by some conscious leaders having a political ideology and struggling for the collective and progressive welfare of peasants, the earlier agitations of peasants may seem to be rather unorganized and spasmodic groupings of the semi-conscious masses in the dark. Yet a brief review of such groupings will be of great interest to us who are anxious to develop a conscious, organized and militant kisan movement bent upon the achievement of Kisan and Muzdoor Raj.

Mass Emigration

The Districts of Cuddapah, Kurnool, Anantapur and Bellary were ceded to the British by the Nizam about the beginning of the 19th century. The local peasants were made to pay in full the excessive land revenue and other innumerable cesses and imposts previously imposed by the Nizam, whereas in the past, the Nizam's collections were not so regular;

the burden of such taxes became too heavy. But all the complaints made by peasants were of no avail and the British administrators were anxious only to increase their collections year after year. In their unholy anxiety to increase their collections, the Collectors insisted upon every ryot taking a particular portion of waste land, whose extent was increasing into cultivation and paying tax on it in proportion to the land cultivated by him whether such land is cultivated or not and desired or not by the peasant. In despair large numbers of peasants of these districts, now known as Rayalasima had begun to emigrate to the neighbouring forests and Mysore, only to escape from these increasing burdens of taxes. They had abandoned their lands and homes and beloved surroundings since at that time, the possession of land became more a burden than an asset. This naturally opened the eyes of the Government. Hundreds of deserted villages and lakhs of acres of abandoned land smote the rulers in the face and threatened the solvency of the Provincial Government. In a hurry, Sir Thomas Munro was sent to settle the land revenue payable by peasants and the Government agreed to his proposals and carried out in 1820-30 the drastic reduction of land revenue and he systematized the survey and settlement and land records. This was the first triumph of our peasants during the nineteenth Century.

Famines and Peasants

Between 1770-1897 there were several disastrous famines all over India; those of Rayalasima were the worst, resulting in the death of lakhs of workers and peasants. Special mention has to be made of the famine years 1770, 1896 and 1897 when millions of poor people died for want of food and water. The advent of railways had only slowly enabled the State to import cereals and pulses to the famine stricken areas and so in most places the prices of foodgrains had gone up and even the higher and lower middle classes were being hopelessly impoverished by their attempts to purchase food and raiment and maintain themselves during times of unemployment. It is a sad commentary on the political capacity of our people that despite such terrible sufferings of the masses and the mass-deaths of workers and peasants and the outbreaks of cholera and other epidemics, in the wake of starvation and consumption of horrible things (ending in cannibalism also) no real and effective mass protest was organized by anyone or any organization against such inhuman state of things.

Yet some dare-devils preferred dacoity to degrading death as a result of starvation and a large number of bandits began to infest the towns and countryside, striking terror into the hearts of not only the townsmen and rich people but also the big landlords and even the local officials. Coupled with the new spirit of philanthropy and public spirit that was slowly manifesting itself in the towns and through the newspapers, this growing danger to the property and safety of the propertied classes was responsible for forcing Government to appoint successive Famine Commissions and to devise and enforce the Famine Relief System. That this system was devised not so much with any laudable philanthropic sentiments as by the anxiety of Government to protect the institution of property and stave off the growing threat to the established order is indicated by the content of this Famine Relief system.

To ascertain whether there is any famine at all in any area, Test Works have to be run for 15 days to employ workers on the hardest and most cruel task of breaking stones for 8 to 10 hours a day in burning sun and blinding winds, on a payment of ¾ anna per day, i.e., a wage which is not enough to give even half of a full meal a day. If the suffering workers flock to such test works in ever growing numbers for those 15 days, then alone is a famine considered to exist. Even after a state of famine is declared to exist and famine relief works are opened, workers are paid only 1½ annas per head per day of ten to twelve hours for work that breaks anyone's strengths and spirit. Thus the most mean minded and cruel relief has been provided for our famished masses with a view just to prevent them from defying the society as a whole because of gnawing hunger and also to tie them down to work, which succeeds in weakening them. Thus the very potential revolutionary capacity of peasants and workers was met first by some relief and next by a process which weakens them every moment.

Famines occurred in 1868 in Northern India.

1876-8 in South India

1888-9 in Madras

Again there were famines in 1891, 1896, 1899, 1906, 1907

1877 famine:- area affected 200,000 square miles

Population affected:- 360 lakhs

1878 N.W.F.P. and Punjab – 220 lakhs of people were affected.

Mortality 55 lakhs.

Expenditure Rs.8 crores and loss of revenue Rs.3 crores

1874 Bengal Famine: Cost Rs.6.75 crores

1875-8 South Indian famine: Cost Rs.9.25 crores

Estimate of annual cost of famine in loss of revenue and actual expenditure made in 1878 - 150 lakhs of pound (sterling).

Three Famine Commissions were appointed in 1880, 1898, 1901.

Recommendations of Famine Commissions

1. Extension of irrigation at a total cost of Rs.44 crores.
2. Granting loans and advances to cultivators to enable them is execute private agricultural improvements.
3. Emigration.
4. Promotion of agriculture

Action taken by Government

1. Famine Code
2. Agricultural Loans Act; Land Improvement Act.
3. Deputation of Sir Frederick Nicholson and his report on Continental Co-operative Movement.
4. Passing of the Indian Co-operative Act 1911.
5. Development of Minor Irrigation and Unproductive Irrigation Works.

Bengal Tenants Outburst

The Bengali Zamindars prospered under the aegis of Permanent Settlement at the expense of the industry and of the hard working peasants. The special gift of nature to Bengal, the culture of jute which came to be in great demand in the world has only enriched these zamindars and served only as another lever with which rents can be forced upon them. Legal and illegal imposts were multiplied and Nazaranas or premiums were heaped upon peasants. Owing to the tightened alliance between the British and Zamindars during and after the Indian Mutiny, even the Courts had begun to decree that the land itself had also belonged to Zamindars and peasants were only tenants-at-will. There seemed to be no limit to the capacity of zamindars and their persecution of the peasants. Just about 1870-80, the economic depression had also contributed its share towards the growth of poverty of peasants. Naturally peasants – the various grades of them began first to fall into arrears of rent, then to be threatened with the loss of lands and eviction from their homesteads. It thus so happened that thousands of peasants came to consciously refuse the rents, disobey the dictates of Courts, obstruct their eviction and finally to fight with whatever weapons were available (the agents of Courts and Zamindars). A regular state of anarchy came to prevail in a large part of Bengal and Santal countryside and a reign of terror was set afoot. The state rushed to the rescue of its allies, the Zamindars, mowed down thousands of peasants and established a counter and more cruel and organized state of official terrorism. Thus in blood and fire was the great uprising of suffering tenants of Bengal and Santhal Parganas suppressed.

But it only served as a warning to the British Government and so an Enquiry Committee was appointed and the first statute the Bengal Tenancy Act was passed, conferring permanency of tenure upon some classes of tenants and thus staying off the immediate danger.

The next agitation came from Mahratta in 1875. The Mahratta peasants to their horror, learnt that according to the British Civil Law, they could be imprisoned for their failure to pay off their debts, whenever demanded by their creditors. They were hard hit by the slump in cotton prices after the cessation of Civil War in America and, so the burden of their debts became too unbearable. Just at that time, the moneylenders began to take advantage of the Civil Laws and purchase the lands of peasants, evict their debtors from their ancestral houses and consign those of them who became unable to pay in time to Civil Debtors Jails. This was the limit for the patience of the warlike Mahratta Peasants. So they rose in their thousands against these moneylenders. They raised the houses of moneylenders, toe away almost in a frenzy the promissory notes and other papers, pertaining to their debts to them. In many places, they were obstructed by some moneylenders and so resorted to violence. Several moneylenders and their supporters were killed or beaten badly. Even a large number of police were severely dealt with, whenever they had tried to save moneylenders or whenever they attempted to harass peaceful peasants. For a time, it looked as if the whole Mahratta country-side was up in arms against the British Raj itself. When the British Government took its cue from this fury of the masses and hurriedly passed the Deccan Agriculturists Relief Act, whereby no peasant of Mahratta could be sent to the Civil Debtors Jail for failure to repay debts.

Protection of Punjab Peasants

A similar uprising took place in the Punjab in 1890-1900 against the growing alienation of peasants' lands to the moneylenders of towns. The Sikh, Muhammedan and Hindu peasants who had till recent past enjoyed an independent Sikh state could not brook the superiority of the moneylenders, conferred upon them by the British Civil Laws. No wonder the murders or assaults on moneylenders began to increase rather alarmingly. The British Government quickly passed the Punjab Land Alienation Act in 1902-03 prohibiting the transferring of land from Kisan tribes or other classes and prohibiting the usufruct mortgages for more than twenty years.

Similarly because the Punjab peasants began to protest against the oppressive, incidence of land revenue, the Government passed the Shaharanpur Rules, according to which the Land Revenue should never exceed 50 per cent of net-income from the original settlement or at any resettlement.

Thus it can be seen that the four major fights apart from the war of Independence put up by our peasants in their crude and primitive fashion have resulted in considerable concessions from Government. The British Government had also shown itself quite capable of meeting mass movements more than half way, lest the masses should either through their struggles develop their political consciousness or fall into the hands of politicians. There were neither political organisations nor class organisations at that time either to stimulate, engineer and develop peasants' risings, or to exploit the spontaneous uprisings of peasants with a view to strengthen any political movement for freedom.

Hence the extraordinary vigilance displayed by Lord Curzon to examine the complaints made by Ramesh Chandra Dutt, C.I.E. that the Land Revenue Assessment was too heavy, that British Government did wrong in undermining the strength and influence of Zamindars and that Government should not have refused to extend Permanent Settlement of land revenue to all parts of India. He obtained fairly detailed reports of land revenue practices from all Provincial Governments and in the resolution of the Governor General in Council, he laid down general principles, to guide, the settlement officers and Provincial Governments in making settlements and resettlements. It was through that resolution that Lord Curzon insisted that in no case the resettlements ought to exceed 18 per cent of the original assessment. At the same time, he laid it down as the policy of Government to protect peasants as against the rapacity of Zamindars. The Resolution of Government of India on 'Land Revenue Policy.' This he did, in 1905 in order to prevent the Indian National Congress, of which R.C. Dutt was the economist, to capture the heart of the peasants. He wanted to make the Government pass for the real champion of peasants. But unfortunately the Indian National Congress did not follow up its advantage by adopting a bold and forward policy in regard to the protection of peasants.

There was, however, one great struggle engineered by our nationalists under the leadership of the Congress on behalf of our voiceless peasants. It was aimed at the abolition of the *Indenture System.* According to this system, lakhs of our peasants and workers used to be somehow or other induced to sign some indenture bonds, agreeing to work for a specified number of years for some specified employer on his estate and in his province or country and consenting to all the penalties that the employer might inflict upon them for any breach of the bonds. Under this system our rural folk used to be recruited for work in South Africa, Malaya, Ceylon and other overseas countries and also for plantation work in Assam, Bengal, Madras and U.P. For years, lakhs of these unfortunate people who had agreed to go and work on the estates of employers, most of whom were Europeans, were persecuted in an unspeakable manner. There was not an indignity that could not be hurled at them and not a punishment that could not be procured by their influential employers from the too willing courts for even petty offences.

The criminal law of our country and the legal systems of other countries were so criminal in their conception and effect that in actual practice, our indentured labourers were converted into virtual slaves of their employers. Against this inhuman system, our Indian National Congress waged a relentless war and the great Bankim Chandra Chaterjee brandished his powerful pen for espousing the cause of these sufferers. At last the Congress had triumphed and the indenture system was abolished by Government which had agreed to shoulder the responsibility for the safety, economic well-being and cultural uplift of all immigrant and emigrant labour. Today Government of India has its agents in Ceylon, Malaya, Burma and South Africa to look after the interests of our emigrants and Protectors in Assam to watch the interests of our plantation labourers.

Struggle during 1905-19

It is however true to say that the Indian National Congress did not lay as much stress on the need for relief for our peasants, during 1905-19 as it did on the needs of our industrialists. There were many causes for this but the most important of them was the predominant voice our industrialists and disciples of Justice Ranade led by Ferozshah Mehta, and Gokhale, were then having in the counsels of the Congress. Our nationalists continued to press for the establishment of permanent settlement of land revenue, the abolition of salt-tax and excise revenue; but since they were preoccupied with their fight for protection for our industries and state assistance to our industrialists, they could not do anything more than formally reiterating these demands on behalf of our agriculturists. Even in this regard, for some reason, not easily explicable, they kept themselves scrupulously silent about the fate of our crores of zamindari tenants of D.P., C.P., Orissa, Bihar, Bengali, Assam and Madras. Lord Curzon's challenge to Ramesh Chandra Dutt, an ex-President of the Congress that it was the Government which had done more to protect tenants from the rapacity of Zamindars, remained unanswered probably because the then leadership of the Congress was so overwhelmingly zamindari and capitalistic in its class content.

Champaran Struggle 1917-18

The next phase in the awakening of our Kisan owed its development and success to the leadership of Mahatma Gandhi and Rajendra Prasad in the famous Champaran struggle against the indigo planters, many of whom were Europeans, who were persecuting the local Bihari peasants to grow indigo against their will on (Tinkathia) pain of paying higher taxes and collecting several illegal exactions. Mahatma Gandhi initiated the method for that time extremely novel and original, of conducting a systematic and authoritative enquiry into the real nature and degree of the sufferings of the peasants at the hands of the planters. Thousands of suffering peasants flocked round the Mahatma and Rajendra Prasad and detailed their woes. But the Provincial Government took fright and prohibited them from pursuing their enquiries. On their refusal to obey this prohibitory order, there arose a crisis, in which the arrest of Mahatma Gandhi and subsequent release were followed by the appointment of an Enquiry Committee with Mahatmajee as one of its members. Eventually the Bihar Government accepted the recommendations of the Committee whose report bears the imprint of Mahatma's personality.

An enactment based on the Report relieved peasants from their most immediate and pressing troubles and freed them from the special impost laid on them by the indigo planters. But just as the earlier Congress agitation led by Ramesh Chandra Dutt against temporary settlements did not embrace the exploitation of our peasants by zamindars, so also this agitation led by the Mahatma in Champaran did not lead up to any fight against the main causes for the terrible poverty and sufferings of Champaran peasants, namely the excessive i'ents and exorbitant incidence of debts. It may be because of Mahatmaji's growing habit which later on came to be considered as one of his political virtues of concentrating upon one thing at a time. But it does strike one as rather significant that both he and Rajendra Prasad should have remained scrupulously silent upon the ravages of the zamindari system and the extreme need for liberating peasants from its clutches. Anyhow, this Champaran satyagraha movement of 1917, i.e. during the Great War had the excellent result of awakening not only of the Bihar peasantry but also the general public of India to the tremendous revolutionary potentialities latent in the bosom of our peasants.

Kaira Satyagraha

Soon the Kaira and Bardoli drought and the consequent failure of crops claimed the attention of Mahatma Gandhi. The half-blind Bombay Government insisted upon its pound of flesh by demanding the payment of land revenue despite the inability of peasants to pay. Gandhiji's Satyagraha came to the rescue of these much harassed kisans and Bombay Government had also to eat the humble pie in the face of this rising peasant revolt led by such an implacable fighter. It suspended the kist collection. It was during this campaign that Com. Indulal Yagnik, now the Joint Secretary of the All India Kisan Committee received his first lessons in field work for our kisans. Even here Mahatmaji did not complicate his campaign by trying to tackle the other troubles of our kisans such as their indebtedness, alienations of lands.

These two campaigns succeeded in establishing Mahatmaji as a magic man of peasant satyagraha and to some extent awakening our peasants to the use of satyagraha for achieving their purposes. It is true that the great majority of our peasantry was still unaware of politics" and was therefore not politically affected by these triumphs. But they did open the eyes of a growing number of the educated kisans, like myself, to the political possibilities of our peasants' mass-action.

Non-Cooperation Movement

But it was left to the great nation-wide Non cooperation movement, which succeeded in drawing in one effort millions of peasants with its magical slogan of 'Swaraj in one year,' into its orbit. It shook our peasants free from their age old political slumber and dragged them, almost against their traditions into the whirlpool of our national political life. For the first time they were told, to their great satisfaction and wonder, that it was quite legitimate for them to refuse to pay land revenue, the payment of which they had come to look upon almost as a religious duty. To them, in those early days of our national movement of direct action and in that first flush of their political awakening, Swaraj meant freedom from all tax burdens and especially the abolition of land revenue. Naturally they hugged to their hearts both Mahatmaji's name and the slogan of 'Non-payment of Taxes.' When therefore Gandhiji commenced his preparations for his open conspiracy of 'Non-payment of taxes' campaign in Bardoli, the whole Kisan India opened its eyes and began to spontaneously refuse or delay the payment of land revenue or rent. Throughout India millions of peasants, believing that the end of the British Raj was within sight, abstained from paying their rents or revenue and began to watch political developments with bated breath. If only Mahatmajee had given the much wanted command to our Kisans not to pay their taxes, as was feared by the British and anticipated by our kisans, who knows if Lord Lloyd's fear of the destruction of British power in India might not have actually materialised. As it was, instead of that command, Mahatmaji suddenly withdrew the whole non-cooperation movement and thus left millions of our peasants as well as the country in mid-air.

With what consequences? Those lakhs of peasants alone know to their bitter cost. They came to be penalised in thousand and one ways by their zamindars, who not so long ago had been so terror-stricken and who were only too glad to wreak vengeance upon their kisans who had the temerity to hope for a better future; those millions of peasants and workers alone can tell what terrible disappointment they suffered when their very first hope of a bright life was frustrated and their aspiration of winning Swaraj was dashed to the ground. With the imprisonment of thousands of active Congressmen whose association with the peasantry was very intimate and with the return to quasi-normal life of the other disappointed and dazed Congressmen, our peasants found so few to fend for them and almost none to lead them in their struggles against the enraged British Government and its more cruel allies, the Zamindars.

Pedanandipadu Campaign

The real revolutionary significance of this first mass upsurge of our peasantry can be guessed from the phenomenal and dramatic success of the following uprisings in particular. One took place in Pedanandipadu area of Guntur District. There for a good few weeks, there was virtually Kisan Raj. In that area even the British mounted police and regular Military forces could not make peasants give them even information regarding the direction to any village pond or well, not to speak of giving any supplies of food or water or payment of taxes.

Oudh Kisan Rising

Laljee made an eloquent mention of this in his autobiography. There lakhs of peasants rose spontaneously against the oppressive zamindars and demanded not only Swaraj but also the removal of their sufferings. It did not subside, even after the Bardoli debacle until the Government hurriedly passed the Oudh Rent Act of 1921 which conferred the permanency of tenure upon the tenants. Luckily for the Government, its ruse, played once before in Maharashtra soon after the Deccan riots of 1897, negotiating with a peasant rising by offering something to appease it, succeeded in Oudh also, with the result that the Agra tenants of the same Province have had to go without the benefit of permanency of tenure until in 1938, the Congress Government has introduced its Bill to that effect.

Two other struggles need a mention in this connection, the No-tax campaign of Karnatak and the Moppl1a Rebellion of Malabar. The former bode fair to become as frightful an affair as that of Pedanandipadu but the withdrawal of non-cooperation movement sabotaged it at its very early stage

Moppl1a Rebellion

The latter proved to be disastrous to all concerned, except the British. In Malabar, Moppl1as who are Moslems by religion are mostly either agricultural workers, or tenants or the most depressed section of intermediary landholders with or without personal cultivation. They were then being exploited mercilessly by the Nambudris who were the virtual owners of the land and who had the absolute right of electing any intermediary peasant, known as Kanamdar or any of the actual cultivators. In fact these Nambudris, who were Brahmins were often aided by Kanamdars, most of whom were Nairs and they were freely exercising their right to evict peasants from their homesteads and raising the rents at their will and pleasure. No wonder an agitation sprang up in the wake of the Religious Revivalist Movement which later on was prostituted by the Justice Party. Its leaders were the late Sir M. Krishnan Nair and Mr M.P. Narayana Menon. One joined the Justice Party and rose to be an executive Councillor of the Madras Government and the other entered the Congress and came to be condemned for transportation for life for the alleged crime of having incited Mopplas to wage war against His Majesty's Government to be released only in 1936.

This rent reduction and permanency of tenure agitation, awakened the peasants, both Hindus and Moslems to the need for political action. It helped Krishnan Nair to be returned to the Madras Legislative Council. It gave a tremendous initial significance to the Non-cooperation Movement of Malabar. But soon a communal turn was given by some very responsible Moslem leaders and all the pent up enemity and disgust of peasants in general and Mopplas in particular burst up like a volcano, and resulted in blood-shed. The frightened Nambudris had in the meanwhile made common cause with' the leaders of Kanamdars agreed with the Justice Party, of which the erstwhile leader of tenants M. Krishnan Nair was an important pillar, over a compromise tenancy legislation and rallied all the Hindus to aid them and thus helped to make the whole thing a communal fight. The poor peasants who were thus mislead by their religious leaders and intrigued by their landlords and deceived by their colleagues, the Hindu tenants who were in their turn humbugged by the Justice Party, rushed headlong with their false religious slogans of hostility and war against Hindus in general and their suicidal means of blood and fire. Thus in a few months the heroic peasants of Malabar were either mowed down by British fire or consigned to Andamans in all their thousands. This fight has become notorious for the train tragedy in which nearly 80 Mopplas died of suffocation in a closed railway wagon and also for the treachery perpetrated upon our innocent peasants by religious leaders, reformist tenant agitators and the withdrawal of all Congress advice, leadership and support from the sufferers just at the right nick of time.

Sitarama Raju's Fight

In the wake of the failure of the Non-cooperation Movement and the six year sentence upon Mahatma Gandhi, a dreadful gloom had set in all over the Country, except in a tiny quarter, it lies on one of the broad backs of the Eastern Ghats, in the Jeypore Zamindari and on the Borders of the Narsipatam Taluk. There was enacted one of the most romantic dramas of revolutionary life of modern India. Alluri Sitarama Raju a Kshatriya of West Godavari District, went there and befriended with the Koyas and other hill-people of that tract. He became a Sadhu, and an expert healer both by spiritual powers and herbs. He saw the sufferings of those ignorant but militant people helpless at the hands of forest and excise officials. His appeals to officials for mercy were in vain. Those hill-tribes were not allowed to carry on their 'Podu' or 'Jungle' cultivation. They were made to pay too many dues upon so many of their activities such as gathering fuel, grazing their cattle in forests, felling fuel, grass, fruit, or gum, gathered in the forest to any outsiders. Thus their very traditional mode of life was threatened by Government. Raju saw no way out of it except through rebellion. When all his appeals for justice were in vain, he welcomed the spontaneous rising of those proud, martial and brave Koyas against the Government. That rising soon became a violent revolution and it was suppressed at great cost to human life on both sides and to the Indian finances, by a merciless and ruthless use of fire and iron by the British Government.

Thanks to the post-autonomy and Congress Governments, M.P. Narayan Menon and hundreds of other Malabar victims, and the few survivers of the Sitarama Raju's 'Pituri' were released recently.

Kamagatamaru

After the war another epoch of our peasant struggle began. Just after the war the magic word went abroad that the British Prime Minister's plighted promise to India that Swaraj would be granted soon after the war was over was broken and that the word came for all patriots to strike their last blow at British Imperialism to wrest from it India's Swaraj. Mahatma Gandhi's weapon of Satyagraha evoked tremendous hopes in the hearts of our nationalists. It was in that atmosphere that hundreds of Punjab peasants flocked to the banner of revolution. Their brethren who had emigrated to Canada, U.S.A. and South America not only sent large sums of money but also despatched a shipload of men, money and ammunition to aid their revolutionary work. Hopes were raised all over the Punjab countryside of the impending struggle and advent of Swaraj. But alas! the British got scent of it, captured those famous Kamagatamaru heroes, clapped many more peasants of Punjab villages into jails and persecuted in an unspeakable fashion many thousands of the brave Sikh peasants for their share in that adventurous scheme.

The Aka movement of Hardoi in U.P. stirred up the peasantry of Sitapur, Raibarelli, Fyzabad and several other Districts in 1922-23, i.e., just after the Bardoli withdrawal of Satyagraha and at the time of the Mopplla and Sitarama-Raju's 'Pituri'. It was led by Nadari Pari, an actual peasant and the whole countryside responded to him to a man. Government found it so hard to tackle it since actual peasants were at its head and the leaders were not specially wedded to the Gandhian ideas of non-violence in regard to every detail. Eventually it was suppressed as all other peasant struggles by the blood and fire of Government.

But all these great and spontaneous risings of our peasants from one end of the country to the other succeeded as nothing else had during the previous sixty years since the great Indian war of Independence, to bestir our peasants bring them into the whirlpool of our national politics, evoked in their hearts great and even extravagant hopes and encouraged them to dream glorious dreams of peace, plenty and prosperity on the advent of Swaraj. If not for anything else, atleast for having opened the eyes of crores of our peasants who would otherwise have continued to vegetate with their, Curzonian contentment and sense of atrophy, and brought them once for all into our political area, the great Non-Cooperation Movement and Mahatmaji's slogan of 'Swaraj within one year' were more than justified. But how one wishes that the Congress had provided some defence forces to protect our peasants on their retreat. How one deplores the failure of our leaders to take a more realistic view of things and prevented such a sudden and almost heartless (one is almost tempted to say, irresponsible) withdrawal of Congress support from our peasants.

Three conclusions force themselves upon our minds as a result of this cursory survey of the effect of introduction of national politics into the life of our peasants, since 1917, by Mahatma Gandhi and his followers, working through the Indian National Congress. That our peasants were taken by surprise, they had either to absorb the political thought of the day even if there were one or were not provided with any political machinery in the shape of a self-confident, self-conscious and local autonomous Congress or Kisan organisation to stand up for them through thick and thin and to constantly guide them. Instead as soon as Mahatmaji withdrew his Non-cooperation Movement and abandoned all aggressive political action, the local Congress committees went limp and Congressmen became devoid of any initiative or leadership. Indeed Congress had fought shy of having anything more to do with Mopplas or Koyas or U.P. or Punjab Kisans or others and Congressmen instantly dropped all Kisan work. Need one wonder then if all over India, our peasantry quickly relapsed into their traditional political somnombulence, nursing an aweful bitterness against our politicians and their own miserable fate.

The second conclusion is that in too many cases were our peasants struggles exploited either by communalists or religious maniacs who had little respect to the creed of non-violence, that our peasants were defenceless against their bad leadership, denied as they had been of any political training, organisational ability or knowledge of the effects and consequences of agitational work, which could be gained only through their active participation in their class or political organisations. Naturally there was too much exhibition of violence at the fag end of our kisan struggles of those hectic days of 1920-23 and it frightened away our Congressmen and thus denied them of any active sympathetic, day to day support and guidance of the Congress, which they then needed much more than at any other time.

The third conclusion is that owing to their abandonment by the Congress once their revolutionary temper went beyond the mild expectations of the Congress leaders and thus upset the calculations of the reformist leaders of the Congress of different provinces of these days by threatening to shake to their roots the very economic foundations of society, our peasants came in for the cruel intentions of Government and zamindars and were persecuted hopelessly for years in many a way.

It was in 1923 July-December, just when the members of Moppla rebellion were dying out and the Sitarama Raju's fight was going on the Ryots Associations (or Kisan Sabhas as they had later on come to be known all over India) Agricultural and Labour Unions in the Andhra were organised. There was instantaneous success in Guntur District with the ryots since they were all disillusioned about the Government and the Justice Party which persuaded them into the belief that no reprisals would be taken against them for their support to the Pedanandipadu's No-tax campaign and later on, inflicted heavy penal-rates of assessment for their having dared to support the Congress to bring 'Swaraj within one year' also helped them to rally to organize themselves into Ryots Associations.

It was just at that time that a very bitter controversy was going on between the pro-changers headed by the late Moti Lal Nehru and C.R. Das and No-changers led by Srijit C. Rajagopalachari as to whether Congress should enter the legislatures or not. Though in several provinces, Swaraj parties were organised the Congressmen went into legislatures under their auspices, in the Andhra and in Guntur District in particular, orthodox Congress leaders succeeded in preventing any great development of the Swaraj Party. Naturally this gave an opportunity to our Ryots Association to formulate its Election Manifesto, set up a selection committee and nominate its candidates and make them sign the peasants pledge and conduct the electioneering on purely peasants' lines. At all the stages, even orthodox Congress leaders cooperated with our Ryots Association. While the Non-Brahmin Party eschewed all Brahmin candidates, our Ryots Association selected a Brahmin candidate, thus demonstrating at its very inception, its non-communal character and politics. Three out of its four candidates were successful. One was sent to the Central Assembly and two to the local council and two of them eventually joined the Congress and distinguished themselves in the country's cause. This unexpected success of the Ryots Association and the splendid response given by peasants to its call excited the fear of Government and jealously of some Congressmen and most of the Justicites. So from all sides we were attacked about the further need for such associations.

We could have gone on developing Ryots Associations all over the province if only we had a sufficient number of workers to carry on propaganda. Unfortunately, we had none and we did not then think of organising a Kisan school to train youths for this work and to develop a self-reliant and independent cadre of comrades for this extra congress work. Since neither the local Congress workers who were themselves few in number and hard pressed for time and resources nor peasants themselves were forthcoming to aid us. Our Ryots Associations marked very little progress between 1924-1926, beyond spreading themselves to West Godavari and Krishna Districts also and spreading and popularising the idea of independent class organizations for peasants and workers.

Bihar and U.P. Kisan Sabhas of 1926-27

In 1926-27, some comrades began to organise Kisan Sabhas in Bengal, Punjab and U.P. on more or less idealistic lines with a revolutionary programme. As they were too often mistaken for communist organizations by the local Governments which were only too anxious to nip in the bud everything that savoured of revolutionary temper, they were banned before they could take deep roots. Somehow the Bihar and U.P. Kisan Sabhas managed to keep up their existence until 1928, when they presented their memoranda to the All Parties Conference presided over by the late Pt. Moti Lal Nehru. So far as one could ascertain, these Kisan Sabhas seemed to have favoured universal franchise, complete independence and fundamental rights. It is significant that when Dr Annie Beasant declined to provide for universal franchise (when some of us suggested it to her in 1925 soon after the Delhi conference) in her scheme for an Indian Commonwealth, the Nehru Committee favoured it, especially when our Kisan Sabhas also pleaded for it.

Andhra Ryots Association

The Andhra Provincial Ryots Association was organised by some of us in 1928 under the Presidentship of B.V. Ratnam M.L.C. and M.B. Needu, M.Sc. One of the Parliamentary Secretaries of Madras Ministry came out with a pamphlet on 'Why Peasants Associations?' and strongly advocated their establishment on the lines of the American Farmers Unions. As he took an active part in that Provincial Ryots conference, he was elected the General Secretary. Even at that time there was a trial of strength between the Justicites and Congressites over the issue of Congress boycott and so the Justicites staged a walk-out saying that Ryots conferences ought not to meddle with politics.

Andhra Zamindari Ryots Association

In 1929, the Ryots Conference met and supported the stand taken by the Congress in regard to politics and concerned itself mostly with land revenue, agricultural indebtedness, unemployment and internal social reforms but did not try to tackle the zamindari ryot problem. That was taken up by the Andhra Zamindari Ryots conference organized by Mr R.M. Sharma. But the conference only demanded a radical revision of the Estates Land Act so as to minimize the sufferings of tenants. Our peasant workers were not then prepared to demand the abolition of the zamindari system, so unprepared was the political world to grapple with such problems at that time.

The 1930 Civil Disobedience Movement, the precipitous fall of prices of our agricultural commodities due to the economic depression and the consequent pressure sudden and stunning brought to bear upon them by moneylenders and landlords and the heroic struggles and achievements of Bardoli peasants in 1928-29 and 1930-31 had all prepared the field for the spread of bolder ideas among the peasantry and for the acceptance by our peasants of our revolutionary lead and also for the adoption by them of our tactics.

1928-29 Bardoli Triumph

It is impossible to overestimate the electrical effect the triumph of Bardoli ryots of 1928-29 had upon our Indian peasantry. There the Bardoli peasants rose against the unjust enhancement of land revenue sought to be imposed upon them by the Bombay Government. They were led by Sardar Vallabbhai Patel and assisted by Mahatma Gandhi and financed by President Vithalbhai Patel. But the chief factor which ultimately won for them their complete success was their own limitless sacrifices and unexampled discipline and determination. At last the Bombay Government had to yield to the demand of peasants to appoint an impartial Enquiry Committee. The Committee gave its award mostly in favour of peasants. This well advertised triumph of Bardoli peasants put heart into the Indian peasantry and evoked again their hopes of being able to successfully rise against the Government.

Unrest in Andhra Pradesh

Unrest among the tribal people of Andhra Pradesh is not a matter of yesterday or today. It has been raising its aggrieved and ugly head now and then in the past 167 years. It is now also active in the Agency Areas of Andhra Pradesh stretching out in a half-moon pattern its agitated arms, indicating a deep seated anguish, resulting from dashed hopes, broken promises and frustrated aspirations. The tribes in this part of the country live both in the plains as well as in the hills and the jungles. While many tribes of the plains are nomadic, landless, homeless and primitive, those in the Agency Areas have their lands alienated, meagre properties heavily mortgaged, and "their health irretrievably shattered, owing to the relentless attacks of malaria, year after year, sapping their energy and thwarting all efforts at better living conditions and purposeful lives".

Most of the South Indian tribes, including the 33 different tribes of Andhra Pradesh, are pre-Dravidian and to some extent share Negroid features. Ecologists assert that the early and the middle palaeolithic civilisation of pre-historic times flourished in the districts of Kurnool, Guntur and Nellore in Andhra Pradesh.

Andhra Pradesh is a large State occupying a fourth place in the Indian Union and covering an area of 106,286 sq. miles, with a scheduled population of 13,24,368 most of whom live in the Agency parts of the State which roughly covers 29,683 sq. miles. In addition to these Agency tribes, Andhra Pradesh has a nomadic ex-criminal and unscheduled population of six more lakhs of tribals who can be classified as primitive. The Scheduled Tribes form 3.68 per cent of the total population of Andhra Pradesh of 3,59,83,447. The numerically largest groups inhabiting both plains and Agency areas are Gonds, Koyas, Hill Reddis, Savaras, Bagatas, Valmikis, Yerukalas and Yanadis, as well as smaller groups like Ronas, Kattunaikars and Bhils. Nearly 52.6 per cent of the total tribal population of Andhra Pradesh consists of Koyas, Yanadis, Yerukulas and Gonds. While Gonds are confined to the district of Adilabad bordering on Madhya Pradesh, Koyas are found in all the Agency districts. Gonds, Koyas, Bagatas and Valmikis are more advanced than Khonds, Savaras, Hill Reddis and Kolams. The Agency tribes inhabit parts of the main districts as mentioned in the following table based on the 1961 Census report:

S.No.	*District*	*Extent in sq. miles*	*No. of tribal villages*
1	Srikakulam	!303.04	462
2	Visakhapatnam	6671.36	1565
3	East Godavari	6637.70	699
4	West Godavari	1492.56	105
5	Khammam	6647.53	888
6	Warangal	980.76	152
7	Adilabad	4534.35	415
8	Mahaboobnagar	1415.63	60
	Total	**29682.93**	**4346**

It is mostly in the first four districts that tribals revolts have been occurring, though in Adilabad a sporadic uprising of the Gonds, led by

Bhimu was summarily put down by the British. Some of the revolts took place during the rule of the British East India Company. The main seat and stronghold of the recent as well as the current 'Naxalite' uprisings is the Srikakulam district which borders on Orissa State, separated only by a long chain of low hills which have been thoughtfully selected by the English-educated Naxalite leaders from Visakhapatnam and East and West Godavari districts for their strategic and logistic facilities. Rebels pursued by the police found a cosy home in the caves and dugouts of these hills access to which is somewhat difficult. Moreover they could easily slip into Orissa. . . .

Tribal revolts in Andhra Pradesh erupted on four occasions. Though the immediate causes were somewhat different, the basic factors that contributed the powder for the guns were on all occasions the same. The first of the revolts led by Rambhoopati took place in 1802-3, now popularly known as the Rampa Fithuri (rebellion), named after Rampa near Chodavaram. The Rampa country is the area covered by the Chodavaram taluk of the East Godavari district of Andhra Pradesh. The second revolt around 1879 led by Chandrayya, Sambayya, Thammandora and Ambul Reddi spread over 5,000 sq. miles in the Rampa country. The third uprising took place in 1922-24 under the leadership of the saint-patriot hero Shri Alluri Sreerama Raju who was murdered, after his voluntary surrender on May 7, 1924, at Koyyur on the orders of a British Major, Goodall, against all canons of justice, national or international. The fourth revolt is continuing since the last two years in the district of Srikakulam, under the guidance of educated pro-Chinese extreme Communists, known as Naxalites, who have taken their name after a village called Naxalbari in the Darjeeling district of West Bengal, where the first outburst took place. . . .

The first two rebellions were due to disputes relating to succession to the Muttadari estates. The Muttadars were petty tribal chiefs who were appointed by the British East India Company's minions for keeping peace and collecting a very nominal land revenue from the tribal people more as a symbol of overall authority of the Company's Government, rather than as a source of revenue to the State. Taking ample advantage of even this limited authority, the Muttadars used all questionable and violent methods to terrorise the poor Koya and Konda Reddi tenants and effect several illegal and unconscionable exactions from the helpless and hapless tribal farmers.

The Revolt of 1879-80

For nearly two centuries the British were in possession of the Northern Circars including the Rampa country, though in Chodavaram Taluk containing the Rampa area, no regular collection of land revenue was enforced till the end of the 19th century. During the period of the cession of the above country to the British, Rampa was ruled by an independent zamindar, recognised by the Reddis as their feudal lord or Mansabdar. During the revenue collection of 1802-3 no settlement was done for Rampa. Ram Bhupati, the Mansabdar seized some villages which were under British control, but was soon repulsed and forced to acknowledge the Company's sovereignty. In 1813, an agreement was reached between the two by which the Company restored the above villages to him free of rent (Peshkash) on condition that he maintained peace in this restless land. Ram Bhupati subleased these villages to his subordinate hill chiefs called Muttadars, on an annual payment of Rs.8,750. After his death his daughter succeeded to his estate though on a hot contest by Ram Bhupati's illegitimate son, she surrendered the property to him. The Muttadars accepted him on condition that he reduced the total rent to Rs.1,000 in 1848. He first agreed to do so but later broke his promise and began to rackrent the Muttadars and make illegal exactions which the hill Reddy Muttadars and the tribal people refused to pay. In addition to this, free drawing of toddy by the tribals was obstructed by the Mansabdar and several types of taxes which were unknown before were invented and levied. The tribals and their Muttadari tribal leaders got vexed with litigation in the civil courts and finally the call to revolt was given as the zamindar obtained *ex-parte* decrees and attached the property of the tribals through the courts at Rajamahendravaram. Cattle and property worth Rs.100 were, attached to realise a debt of only Rs.5. All the attached goods were taken away with the police helping the Mansabdar and the Courts decreeing for him. This left no alternative to the tribals except to revolt and they did it in right earnest perhaps knowing fully well the consequences thereof.

The first outbreak of the rebellion occurred in March 1879 when the tribals captured 6 policemen under Thammandora's leadership near Boduluru, 22 miles from Chodavaram, kept them in custody for several days and finally took them to Kodigandi where a head constable and one constable were kept tied under a tamarind tree. Thammandora himself severed their heads as a sacrifice to the Goddess in the presence of 200 tribesmen. The rebels then attacked the Chodavaram police station and reduced to ashes the station at Addatigala. Soon the Rampa country was ablaze and the rebellion assumed serious proportions.

The disturbances spread to Golugonda hills in Visakhapatnam in April and to Rekapalli country in Bhadrachalam in July. Here the immediate cause of the revolt was the sudden increase by the Madras Government of the assessment of Podu lands by three times while it was only four annas an acre hitherto. Further, the ryots were excluded from certain areas and a tax was newly levied on the felling of certain varieties of trees. The fight with the tribals who could penetrate unseen into the jungles and launch surprise attacks— the manner of guerilla warfare avoiding direct confrontation—made the task of the Government troops very difficult. Towards the end of 1879 the Government despatched from Madras, 6 regiments of the Madras Infantry, 2 Companies of Sappers and Miners, a Squadron Cavalry, one wing of Infantry, besides several hundreds of Police. The war with the tribal insurgents lasted till November 1880.

Peasant Resistance and Revolt in South India

With a third of the world socialist, and guerrilla movements active in more than a dozen countries, some social scientists in the West have turned their attention to the role of peasants in revolution.[100] This article stems from work by Hamza Alavi, Eric Wolf, and A.G. Frank.[101] It tries to supplement Alavi's analysis of peasant revolts in two areas of India—Telengana and Bengal with an account of some peasant actions in the northern part of the state of Kerala, with references for purposes of comparison to Tanjore, a district in southeast Madras.

The questions of principal concern are, First: is rural class struggle endemic in these South Indian regions, or is it engendered by self-interested political parties, especially the communists? Second: in modern peasant insurrections, what have been the respective roles of landlords, rich peasants, middle and poor peasants, and landless labourers? Third: what is the potential for future peasant revolt?

Kerala has a large number of types of land tenure, which vary, moreover, as between Malabar, Cochin, and Travancore. The most common traditional tenure has been 'kanam', in which the tenant surrenders a fixed rent, often about a third of the crop, to the landlord, in addition to a cash renewal fee every twelve years. In pre-British times this 'superior' tenure was confined to Nayars and other high caste Hindus of similar rank and to relatively high ranking Muslims and Christians. The most common 'inferior' tenure is 'verumpattam', in which the tenant pays a fixed rent, usually amounting to about two-thirds of the net produce, to the landlord or the 'kanam' tenant, whichever is immediately above him. 'Verumpattam' and similar tenures have traditionally been accorded mainly to members of the large, relatively low ranking cultivating caste of Tiyyars or Iravas; very seldom to the lowest, 'Untouchable' castes such as Pulayas and Parayas, almost all of whom are landless labourers.

In Tanjore the most common types of tenure have been 'kuthakai', in which the tenant traditionally paid a fixed rent usually amounting to about three to four-fifths of his net produce, and 'varam', an older, share-cropping tenure in which the tenant retained one-fifth of his net produce each year, regardless of the size of his crop.[102]

This analysis cuts somewhat cavalierly through the details of land tenure to apply Mao Tse-tung's categories, which are useful for the sake of comparison with other areas. Thus, in 1933 Mao analyzed the classes in rural Chinese society as follows:

A landlord is a person who possesses land, who does not engage in labour himself or merely takes part in labour as a supplementary source of income, and who lives by exploiting the peasants. The landlord's exploitation chiefly assumes the form of collecting land rent; besides that, he may also lend money, hire labour, or engage in industrial or commercial enterprise. (2) The rich peasant as a rule possesses land. But there are some who possess part of the land they farm and rent the remainder. . . . The rich peasant as a rule possesses comparatively abundant means of production and liquid capital, engages in labour himself, but regularly relies on exploitation for a part or the major part of his income. The exploitation the rich peasant practises is chiefly that of hired labour. In addition, he may also let a part of his land for rent, lend money, or engage in industrial or commercial enterprise. (3) In many cases the middle peasant possesses land. In some cases he possesses no land at all and rents all the land he farms. . . . The middle peasant relies wholly or mainly on his own labour as the source of his income. As a rule he does not exploit other people; in many cases he is even exploited by other people and has to pay a small amount of land rent and interest on loans. ... The middle peasant as a rule does not sell his labour power. (4) In some cases the poor peasant possesses a part of the land he farms. . . in other cases he possesses no land at all, but only an incomplete set of instruments. As a rule the poor peasant has to rent land for cultivation. . . While the middle peasant need not sell his labour power, the poor peasant has to sell a small part of his—this is the principal criterion for distinguishing the middle peasant from the poor peasant. (5) The worker (including the farm labourer) as a rule does not possess any land or implements. . .. A worker makes his living wholly or mainly by selling his labour power.[103]

Alavi distinguishes three sectors of the rural economy in India. In the first sector, land is owned by landlords who do not themselves undertake cultivation. They rent land to poor peasants, mainly sharecroppers: In the second sector are independent small-holders or middle peasants, who own the land they cultivate and do not exploit the labour of others. In the third sector, land is owned by capitalist farmers or rich peasants, who manage the land themselves and employ hired labour. Alavi's argument is that it was the independent middle peasant who, in Russia and China, played the most active role in the early stages of revolution; the poor peasants, both more backward and potentially more militant, were drawn in along with the middle peasants in later stages. In India, he sees the poor peasants as having been most active in the Bengal and Telengana movements of 1946-48; he attributes their failure in part to a failure to draw the middle peasant into the struggle.

This analysis differs from Alavi's on two counts. First, the situation in Kerala and Tanjore do not allow a clear distinction between the 'landlord' and the 'capitalist' sectors, nor can either of them be separated from the sector of the middle peasant. In both regions there has been, over the past hundred years, a gradual increase in the proportions of landlords and rich peasants who employ hired labour, and in the proportions of hired labourers to poor and middle peasants. This tendency has not declined, and may even have been stepped up, with the land reforms of the past decade. At least since the late nineteenth century, however, it has been common for both landlords and rich peasants to lease out portions of their lands to poor peasants and to have other portions cultivated by labourers. It is, moreover, common in these regions for both rich and middle peasants to lease at least part of their land from landlords, a fact which makes it virtually impossible to separate Alavi's three 'sectors'. The attempt to do so probably stems from a 'dual economy' (in this case 'triple economy') thesis which sees the capitalist and pre-capitalist (sometimes called 'feudal') sectors of the economy as existing side by side, with the former gradually overtaking the Jatter. But while some 'features' of pre-capitalist relations (payments in kind, debt-labour, special levies, etc.), may undoubtedly continue to exist here and there in rural India the system as a whole has been a colonial capitalist system, incorporated into, and affected by, the fluctuations of world markets, since at least the last third of the nineteenth century.

The distinction between landlords and rich peasants rests, therefore, not on whether tenants or hired labourers are engaged, although it is true that rich peasants tend to have most of their land cultivated by labourers, and that big landlords rent out substantial amounts of land. Instead, the distinction is made in terms of whether or not the owner or holder actively engages in management of his lands and contributes some of his own manual labour to their cultivation.

In Kerala and Tanjore, a landlord is thus a land owner ('janmi' in Kerala, 'mirasdar' in Tanjore) who himself does no cultivation, who almost always rents out part of his land, but who in addition often employs hired labourers; the latter are usually managed by overseers. A landlord may own anything from about eight to several thousand acres; if he own less than eight acres, he is likely to have clerical, professional, or mercantile work in addition, and will thus not be primarily a landlord. A rich peasant is likely to own or to lease from about eight to thirty acres of land. He manages most of it himself, usually does some manual labour, and regularly hires a number of labourers; he may also rent out small plots to tenants. Rich peasants in Kerala are likely to be either 'kanam' tenants or to own some acres and to lease more on 'kanam'. In Tanjore they are usually small 'mirasidars' who may in addition lease land on 'kuthakai'. Middle peasants in Kerala and Tanjore may own a little land of their own, but almost all lease some from landlords, on 'kanam' or 'verumpattam' in Kerala and on 'kuthakai' in Tanjore. 'Pure' middle peasants who hire no landless labourers are actually almost non-existent in these regions. Most have one or two regular workers and engage more at peak seasons. They are thus somewhat hard to separate from the rich peasants and are involved in both of Alavi's first and third sectors—as tenants and as hirers of labour. Poor peasants in Kerala lease all their lands, usually on 'verumpattam' or one of the less favourable variants of 'kanam'; in Tanjore they may be 'kuthakai' or 'varam' tenants. They are too poor to survive on these lands and work either half-time or seasonally for landlords, or for rich or even middle peasants. Most poor peasants come from relatively low or 'backward' castes (in Kerala, Iravas or low-ranking Muslims or Christians; in Tanjore, Konar, Nadar or relatively low-ranking subcastes of Kallar or Vanniyar) whose ancestors have traditionally served as tied labourers or semiserfs of landlords. Substantial numbers of high caste people such as Vellalas and Naidus in Tanjore, or Nayars and Syrian Christians in Kerala, have, however, become middle or poor peasants in recent decades. Landless labourers, finally, include almost all members of the Harijan or 'Untouchable' castes of former agricultural slaves: Pallas and Parayas' in Tanjore; Pulayas, Cherumas, and Parayas in Kerala. Many Muslims and Christians in Kerala, and many 'clean' caste Hindus in both Kerala and Tanjore, have, however, become landless labourers during this century. Landless labourers possess no land, and lease at best only a minute plot as a house-site. They work full time for wages, either in cash or kind, and either for long periods or casually by the day.

A second difference from Alavi's analysis derives from the different course taken by the revolts in Bengal and Andhra as described by Alavi, and those in Kerala and Tanjore. In the latter, while poor peasants and also landless labourers were drawn into the struggle, there was still a tendency on the part of the communists to rely on the middle peasants for local leadership. It is true that it has always been difficult to combine middle and poor peasants and landless labourers in a united struggle. Nevertheless, in these regions, the failure of the revolts of the late 1940s was due more to vacillations of policy on the part of the communist leadership, and to the fact that only isolated sectors of India were at that time ripe for agrarian revolt, than to a 'sectarian' preference for poor peasants and landless labourers on the part of the communists. If anything, it would seem that the communists have so far failed fully to utilize the militancy of poor peasants and landless labourers in Southern India. Today, the increasing proportions and restlessness of these agrarian classes are causing some communist groups and leaders to reconsider their policies in this regard.

Collective acts of violence or non-violent resistance by Indian peasants against landlords and higher authorities were common during British rule. They included spontaneous killings of landlords or officials by small groups of peasants; organized nonviolent strikes; and prolonged armed attempts to seize the land and establish peasant self-government. The largest revolts were the Mappilla (Moplah) or Muslim rebellions of Malabar District in North Kerala of 1836-98. Muslim tenants revolted twenty-five times, killing many Hindu landlords, British officials, and soldiers. Before 1920, such actions emerged from the peasants themselves, with some of them focusing around local charismatic leaders. After 1920 peasant revolts tendered to come under the guidance of regional, national, or urban-based political movements.

Peasant revolts during British rule appear to have stemmed from the increasing exactions of the colonial economy. During the first two-thirds of the nineteenth century the British instituted capitalist agrarian relations throughout most of India. These relations involved private ownership of land by its former managers, the right of the landlord to sell his land in the market, the right to evict unwanted tenants and freely to undertake contractual leases, the freeing of serfs and slaves, and their conversion into landless wage labourers.[104] The sale of cash crops, whether for foreign or local markets, developed in both Tanjore and Kerala in response to the government's extraction of a heavy revenue from the landlords. In Tanjore's deltaic rice area, landlords began to sell grain to other' regions, retaining enough to feed their families and labourers.

In Kerala the second half of the nineteenth century saw a great increase in the agricultural population and a vast expansion of export crops such as coconuts, spices, lumber, and later tea, rubber and cashewnuts. Much of this expansion took place in former forest lands but long-settled villages were also affected. Pulled by the rising prices of export crops and pushed by the need to pay high revenues, landlords extracted more and more produce from their too-numerous tenants and labourers and evicted them when they were unable to pay their rents. Many of those evicted starved. Others eventually found work in the towns, in the new lumber industry in the forests, or on the export crop plantations developed in the last third of the century by British firms. Tenancy Acts passed after 1887 gave increasing security to those holding superior tenures—often themselves non-cultivating middlemen—but did little to stay the insecurity of the poorest tenants and landless labourers.[105]

The first modern politically-sponsored revolt took shape under the Congress-Khilafat movement of 1920-21. Guided by the Indian National Congress and the Muslim League, Kerala's new middle class of students, rich peasants; middle ranking merchants, and professionals encouraged cultivators and hand-mill workers to engage in non-violent strikes and boycott of British goods. The goals were Home Rule for India and for Turkey, at that time struggling against European hegemony. The British responded with violent repression. At this, poor Muslim tenants, heirs of the nineteenth century rebels, organized in village assemblies round their religious leaders and with knives, spears, clubs, and homemade firearms drove out or killed both Hindu and Muslim landlords, government servants, and police. Muslim leaders of middle peasant rank took over the government of 220 villages for several months. They killed five to six hundred landlords, police, and others who had aided the British military. Once violent revolt occurred, Congress leaders under Gandhi withdrew their support. The British defeated the movement and deported or executed many rebels. About 10,000 died in this rebellion.[106]

In the 1920s and 1930s, a gulf widened between rightwing Congressmen who wanted Home Rule with a minimum of internal changes, and left-wingers, often of Marxist persuasion. The latters' bases lay in the modern labour unions they had formed among handmill, industrial, and transport workers in the coast towns, among peasants in villages of the midlands, and among wage earning plantation workers on the large British-owned tea and rubber estates in the highlands. In 1934, leftwing Congressmen formed the Congress Socialist Party within the Congress Party. The socialists dominated the Kerala Provincial Congress Committee until 1940, when they were expelled by the national leadership and openly declared their affiliation to the Communist Party.

This period of the late 1930s, together with the post-war period of 1947-50, saw the most intense politically sponsored activity among middle and poor peasants that has occurred in South India. Most of it was organized by communists, although socialist, Congress and independent peasant unions sponsored some peasant boycotts and strikes. Communist peasant actions were inspired not only by immediate economic goals but also by a belief in revolutionary class struggle. Peasants came to hope and expect that it would eventually culminate in seizure of the land by its cultivators and of the country by the Communists.

Communist influence strongly affected the Kerala branch of the Socialist Party by 1940. In that year the communists tried to precipitate Indian independence by paralyzing the British wartime administration. The national bourgeoisie within the Congress was now seen not as allies but as 'cowards' to be 'isolated',[107] and the urban proletariat was expected to lead the struggle. There were urban strikes and sabotage throughout India, and supporting actions by peasants. On September 15, 1940, during widespread demonstrations, a number of police, socialist leaders, and peasants died in armed clashes in several towns and villages of Malabar. Responding to these events, the national Congress leadership expelled the Kerala socialists from the party. All of them thereupon joined the

Communist Party. Those communists who escaped imprisonment went underground, and the 'proletarian struggle' petered out in early 1941.

Shortly after the Soviet Union entered the war in mid-1941, Indian communists opted to support the war effort and entered into limited collaboration with the British. Until the end of the war, they refrained from militant struggles. At the same time, with the Congress leadership in jail for non-cooperation, the communists expanded their leadership in labour and peasant unions in Kerala, and at war's end they emerged in control of most of these bodies.

In 1946-47, revolts broke out in the Indian Navy, among the urban classes in many cities, and among the peasants in large regions of Bengal, Te l engana, Tanjore, and Kerala.[108] The CPI national office did not support these revolts, for its leadership' was divided and its official policy was now one of cooperation with the Congress in the transition to independence. Rural communist leaders were, however, active in the revolts. In Telengana in the princely state of Hyderabad (now part of Andhra State) guerrilla warfare led to the seizure of some 3000 villages in two whole districts, and to their administration for six months by peasant' soviets. These revolutionary institutions were crushed by the Indian Army, which under orders from the new Congress government invaded Hyderabad and annexed it to the Indian union in 1948.

The Communist leaders in Telengana were influenced by the Chinese theory and practice of peasant guerrilla warfare. This differed both from the path of proletarian uprising and from that of United Front constitutional opposition which the Indian communists had hitherto alternately pursued. Chinese influence also affected the leadership of Tanjore and Kerala. In these regions the struggle never attained. The proportions seen in Bengal and Telengana. Nevertheless, communist-organized groups of middle and poor peasants did drive out the landlords and take over a block of villages in eastern Tanjore for several weeks early in 1948.[109] In many other villages, unions of tenants and labourers struck during the harvest season until they had compelled the landlords to halve rents and double wages. The Tanjore revolt was put down by armed police in the course of 1949. In Kerala, too, there were strikes of tenants and labourers for lower rents and higher wages, large demonstrations, and organized seizures of black market grain-stocks from rich landlords and merchants. Both in Tanjore and Kerala, landless labourers as well as poor peasants were now drawn into the struggles and played a militant role. Many of them came from the lowest castes of Harijans, hitherto ostracized and exploited by the somewhat higher Hindu castes of middle and poor tenants.

In Tanjore, Harijans (called Adi Dravidas) form about one-third of the population and live in segregated streets on the outskirts of villages. The communists organized these streets into unions on the basis of their existing caste-assemblies. The Adi Dravidas acted separately, although in alliance, with the unions of higher ranking middle and poor peasants, thus raising the struggle to new heights of militancy. In Kerala, thousands of Harijan and Backward Caste landless labourers struck for the first time on the cash crop farming estates of big village landlords in 1947. Both men and women came out. Their discipline and militancy were remarkable. In one North Malabar village sprawling over four square miles of mountains and valleys only one labourer went to work on the first day of the strike. He had heard of it but did not really think the people would be united. His caste members approached him before the second day and he stayed away thereafter.

The peasant revolts of 1947 took place without support from the central leadership of the Communist Party. In 1948, however, as in 1940, the CPI line changed to one of revolutionary upsurge led by the urban proletariat. In theory, the peasants were still neglected. B.T. Ranadive, the Party's general secretary, in fact described Mao's theories as 'horrifying', 'reactionary', and 'counterrevolutionary'.[110] In practice, however, communist revolutionary action in this period was more successful in the countryside than in the cities, and South Indian rural leaders clung to the Chinese line. Finally, in mid-1950, a reconstituted central committee briefly adopted the Maoist approach of armed revolution based primarily on guerrilla warfare. By this time, however, the main revolts had been crushed. The Congress government was firmly in control and most villagers appear to have been made hopeful by the prospect of universal franchise under the new constitution. In 1951 the communists changed their approach to one of parliamentary opposition. They renewed their attempts to unite the workers, all classes of peasants, and the "patriotic" bourgeoisie to bring about a mixed economy under government regulation, with a democratic parliamentary structure. Beginning with the Indian elections of 1952, the communists have followed the parliamentary road up to the present time, in spite of the party-split of 1964 and a variety of fundamental disagreements on international and national problems.

During the period of parliamentary democracy, many communist peasant unions have been allowed to lapse. In 1964, Kathleen Gough found that local communist leaders in Kerala absorbed in electioneering, legal work, and ideological meetings and conflicts, often had little time for day-to-day organization in their villages. Union meetings were infrequent and in many villages peasants had ceased to pay their dues. Some militant struggles had been waged by the communists, however, and also by a new Christian Peasants and Workers' Party which has since joined a United Front with the communists. These struggles were especially prominent among some 30,000 peasants in hill areas, who had occupied government and private forest lands and whom the Congress government of 1960-64 had tried to evict.

It is important to note that even in the absence of their communist leaders, peasants often revert to their traditional forms of joint action and resistance in crises. Two examples illustrate this point. In eastern Tanjore in late 1948, after the peasant revolt had been crushed, police arrived one day in a village to see that everything was under control. The Village Headman, a high caste landlord, summoned the elected headman of the Untouchable landless labourers' community. He intended to impress on the low caste headman the fact that the revolt was over and that the labourers should peacefully resume their tasks. On hearing the summons all the landless labourers of the village downed tools and marched to the landlords' street with the communist flag, fearing that their leader might be intimidated or beaten. When they saw the police trucks they angrily climbed into them, shouting that their lives were wretched and that they wished all to be taken to prison. In the ensuing melee the police drove off with thirty of them. They were sent to jail in Trichinopoly, some hundred miles away, and held without trial for four months. A deputation of local landlords eventually went to plead for their release so that the harvest work could go on. Labourers in this region continued with periodic strikes, stackburning, and even attacks on the homes of landlords until 1952, when their communist leaders were released from jail and the peasant unions were formally reconstituted. Under communist leadership the unions then pressed, through strikes and legal channels, for implementation of a newly enacted land regulation.[111]

In Kerala my Irava cook, who hailed from a British tea plantation, told of an incident in 1962. A woman in a nearby house in the plantation coolies' barracks began to give birth to a child and was taken to the plantation hospital. The surgeon refused to leave a movie he was attending and the nurses gave the woman injections to try to delay the birth and to ease her pain. She became unconscious and seemed at the point of death. The cook summoned one hundred of his street fellows and they marched to the cinema, dragged out the doctor, and forced him to return to the hospital, where he safely delivered the child. 'If you act thus again we shall kill you next time', they told him. This pattern of 'encirclement' or 'gherao' by groups of labourers of an official or landlord until he submits to their demands has recently spread throughout India and is currently a potent form of direct action.

In Kerala, as is well known, the Communist Party came to power in the state government in 1957 with 41 per cent of the vote. It was ousted by the Central Government in 1959 on grounds of inability to maintain law and order. Through its policies of land ceilings, minimum wages, rural debt cancellations, and welfare provisions, the Party increased its support among the poor tenants and the propertyless classes. Even while pursuing the parliamentary road, the communists deepened the class struggle, by encouraging the poor to put forward their claims. In the sixteen years of parliamentary struggle the communists have continued to help tenants and landless labourers by filing suits on their behalf, leading strikes and boycotts within the constitutional framework, and counselling them on their rights under the various land reform laws.

In 1964, Left and Right communists split on the fundamental question of approaches to the Congress Party. These were in turn, of course, linked with Rightist support of the Soviet Union, which gives aid to the Congress government and hopes for a peaceful transition to socialism. The Left communists (CPI-M) oppose Soviet revisionism and any compromise with the Congress Party, and give critical support to China. They foresee the possibility of armed revolution if the Indian government succumbs to American penetration and closes all avenues to constitutional and parliamentary struggle. At the same time, the CPI-M continues to participate in elections. In Kerala, the Right communists have rather weak support from the urban lower middle classes and the industrial unions; the Left communists have much stronger support from middle and poor peasants and from landless labourers in villages and export crop plantations. While bitterly opposing each others' ideology, the two parties have forced electoral or post-electoral alliances in a number of states.

Communist-led United Front governments came to power in Kerala and Bengal in the Indian elections of early 1967. The Bengal government was ousted by the Centre in the autumn of 1967 after defection from the Front of some individual non-communist legislators. In Kerala the Front remains in power but in deepening trouble because of food shortages. With over 40 per cent of its land under export crops, Kerala must import half its food. In the general food crisis in India the Central Government has failed to maintain supplies. Adults in Kerala consider twelve to seventeen ounces of rice per day an adequate diet. Under the present informal rationing scheme they receive only three ounces in ration shops and must obtain the remainder at prices which exceed the wages of landless labourers.

Meanwhile, further serious divisions of policy have appeared among Left Communists. In May 1967, a revolt broke out among sharecroppers and landless labourers in the mountainous district of Naxalbari in West Bengal. It arose because landlords refused to cede land taken from them by the government under the land ceiling laws, and sent police and armed bands against the cultivators when they tried to occupy the lands. Many of the cultivators were Santal tribes people who countered the landlords' attacks with bows and arrows. Plantation workers on nearby foreign tea plantations struck in sympathy. The revolt was led, or at least supported, by local Left Communists. It appears to have followed traditional patterns: expropriation of the land, driving out of the landlords, attempts to set up peasant soviets and to immobilize local government officials. One policeman and ten peasants were killed. The West Bengal Minister of Land and Land Revenue, a Left Communist, tried to bring about a compromise but it was foiled by police who continued to attack and by local Left Communists and peasants who continued to defend themselves. The revolt at one point affected some 42,000 people in 70 villages over an area of 80 square miles. It appears to have been temporarily put down by the police, although rebel Left Communists claim that a revolutionary framework has been maintained. The United Front government condemned the revolt as adventurist, and the Left Communist Party expelled the rebels.[112] The United Front Government was however, ousted by the Central Government in November, 1967.

The rebel policy has since triumphed in the Left Communist Party-plenum in Delhi, and spread to a number of Left communist district and village committees in Bengal, Orissa, Bihar, Punjab, Uttar Pradesh, Maharashtra, Andhra, Mysore, Madras, and Kerala.[113]

The rebel approach includes the following: the organization of peasant-based guerrilla warfare as the main path to revolution in India, with the assistance of the urban working class; rejection of parliamentary participation as revisionist; and an analysis of Indian society which sees the Congress Central Government as the captive of American imperialism, and India as already a neocolonial state. This last contrasts with the orthodox Left Communist view of India as under the class-rule of the landlords and the bourgeoisie, led by the big bourgeoisie which, so far, is only 'increasingly collaborating' with imperialism.[114]

The rebels accept the Left Communist distinction between a 'feudal' sector of the economy dominated by the landlords, an 'imperial' sector dominated by foreign monopoly capital with the assistance of an Indian comprador bourgeoisie, and a 'national capitalist' sector led by an independent national bourgeoisie, at least part of which is seen as a potential revolutionary ally. I would question such distinctions, arguing instead that the various sectors of the economy are fully integrated with one another in a colonial-style capitalism which is itself part of world capitalism and whose main features of underdevelopment derive from its satellite relationships with the metropolitan powers.[115] Correspondingly, it is questionable whether there is, or is any longer, a sizable independent national bourgeoisie in India, for the increasing penetration of the economy by American and European capital since the Second World War has co-opted to the imperialists' side virtually the whole Indian bourgeoisie, whether mercantile, farming, or industrial. This means that while private industry and trade would, as in China, probably need to be retained for some time after a revolution, no substantial section of the Indian bourgeoisie can realistically be relied upon as potential revolutionary allies at the present time.

The rebel analysis does, however, give greater weight to foreign penetration of the Indian economy than does the orthodox Left Communist nalysis. Thus the rebels, like the Chinese Communist Party, argue that substantial elements of the Indian industrial bourgeoisie are part of the comprador bourgeoisie as a result of American, British, and other foreign penetration of Indian industry.[116]

It seems probable that much of the rebel Left Communist analysis will appeal to poor peasants and landless labourers in Kerala. In 1964, I found on the one hand that support for the communists, especially the Left Communists, had become virtually universal among landless labourers and had increased among poor and middle peasants. This resulted from the deterioration of food supplies and real wages in these classes in the 1960s and from the communists' record of 1957-59. On the other hand, there was a growing impatience and a wish to return to the militant actions of the late 1930s and 1947. My fieldnotes abound in statements by poor peasants and labourers that nothing will solve Kerala's problems except armed revolt against the landlords and sharing of land among those who cultivate it. Similarly, workers on the foreign export crop estates insisted that programmes for improved wages and benefits were at best temporary. Eventually, they held, a communist government must expropriate the planters and either divide the land among the plantation workers or run it cooperatively for their benefit. These and similar sentiments were shared by many of the village level communists whom I interviewed. A number of them complained about what one communist called 'this confusing, treacherous period of bourgeois democracy'. Many admitted uneasiness over opportunistic electoral alliances and though that eventually the Left Communists would be forced by repression to abandon the constitutional road and to arm and organize the peasantry. With this background, I was not surprised to read that a majority in four out of nine district committees in Kerala tend to favour the 'rebel' path. Is the party-plenums in Kerala in January 1968 re-endorsed E.M.S. Namboodiripad's communist-led United Front government, but this unity is apparently precarious. The All-India Peasant Union President, A.K. Gopalan of North Kerala, has since called for intensive organization among peasants, especially landless labourers, recruitment of peasant and worker volunteer forces, and psychological preparation of the peasantry for a prolonged struggle against the landlords and the imperialists.

What conclusions can be drawn from this analysis? In Kerala and Tanjore, peasant revolts occurred frequently during British rule. These revolts appear to have been responses to increased exactions from poor and middle peasant brought about by colonial capitalist relations. When they achieved scope and intensity the revolts aimed at throwing off the authority of the state and of landlords, and at setting up a local government drawn from the peasantry.

When modern reform or radical parties have coordinated the peasants without constricting them, peasants have tended to follow the same pattern of overthrow of landlords, seizure of the land, and removal or neutralization of officials of the existing state. The difference has been that radical parties, especially the communists, have been able sometimes to link these revolts over wider areas and to infuse them with a revolutionary ideology and a new conception of the state.

In relatively traditional villages, peasants have readymade bases of organization in their caste assemblies, composed of the heads of households of one caste within each village or group of villages. These assemblies were traditionally organized for the settlement of internal disputes; in addition, the assembly of the dominant high ranking caste usually governed the village as a whole. During British rule, the assemblies of middle or low castes of tenants or laborers often provided a framework for revolt or resistance. The communists have appreciated the value of caste assemblies and, especially in Tanjore, have managed to unite the assemblies of several middle and low ranking castes in groups of villages to form labour unions capable of either organized revolt or constitutional agitation. Caste assemblies have their greatest strength and unity on large village estates where a majority of poor tenants or landless labourers fill the same role and are exposed to the same forms of oppression. Such assemblies are especially strong, egalitarian, internally democratic, and militant among Untouchable landless labourers. On foreign export crop plantations, in spite of caste, linguistic, religious, and kinship diversity, workers of the same street or barracks tend to form assemblies to settle their internal disputes along lines similar to their old caste assemblies. Such multi-caste, local assemblies also provide a ready basis for union organizing by leftwing parties.

Communist Party cadres operating in villages have come mainly from families of less successful landlords and rich peasants, from the children of priests and literati whose authority had been challenged by new bureaucratic and market-oriented institutions, and from such local and low-paid intellectual workers as school teachers and village clerks.

The communists were first able to recruit tenant cultivators of middle peasant rank into their peasant unions, and have hitherto tended to rely' on the village leadership of this class. In Kerala and Tanjore, middle peasants come mainly from the middle to high castes of Hindus, Christians, and Muslims. Their early responsiveness to socialist ideas can probably be attributed to various factors mentioned by Eric R. Wolf. These include their comparative literacy and knowledge of the wider society, their enjoyment of relatively greater security and autonomy than the poorest sharecropping tenants or landless laborers, yet their experience of uncertainty and of new kinds of exploitation in the market economy. In the agitations of the 1930s, as apparently during Malabar's 19th century peasant revolts, Kerala's middle peasants were able to organize large numbers of poor peasants to throw off some of the more traditional exactions of landlords. From about 1947, landless labourers were also, apparently for the first time, drawn into political struggles and organized into unions on a large scale. Difficulties exist because middle peasants themselves often exploit landless labourers. In many contexts, the interests of the two classes are opposed, and landlords have used every opportunity to keep them at enmity. In South India the extremely deep social and ritual barriers between middle or poor peasants of middle to low Hindu caste on the one hand, and those landless labourers who are of the lowest, Untouchable castes on the other, made the rapproachment between tenant and landless labourer peculiarly difficult. By the late 1950s, however, both in Kerala and Tanjore, the two were beginning to amalgamate within the same peasant unions and thus to reinforce each others' demands.

It is noteworthy, moreover, that the communists (and since 1964, 'the Left communists) have drawn their greatest support from states and districts where landless labourers are numerically most prominent, for example Bengal, Kerala, Andhra, and Tanjore. In Tanjore and Kerala, further, it is to my knowledge the landless labourers who, once they are aroused, most completely and consistently vote for the communists. In Tanjore, landless labourers, chiefly Untouchables, formed about one-third of the total population in 1952; their proportion has certainly increased since then. In Kerala, landless labourers and their families increased from 12.5 per cent of the total population in 1931 to 21.6 per cent in 1951.[117] This figure is much higher today, even excluding the hundreds of thousands of workers on foreign export-crop plantations. In Malabar (North Kerala), the proportion of landless labourers to the total agriculturally dependent population increased from 38 per cent in 1931 to 44 per cent in 1951 and 47 per cent in 1961. In contrast to Alavi, I would argue that the Indian communists have never accorded sufficient weight to the poor peasants and landless labourers in their organizational and revolutionary efforts. A change may, however, be underway among both rebel and orthodox Left Communists. In a recent speech to the All-India Left Communist Kisan Sabha (Peasant Association), A.K. Gopalan stated that agricultural labourers now form 25-40 per cent of the population in most of the states of India. Gopalan's conclusion seems warranted, namely, 'We have to make them (the landless labourers) the hub of our activity. Reluctance to take up their specific demands, fearing that this will drive the rich and middle peasant away from us, will have to be given up.'[118]

Over the past sixteen years, the communists' pursuit of the parliamentary path has allowed them to increase the numbers of their supporters in several states. At the same time, it has placed serious difficulties in the way of organizing peasants and workers 'from below'. Concern with canvassing for national, state, and village elections takes village communist workers away from day-to-day organizational work among the propertyless. It causes even village communists, let alone national leaders, to focus on budgetary problems, short-term reforms; and the arithmetic of seats and votes. As a result, they tend to neglect socialist education and the deeper political and ethical problems of class struggle. In one North Kerala village, for example, a Left Communist Party member and panchayat president admitted to me that his task had become difficult because of electioneering. Between elections he tried to persuade Muslim poor peasants that the Communist Party had more to offer them than the non-socialist Muslim League. In the 1963 panchayat elections, however, the communists supported a number of League candidates, as the Left communists did later in the state elections of 1965 and 1967. In such ways, the policy of "unity from above" through electoral alliances and adjustments with nonrevolutionary social democratic-or non-socialist ethnic parties seriously damages the potential for class unity, with clear ideological direction, from below. It makes many peasants cynical about the sincerity of communist analyses of class struggle and suspicious that the communists, after all, are interested less in revolution than in power. When communists have actually attained power at the state level, as in Kerala in 1957-59 and, in 1967, their efforts to protect and to redistribute benefits to the poorest classes have brought them the gratitude of poor and middle peasants, landless labourers, and urban workers. These efforts are, however, too meagre to make a substantial difference. Confined within the provisions of the Indian constitution, it is impossible for the communists to transform property relations, allocate resources, and plan production. This means that they can compensate the propertyless only at the expense of the petty bourgeoisie, the rich peasants, and even some of the middle peasants, without increasing production. Further, their welfare-state efforts foster dependency and helplessness rather than active self-organization among the common people.

Meanwhile, during the last sixteen years, India's socio-economy has changed so that its problems are not the same as those of 1952. Although they have not given land to the tiller, the Congress Party's land reforms have changed relations in the countryside. As A.G. Frank suggests for Brazil, there seems to be some likelihood that social democratic land reforms can actually help to polarize property relations with regard to land. The upgrading of superior tenures and the guarantee of security of tenure mean that a small proportion of middle and rich peasants improve their position. With inflation such as has occurred in Kerala in recent years, however, many more peasants have to sell out to usurers, landlords, merchants, or bureaucrats to keep their families alive. Again, landlords manage to evict large numbers of poor peasants and turn them into wage labourers before land reform laws come into effect, in order not to lose control of their land to their tenants. Similarly, measures to get rid of non-cultivating middle-tenants and rent-collecting landlords both produce a higher proportion of landlords and rich peasants farming with hired labour. The fact that most export crops are exempt from land-ceiling means, finally, that in an export-crop producing region like Kerala, an increasing proportion of the land is turned over to cashewnuts, rubber etc. The swelling numbers of poor tenants and landless labourers are thus left stranded, are crowded on to ever smaller plots, or are forced into squatting on forest lands, where they must fight an uneven battle against landlords, plantation managers, and government. Finally, the failure to industrialize with sufficient rapidity means that an increasing proportion of the population becomes dependent on agriculture and that landless labourers become the largest section of these.[119]

These conclusions are amply borne out in the North Malabar village that I surveyed in 1948 and 1964. In spite of all the land-reform acts that have been passed in Kerala, the biggest landowning Nayar matrilineage has increased its share of the ownership of the total village lands from 31.5 per cent in 1948 to 44.6 per cent in 1964. Its holdings in this village now form part of a total estate of about 30 square miles. In the same village, 21.9 per cent of the land has remained in the ownership of a Hindu temple located some ten miles away and managed by a small number of wealthy high caste Hindu families. The remaining 33.5 per cent of the village land was, by 1964, divided between 206 other owners of middle and poor peasant rank. The total acreage of the village was 1,351 acres, and the population had increased from 1,176 in 1949 to 1,478 in 1964.

Among the villagers, the percentage of landlords and rich peasants had dropped from 4.3 per cent in 1948 to 2.6 per cent in 1964. The proportion of middle peasants, together with persons of middle peasant rank who retained a little land and ran some other occupation, had fallen from 23.6 per cent to 9.2 per cent of the total. This meant that in 1964 only 11.8 per cent of the villagers owned or leased enough land to maintain themselves and their families, while 27.9 per cent could maintain themselves from their lands in 1948.

Coming to the poor peasants and landless labourers, we find in this village that poor peasants, that is, persons who lease or own one substantial garden for their own use but hire themselves out as labourers for at least half of each day when they can, formed 36.7 per cent of the villagers in 1964, as against 41.7 per cent in 1948. This does not mean that some poor peasants have risen in wealth since 1948. It means, rather, that while the poor peasants category has received some new people from the former middle peasant rank, a larger number of poor peasants have completely lost their land since 1948 and have become landless labourers. Such people lease no land and own only a small shack together with the use-right of one-tenth of an acre of garden on their landlord's property. Even this latter privilege they owe to the communist government of 1957 -59 and they are not always accorded it in practice. In all, 29.3 per cent of villagers were landless labourers in 1948,51 per cent were landless labourers in 1964.

Increasing polarization between agricultural classes knocks out the middle peasants as a significant social category. It breaks down the barriers between poor peasants and landless labourers, and, among these classes, between "clean" castes, 'backward' castes, and Harijans. There are definite signs that increasing polarization of agrarian relations also breaks down religious barriers between Hindus, Muslims, and Christians among the propertyless in villages. The prolonged food shortage and the ever growing inflation in Kerala of the last five years have brought these rural classes, and their urban counterparts, to a pitch of anger and militancy in which they take action independently along traditional lines or along lines laid down by their Marxist leaders of the 1930s and 1940s. Strikes, 'encirclements' of cabinet ministers and government officials, attacks on transport and food stores, and threats or assaults against landlords and plantation managers have become common, and a fairly large revolt occurred on the Munnar tea plantation in Travancore in January and February, 1968. Incipient revolt among the peasants in turn produces counter-attacks by the landlords, usurers, and big merchants, poses problems of "law and order" for the United Front Government, and brings on the threat of intervention from the Central Government.

The precise details of ideological and policy crises within the Left Communist Party and between the Party and its expelled rebels cannot be fully assessed by observers from the outside. In the past few months, however, communist leaders in Kerala while officially endorsing the United Front Government, have formed volunteer corps among the peasants and urban workers to carry out public works projects and to fend off violent attacks. With Indonesia, 1966, as an object lesson, it is possible that these measures are being taken none too soon.

Indian Peasant's Struggles and Achievements

War of Independence

In all the areas in which the first war of Indian Independence was in progress (1857-60) peasants played quite a heroic part, suffered terribly, displayed great military skill, prowess and achieved victories. But they were made to pay bitterly for their display of patriotism. To this day, the peasants of Meerut Division pay certain *abwabs* which were then levied as punitive imposts for their participation in that revolution.

During that struggle, large numbers of peasants threw themselves valiantly into the fray with such abandon that they did not mind leaving their holdings in the care of their landlords. So many of them forgot the wrongs done to them by their landlords and made common cause with them in fighting for freedom. But alas, when later the British had triumphed, their lands were treated as the property of the Zamindars since the latter were found in actual control and they were reduced from the status of proprietors to that of tenants-at-will of their own former lands; so heavy were their sacrifices. And the Zamindars had no scruples in grabbing their lands so unjustly.

Unfortunately, they could not rise beyond the limitations of their feudal environment and hence were reduced to dust before the British arms. And as yet, they had not developed the political aspect of their cultural and traditional conception of unity of the whole of India nor could they anticipate the later twentieth century idea of achievement of a nation-wide organization, consciousness and unified patriotic endeavour.

We can understand the magnitude of the sacrifice offered by peasants in that struggle when we remember from what a high state of customary rights, individual and collective, Indian peasants fell by deciding to join the war against the British. They had been members of village communities which, according to Elphinstone, contained 'in miniature all the materials of a State within themselves and are sufficient to protect their members if all other Governments were withdrawn'.

That the lands were recognized even by the Mughals to be the property of kisans is proved by the fact that Akbar and Aurangzeb had to purchase lands from cultivators.

Todar Mal's revenue settlement conducted under the order of Akbar was made with individual peasants and not with any of the Zamindars or even the headmen of a village. No wonder Holt Mackenzie grew eloquent over the permanence of the rights of these peasants. He observed 'the village Zamindars. . . were the immemorial occupants of the soil. . . . They sold, and mortgaged their lands at will. They may have been bound in some cases to a lower class of cultivators, who had by distinct engagements or long usage acquired the right of occupancy so long as they paid the customary rent . . . . Nothing but violence appears to have disturbed the tenure of the village Zamindars; neither the exile nor the longest absence, dissolved the tie that bound them to the fields of their ancestors, nor destroyed their right to resume possession when they returned.'

The British came to upset all this. Their early administrators recognised the Taluqdars as the prototypes of English landlords to subserve their political ends. But when they found that these Taluqdars were also undependable, Lord Dalhousie decreed that 'the settlement should be made village by village with the parties actually in possession but without any recognition, either formal or indirect, of their proprietory right so as to deal with the actual occupants of the soil'.

Thus, the U.P. peasants were being re-instated in their traditional rights and holdings by the British who were losing faith in the so-called landed aristocracy, as a political stabilising force. Lord Canning who was no friend of the peasants had to confess that 'as a question of justice the lands and villages taken from the Talooqdars had, for the most part, been usurped by them through fraud and violence.'

Naturally the British expected gratitude from those U.P. kisans. They hoped that the kisans who were being helped to get back to their lands from which they had been forcibly ejected by the Taluqdars would betray the national cause and side with them, the new beneficent rulers.

Lord Canning observed in 1858 that 'it might have been expected that, when insurrection first arose in Oudh. . . the village occupants who had been so highly favoured by the British Government and injustice to whom it had initiated a policy distasteful to the most powerful class in the province, would have come forward in support of the Government who had endeavoured to restore them to their hereditary rights and with whose interests their interests were identical. Such, however, was not the case. So far as I am informed, not an individual dared to be loyal to the Government which had befriended him.'

On the other hand, lakhs of peasants made common cause with that war of independence. The British naturally decided that 'the lands of men who have taken an active part against us should be largely confiscated in order, among other reasons, to enable us to reward others.' The Governor-General proclaims to the people of Oudh that... the proprietory right in the soil of the province is confiscated to the British Government which will dispose of that right in such manner as to it may seem fitting.'

The consequence was that the great class of kisans fell, the Taluqdars who were the usurpers and adventurers, rose and within the course of a year, the kisans' 'rights had ceased to exist or were reduced to a mere shadow; they were completely in the power of the Taluqdars and were 'subject to every kind of oppression, tyranny and exaction.'

Such was the bitter price paid by kisans for having made common cause with Taluqdars in that first war of independence and such indeed was the reward reaped by the faithless Taluqdars for their rebellion against the British and their eventual submission to the foreign rulers. Is this net typical of what happened in England after Cromwell's yeomen's revolution, in the U.S.A. after the attainment of independence and in the U.S.S.R. after the 1917 revolution and 1920-21 counter-revolution? Wherever and whenever peasants have gone into any revolution without their own leadership, ideological stand and definite political objectives but under the leadership of other classes, they have uniformly been cheated of the fruits of revolution or been the worst victims of the failure of a revolution.

Santhals' Revolution

Later came the 1855-73 Santhal and Bengal revolts, this time not only against the British Raj as such but also against the Zamindars who were invested with unjustified and undreamt of powers of ownership of land that peasants had customarily considered and cultivated for millenniums as their own and also against moneylenders who were given powers to get peasants imprisoned for failure to repay their debts and against the autocracy of officials. The Santhals never thought that they could be evicted from their ancestral homesteads, holdings and forests for failure to pay taxes and debts but that had come to happen.

The self-respecting, proud, if unorganized, Indian peasant never could reconcile himself to the preposterous right conferred by the British Government on the Zamindar to distrain his properties, including his draught cattle, grain crops and that too came to be the order of the day. So he rose in revolt against that unjust order of the day, imposed upon them by British imperialism through the convenient media of its allies, the Indian Zamindars and moneylenders.

The peasants 'banded themselves (especially in Patna District) to resist short measures; illegal cesses, and forced deliveries of agreement (one-sided) to pay enhanced rents.' And also 'there had been combination of Raiyats (peasants) in East Bengal, refusing to payments except what they considered just.'

The Santhals found their leaders in two brothers who claimed to have received some occult blessings from the gods to put an end to the *zhulum* of officers and to the deceit of merchants. As many as 35,000 Santhals formed their bodyguard. They armed themselves with their traditional weapons of bows, arrows, axes and swords. They began to march to Calcutta to place their petition before the Governor to free them from their oppressors. But one Government Inspector obstructed their march and provoked them on 7-7-1855 into violence. Thus had commenced their rebellion and their resultant massacre at the hands of the British. The British officers who had been smitten with remorse later confessed that 'it was not war, it was execution; we had orders to go out whenever we saw the smoke of a village rising about the jungle. The Magistrate used to go with us. . . I surrounded the village with my sepoys and the Magistrate called upon the rebels to surrender.' To such an unjust and peremptory order, the brave Santhals knew only one answer to give. That was defiance. There upon they were brutally fired upon and butchered *en masse*.

The Santhals displayed such exceptional courage and military discipline that they faced successive vollies of British bullets with reckless heroism and abandon.

Government had however to yield to these peasants, despite its gratitude to the Bengal Zamindars for their treacherous betrayal of the War of Independence and pass the Bengal Tenancy Act which had come to re-establish the lost permanency of tenure and fixity of feudal exactions.

Mahratta Peasant Awakening

With equal fury and fervour rose the Mahratta peasants in the same generation, against the oppressions of moneylenders. They could not brook the idea of obedience to the new laws which gave such coercive powers to moneylenders that any moneylender could with impunity move a court to imprison anyone of his peasant debtors. So they revolted, burnt down the houses, destroyed other properties of moneylenders, killed a good many such oppressors and even attacked those Government officials who were supporting their oppressors.

Bombay Peasants' Revolts in 1871-75

These revolts were not well planned, nor were they widespread. They took place haphazardly and in many districts like Kaira, Ahmednagar, Poona, all unconnected with each other. The peasants aimed their blows not on Government, but on moneylenders and even when whole villages were in revolt, great care was taken not to harm anyone else but Marwari moneylenders. Generally 'object of the rioters was to obtain and destroy the bonds, decrees, etc., in the possession of their creditors; when these were peaceably given up to the assembled mob there was usually nothing further done. When the moneylender refused or shut himself up, violence was used to frighten him into surrender or to get possession of the papers'.

Again the might of British Raj came down on them and suppressed their risings. Yet it had to yield and redress their grievances as least in part. Hence the passing of the Deccan Agriculturists' Relief Act, whereby an exception was made for the Mahratta peasants from the operations of the Civil Procedure Code in that they could not be imprisoned for failure to repay debts—a great concession indeed.

Punjab Discontent

Similarly, the Punjab peasants too agitated and threatened to revolt to prevent the rapid alienation of their lands to the urban moneylenders for failure to repay debts. The British Government could not await a similar rebellion as had taken place in Bengal and Maharashtra since the armed and martial Sikhs might make a formidable enemy. So it hastened to pass the Punjab Land Alienation Act to prevent the alienation of peasants' lands to non-agricultural sections.

South India in Ferment

Similarly, the Krishna and Godavari Deltaic peasants and the Karnataka and Rayalaseema peasants too revolted several times from the beginning of the 19th century to protest against the exorbitant land revenue exactions, the neglect of irrigation facilities and the extortionate method of tax collections. G. Lakshminarasu Chetti organized a grand constitutional agitation against the Madras Tortures Act and succeeded in getting it repealed and this saved the South Indian peasants from being put to several cruel and inhuman tortures for failure to pay taxes. The South Indian peasants resorted to their ancestral method of *satyagraha* by abandoning their lands and villages (a method of satyagraha adopted by the Lohara peasants in 1936, and by those of the Orissa States in 1939 with much less success) and migrating to the neighbouring Indian States or even British districts. Since peasant solidarity was so great in those days and also since the cultivation of land under the then prevailing tax burdens was such an unwelcome task none would go and occupy their lands and houses and Government had to climb down and agree to a reduction of their tax burdens in order to persuade them to return to their lands and villages.

Contribution of the Indian National Congress

With the beginning of the 20th century, the Indian National Congress began to champion the cause of the oppressed peasants. It imported a political significance—common cause with the nation-wide freedom movement and anti-imperialist bias—into every one of the struggles that peasants have had to wage in order to free themselves from new imperialist impositions and machinations. Thus country-wide campaigns were organised with nationalism as their dynamo and economic pressure as their propellers against the vicious indenture labour system, contract labour in plantations, exploitation by European planters in India and other parts of the British Empire. Now that political consciousness and organisation were added to economic grievances, success began to dawn on the horizon of Indian peasants. The indenture system was abolished and some relief was got for plantation labour. A large number of risings took place in

Malabar both in the last and present centuries. They were misnamed communal riots and their basic causes, the political and economic grievances of peasants against the local landlords were not sought to be removed. Of course, there was always the tendency for communal leaders to exploit these basic factors. But thanks to the sacrifices made by the Mopilla (Moslem) peasants, the Madras Government had had to pass the Malabar Tenancy Act which conferred permanency of tenancy upon a very large section of peasantry.

Gandhiji and Peasant Satyagraha

An entirely new dynamic and political revolutionary tendency has come to be imported into peasant struggles by Mahatma Gandhi since his advent on the Indian politico-economic theatre in 1916. He familiarised the peasants of Champaran in Bihar and Kaira in Gujarat with his new weapon of Satyagraha, an open, non-violent, organised, politically alive revolt against injustice—in their struggles against the indigo planters and land revenue collectors respectively. He introduced the technique of first enquiring into the essential facts of the peasants' grievances, then formulating their demands, educating them as to the nature and magnitude of their needs and immediate demands, training them in the art of internal self-sufficiency pointing out the need for economy in case of a prolonged struggle against the authorities and steeling their mind to the rig ours to jails, and other harassments of imperialism. He would convince the peasants that the satisfaction of their carefully moderated minimum demands was most urgently called for by Dhanna or social justice, and that it would be their sacred duty to force the authorities to perform their Dharma towards them. The injection of this inspiring and ennobling conception of serving Dharma by revolting against injustice and by seeking redress for their own grievances, would steel the determination and fighting morale of the peasants. As the champions of Dhanna, peasants would go ahead, to face all their enemies without fear and with perfect confidence in their own cause and in their duty to and capacity for teaching their opponents how to conform to Dhanna. As Calvin strengthened the bourgeoisie by his casuistry proving that they were helping society by helping themselves; as Marx put new life into the proletariat by demonstrating that they were the heirs of capitalism, chosen by Dame History, so Mahatma Gandhi invested the peasants as well as the colonial peoples with the saintly staff of satyagraha to achieve the protection to Dhanna for themselves and to oblige their opponents to conform to Dhanna and thus save humanity from injustice.

Bardoli Satyagraha

With the blessings of Mahatma Gandhi, his greatest kisan disciple, Vallabhbhai Patel organised and led the Bardoli peasants against the resettlement enhancements proposed by Government. Under his inspiring guidance, peasants braved all risks, faced with courage the loss of their beloved cattle and ancestral lands and even risked eviction from their villages. At last, they triumphed over the Government. That was in 1929.

Again in 1930, when Mahatmaji gave this call to the people to rise against Imperialism to achieve national independence, the Bardoli peasants rose to a man, refused to pay taxes, faced the auction sales and eventual loss of almost all their lands and refused to have any truck with Government. Such was the marvellous strength of their political revolt led by their great Sardar. When the Congress was in Ministry in 1937-39 the loyal Sardar saw to it that all their lands were returned. Thus did our peasants gain their initiation in both economic and political Satyagraha.

Vizag Revolution and Raju's Leadership

The Vizag Agency tribes waged a two-year war against British imperialism with the help of an extraordinary revolutionary leader Sitarama Raju. They made the fullest military use of the strategic advantages of the hills and valleys and impassable gorges and their own special knowledge of the terrain. They were strictly nonviolent. They made full use of their traditional weapons. But strangely enough, they pursued the Hindu Dharmic way of liberating their enemies, once they fell into their hands and asked for excuse, with the result that their secret dens came to be known and their ways of organisation understood by their enemy.

What did they fight for? At first they started asking for free use of the forest lands and produce. Rapidly their demands went up and they wanted to establish Swaraj for the whole of the Agency area, if not for the whole of India.

The tragedy of it all was that their struggle came off a year after the great Non-co-operation Movement (1920-22) was over and when nationalist India was just recovering from the shock of reaction. The British Government was very cruel towards those brave tribal people. It used all the modem weapons and killed thousands of those unfortunate Koya and Savara people.

Great trouble set in upon these people after their noble and resourceful leader Raju was killed. Most of their other leaders were killed, several others were sent to jail and great reprisals were hurled upon the masses. Yet the spirit of resistance of these hill tribes did not die. It only awaited another inspired leader and a suitable opportunity. This became clear in the August 1942 Revolution when again these people gave a fine account of their anti-imperialist spirit.

But owing to the special attention paid by the police to this area and its people, even such Congress constructive work as hand-spinning was not allowed. Government encouraged the local Muthadars or village tribal chiefs to tyrannise over the people and thus destroy their will to revolt. Despite all such repression, Congress-men like P. Kodandaramayya and R.M. Sarma had been doing yeoman service to these people. As a result of their work, the Gothi system by which the hill tribes were kept down as hereditary servants (bordering on slavery) of those Muthadars and others who advanced small sums of money to these ignorant and helpless people either for marriage or for drink has come to be abolished since 1940. Yet so many of these people are even now unable to take advantage of it. Secondly, the last Congress ministry has declared their lands inalienable. But during the war, the Advisers' regime again had allowed alienation of their lands subject to the Collector's permission.

The present Congress Ministry is trying to help these tribal peoples. The All-India Adibasis and Excluded Areas Association was founded in 1936. It has now become a powerful organisation developing the political consciousness of these 20 million Adibasis in our country.

Satyagraha Struggle between 1921-30

Ever since the Non-cooperation Movement a number of Satyagraha campaigns have come to be organised against so many unjust laws and imposts; such struggles as those of Bardoli and Pedanandipadu and Duddukuru in 1921 against the land tax; the struggles against Karnataka forest laws in 1921 and 1931-34; the rent exactions in U.P. and Bihar in 1921 and 1931-33; the antiresettlement campaigns of Godavari and Kistna Deltas and a number of peasant struggles against landlords of Venkatagiri (1931) Tsadumu and Munagala (1939) were organised in the South by some of us. There were also the Land Satyagraha in Bihar (1939), the anti-Zamindari fight in Bengal, and Andhra, and Canal Duties struggle of the Punjab and Bengal (1939), the Jute Prices Struggle (1937-42), and the Debt Relief Agitation of Bengal. All these campaigns shared the same new features.

Aboriginal Kisans

There are more than 200 lakhs of aboriginal kisans in India. The Santhal rebellion of the last century and the Koya revolt of the thirties of this century and the recent agitation among the Bhils of Dahanu, the tribes of Mymensingh, and Mayurbhanj have shown that these aboriginal tribes too have in them the irrepressible spirit of revolt that can shake up modern capitalist hegemony to its very roots.

The pity is that the Santhal tribal people are not fully aware of their legal rights accruing from the Chota Nagpur Tenancy Act. 'Even were they aware of it, not one in a thousand would have the means and the courage to risk the Rajah's displeasure by having recourse to the law. Hence, Rajahs and landlords ruthlessly exploit this helplessness of the ryots' observed Rev. Kanjiya in 1946. (*Modern Review).*

These Santhals are losing their lands to the plainsmen, whether they be moneylenders, landlords or touts. Many are the causes for this. The following are mentioned by Mr Ece Mculder in his article in the *New Review* of February 1947.

(i) Rent suits and executions, (ii) loans, (iii) surrender by fraud, (iv) wilfully defective settlement, (v) *zhulum* and brute force of landlords, officials, etc., (vi) illegal mutilation of kisans' names on landlords' registers, (vii) misunderstanding of the tribal peoples' rights by the courts, (viii) starting pen shops on aboriginal land and then quietly or suddenly rebuilding these shops into pucca buildings, (ix) covering aboriginal areas with grogshops, instead of providing wells, tanks and other forms of irrigation, (x) the threat of leasing out forest and grazing lands to companies of financiers, bankers or landlords.

As a result of the growing but forced landlessness of kisans caused by the above methods pursued by moneylenders, landlords and corrupt officials, the area of *bakhast* lands is increasing almost in every tribal village, on which the landlord comes to have the right to settle new kisans.

These complaints are to be met with in every tribal area all over India. I conducted enquiries into the conditions of tribes in Hyderabad in

1927 and in Nilgiris in 1929 and in the Andhra hills in 1931-33 and again in 1936; everywhere the same vicious economic forces were found to be at work to deprive the tribal kisans of their rights.

To relieve their social and economic distress and win for them the same political freedom and status as was being granted to the other peoples of India, there was founded in 1936, the All-India Excluded Area and Tribal Peoples' Association and Sri P. Kodandaramayya has been its soul ever since. A number of provincial conferences also have been held. The Provincial Congress Ministries, notably of Orissa, Bombay, and Assam have been trying to improve educational facilities for these tribal peoples. A few co-operative societies too have been formed. But because we have not yet succeeded in grafting our new organisations on to the traditional love of their own martyrs and heroes who had fought for their freedom and their tribal democratic organisations, as apart from their so-called Rajahs or Chiefs or Muthadars, our modern organisations have as yet remained largely beyond the affections and reach of their masses.

Recently, we have put ourselves in touch with the natural leaders of some of these tribes, such as Samant, Jaipal Singh, Nichols Roy and with the Tribal or Adibasi organisations they have been building up and we trust that very soon these tribal peoples too will be able to march hand in hand with all other sections in our revolutionary attempts to achieve Kisan Mazdoor Praja Raj.

We are encouraged in this hope by our recent discoveries of the revolutionary traditions, legends and ballads that some of these tribal people have built up. For instance, the Manipuri kisan women became so adept in the modern intricacies of markets for their agricultural produce that when the merchants and consumers of Manipur refused to pay them reasonable prices, they organised and went on a strike. For weeks, they maintained their strike and saw to it that there were no black legs. In the end, the Manipuri merchants had to accept the demands of those worldly-wise tribal women.

Secondly, when I visited Akola in 1945, and again Udaipur in 1946, I came across the inspiring dance recital of a Bhil kisan cum tribal revolt against their Jaipur and Udaipur Maharanas. According to this recital, which, by the way, is based upon a popular ballad woven by the Bhil poets several centuries ago, the Maharana heaped so many taxes on the Bhils, oppressed them so much and in the end his officers violated their hearths and the modesty of their women, that they rose against his oppression.

Their leader, Ram Gopal, organized them for an armed rebellion. For weeks, a guerilla fight went on between the State troops and the Bhils. In the end, their leaders were killed, many of their ranks too fell on the battlefields and out of disgust they left the State in a mass exodus. But after a time, the son of the Maharaja, when he came to the gadi, repented for the sins of his father and begged the Bhils to return to the State.

This legend is woven into such a powerful and eloquent ballad and it is sung, to the tune of a mass dance which inspires the Bhils even today into such crescendoes of emotion, anger and abandon that one can easily get an idea of the passionate mass movement their rebellion must have been in its own day.

The Adibasis who could organize such a movement and who could perform such heroic deeds in an organized manner not only in the Bhil area under their own Bhil leadership, and in the far distant Manipuri under the leadership of their women but also under the inspiration of an outsider like Sitarama Raju on Koraput hills of the Andhra can be expected to take once again their place in the vanguard of our present-day revolutionary struggle for the democratic Kisan Mazdoor Praja Raj.

Indian States Peasants Rebel

Between 1937-46, the peasants of a number of Indian States were in revolt against their horrible conditions of life, which were not in any way different from the intolerable conditions, prevalent in the days of Charlemagne, as described in the chapter on 'The Peasant Bodo,' in medieval Europe by Eileen Power.

The following few quotations from her book on Bodo's life will give us a realistic picture of a part of the misery of the Indian peasants in almost all our Indian States and also in a number of Zamindaris of British India.

'Every year each man was bound to do a fixed amount of ploughing on the domain land and also to give-Carvee-an unfixed amount of ploughing every week when it was needed.'

In addition, there was 'handwork-he had to help repair building or cut down trees or gather fruits or make ale or carry loads. It was by these services that the monks got their own seigniorial farm cultivated.' . .... (p. 16).

The farmers 'had to carry a load of wood to the big house (of the landlord) in return for being allowed to gather firewood in the woods; they had to pay some hogsheads of wine for the right to pasture their pigs in the same precious woods; every third year, they had to give up one of their sheep for the right to graze upon the fields of the chief. Every farmer had also to pay other rents in produce; every year he owed the big house three chickens and fifteen eggs and a large number of planks to repair its buildings; often he had to give it a couple of pigs; sometimes corn, wine, honey, wax, soap or oil. Even the wives of the farmers were kept busy, if they happened to be serfs; for the servile women were obliged to spin cloth or to make a garment for the big house every year.' .... (pp. 16, 17).

The sufferings of the peasants in the Indian States were even more intolerable and they have had to bear the burden of the continually accumulating illegal *abwabs* or imposts. Their feudalism has inherited all the evils of the Mughal empire and had been maintained by British arms and the Indian princes!

Against this terrible order, Indian peasants began to protest. At first the Loharu, Patiala and Nabha peasants revolted. They organized a 'Farm Strike', abandoned their villages and ran into the neighbouring forests. The States sent out their armed police and military on horse-back, to hunt the peasants as it were, and force them to go back to their villages and cultivate their lands. After some fight, the peasants gave up their Satyagraha. There came the prolonged Mansa Peasants' Satyagraha for rent reductions. Partial success came their way after a three month struggle.

The Mysore and Travancore State peoples waged their statewide struggles for responsible governments. Many were the atrocities committed by the governments. Hundreds of peasants and workers died in those shooting outrages. Only a few political concessions were made and the feudal dues were reduced.

The struggle then spread to the Orissa States. For a while some of the princes fled their states, so furious and all-enveloping were the peasants' revolts, and so helpless were their local police and military forces. The princes hastened to promise to abolish a number of feudal dues, such as forest fees, free supply of fuel, wood, grass, forced labour and supply of animals. Rents too were offered to be reduced. Soon the British forces went to their rescue and the former concessions were mostly withdrawn. Thereupon, the peasants again rebelled, and marched on the princes' capitals and demanded various economic and political concessions. But the British military fired on them, killed large numbers and suppressed their risings. Cruel reprisals were thereafter instituted by the princes. I had an occasion to see large numbers of peasants who fell victims to those barbarities and they were such as to bring shame upon the princes and their protectors, the British. Women were raped, young boys were whipped on their tender parts, peasants were immersed for many moments in rivers, houses and villages were burnt down and grain was looted and cattle confiscated.

Unable to bear these indignities, more than 30,000 peasants left their villages in a number of States including Nilgiris, Dhenkenal, and marched into the neighbouring forests of Orissa Province; built small huts out of the forest leaves and branches and lived in those improvised camps for many months. At long last, the States had to agree not to resort to any reprisals or indulge in incendiarism or looting and also to abandon their demands for forced labour and some of its more oppressive forms before those peasants could be persuaded to return to their villages.

I visited their camps and interviewed their men, women and leaders. It was an eye-opener to us. Those camps were perfectly orderly. They were built according to the traditional village planning of our peasants. They were ruled by their peasant panchayats. A number of their leaders were women—old and bold. They displayed their inherent qualities of leadership, organisation, discipline and unity. Under the stress of that revolution, their traditional caste distinctions were gone and untouchability was abolished and they learnt to live as one united equalitarian society.

In the wake of these revolutions, rose the peasants of a number of Maharashtra and Karnatak States. They too achieved a number of triumphs and concessions.

Then rose the Jaipur, Gwalior and Udaipur peasants against their local Thakors and other feudal lords. They made use of the internal quarrels and contradictions between the States, princes and the Thakors of Jaipur. They were led by the late Jamnalal Bajaj, a merchant prince and a great follower of Mahatma Gandhi. They achieved victory on their economic front. The Udaipur revolt was put down cruelly. But forced labour had to be abandoned.

During the latter half of 1946, the Hyderabad peasants have risen against their local feudal chiefs, the Deshmukhs. The Communists and Congressmen provided the requisite leadership. But as it is always the case with Communists, they tried to elbow out the Congressmen and achieve a 'closed shop' for their organisation, with the result that the ranks of the peasants were split and a large section of the middle classes and merchants were forced to join hands with the State authorities in order to save themselves from Communist repression.

The State authorities and their local feudal and other allies perpetrated many horrors on the Warangal, Nalgonda and Bidar peasants. Lootings, rapings, incendiarism and murders of peasants became the order of the day. It was after the States' Peoples' Organisation and the Andhra Congress had begun to champion the cause of these peasant sufferers, that the State has called a halt to its campaign of repression. But this freedom from the feudal lords of the States is being won at great cost by States peasants. All over the Rajasthan States, peasants have had to struggle hard for months after August 1947 to get rid of forced labour, *abwabs* and eventually the Jagirdari or Thakurdari systems.

The sufferings of Hyderabad peasants were of a sterner type. Owing to the intransigence of the Nizam and his ministry, the States people had to offer heroic resistance to the Nazi terrorism of Razakars, a gang of power-mad Moslems. The tribal people, known as Koyas of Palvancha Taluk, the kisans of Nalgonda, Warangal, Mahaboobnagar districts struggled heroically against the State's campaign of violence and repression. The Koyas offered many pitched battles in their mountain fastnesses on the banks of the Godavari.

Fortunately, the statesmanship and strong 'Police Action' organised by Sardar Patel, the hero of Bardoli peasant Satyagraha of 1928, forced the Nizam to surrender. With his fall has come down the Razakar terror and the power of the landlords.

The liberation of practically the whole princely order and the consequent liberation of 70 million States peoples and their attainment of democratic government is the biggest and most romantic achievement of post-partition India and it is significant that it has been achieved by Sardar Patel, the kisan statesman. The Indian States' peasant masses have been in the vanguard of the States' peoples fight for economic and political freedom and thanks to the attainment of freedom by India on 15th of August 1947 and the statesmanship and revolutionary capacity of Sardar Vallabhbhai Patel, the States peoples have also attained control of the government and the feudalism of the zamindari and jagirdari orders is being liquidated

Veera Gunnamma

An indomitable spirit of revolt and Satyagraha was displayed by Veera Gunnamma of Mandasa. On the 31st March 1940, even as I was being interned and imprisoned by the Madras Government, the local police and Magistrate were arresting seven of the local peasant leaders of Mandasa on very flimsy grounds. The gathering of peasants consisted of more women than men, since the village was stormed by surprise while men were at work in the field. The women protested against the unjust arrests. The police insulted them. Gunnamma roundly abused them for their behaviour. They fired on her. She sprung upon them like a lioness. She was being shot at and she continued to vigorously protest against that police brigandage and injustice until she was felled by the sixth gunshot wound. Today the Vizagapatam peasants cherish the memory of this great heroine, who, unarmed as she was, put to shame, without flinching under the fusillade of shots tearing at her body, the whole beastly might of British Imperialism. When on the Istof September 1941, Bharatidevi, the peasants' president was offering to Gunnamma's memory at her grave, the highest honours due to a peasant martyr, there was a gathering of one hundred thousand peasants. Peasants have learnt how to die nobly and heroically and also how to honour their martyrs. It is in the fitness of things that a woman, Gunnamma should preside over their growing lists of martyrs.

Even in the realm of practical politics, peasants have achieved quite a lot. Between 1937-40, a number of Provincial Governments had to declare moratoria for rural debts, scale down debt burdens improve the rights of Zamindari tenants, reduce rents and land revenue burdens for all peasants and grant educational and cultural facilities for landless Harijans and prohibit the alienation of the lands of the aboriginal peasantry and so on.

August Revolution and Peasants

During the 1942 August Revolution, it was the Indian peasant who played the most heroic, dynamic and effective role. Students and urban middle classes too contributed much. But peasants excelled themselves. They rose spontaneously and simultaneously, as if by design and upset the means of transport of the British war machine. Police stations and other local officers of Government were captured. Wherever they succeeded in overcoming the local governmental forces and agencies, they proceeded to establish their panchayats and in several areas in United Provinces, Bihar,

Bengal, Maharashtra and Tamilnad, they established their rival Governments. The most famous achievements were witnessed in Midnapore and Satara Districts where for years, the British were unable or regain their control over whole regions consisting of the masses of peasants.

Thus the 20th century and post-August revolutionary peasants have shown that they are bent upon achieving political power and that they are no longer content with mere looting and occasional displays of their discontent and fury. One remarkable feature of this peasant regime of post-August revolution is that no harm was done to private properties, ordinary individuals or their interests and only Government agents and properties were attacked. Underground activities were highly developed and both criminal and civil agencies of their Panchayat Raj were used to maintain law and order in their emancipated peasant India. Thus the peasant became the central figure of the 1942 revolution.

One other interesting feature of peasant revolution is the rapidity with which peasant revolutionaries were able to construct the whole edifice of separate panchayats for political, administrative and judicial purposes and make them all work efficiently and in harmony. In Satara district from the villages right upto the district level, these tiers of panchayats were built up. And they did remarkable work. They were able to make and enforce laws. They could collect taxes and cesses and administer public funds. All this was possible because the hoary traditions of Panchayat Raj and democracy were still there with the peasants in their folk-lore and day-today settlement of village affairs and disputes. And they served as foundations. So, neither the exercise of political power through panchayat democracy nor the management of administration were new. This is another proof, if proof were needed, to demonstrate the capacity of Indian and Chinese and African peasants to run their administration, if and when they capture political and economic power.

No longer are our peasants' satyagraha campaigns isolated struggles unobserved by the peasants of other parts, as Lenin found Russians to be. Wherever there was a struggle, the peasants of the whole of India came to be interested in it, collected funds, observed sympathetic All-India Days and helped the sufferers in every possible manner. Thus the Mandasa State subjects, the Orissa State subjects, Refugee Camps, the Bengali Flood victims, the Rayalaseema famine-stricken peasants, the Malabar peasants and so many others were helped on an all-India basis. True, the All-India Peasants Congress had come to knit all the peasants together under the aegis of a National Peasant unity. But it was Mahatma Gandhi and the National Congress which laid the foundations for the growth of the new consciousness and familiarized the peasants with the potent idea of their national unity.

Peasant Mobilization

When Romesh Dutt, who set the pattern of nationalist criticism of agricultural policy, argued at the beginning of the century in favour of the permanent settlement of land revenue and drew attention to the high incidence of the land tax and the poverty of the peasants in ryotwari areas, Curzon did not fail to point out that the peasants in Bengal did not live in "exceptional comfort and prosperity", and that the victims of famines who flocked to the relief works came mostly from "labourers on land, whom the land revenue assessment practically in no way affects."[120] Indeed, the agrarian policy of the Congress centred on the interests of landlords and rich peasants who were primarily concerned with the reduction of land revenue. As two contemporary peasant leaders put it, the nationalist leaders "kept themselves scrupulously silent about the fate of our crores of zamindari tenants of V.P., C.P., Orissa, Bihar, Bengal, Assam and Madras."[121] Over the years the Government undertook tenancy legislation which was designed to safeguard the interests of the new elite in the villages at the cost of rent-paying tenants. It was not fortuitous that agrarian movements from 1920 onwards took the form of tenant struggles, particularly in zamindari areas. In fact, agrarian movements were intense in zamindari areas until the advent of independence. The main thrust of the tenant struggles was directed against the agrarian system.

It was in the Gandhi era that the Congress embarked upon peasant mobilization. At last the Congress became linked with the peasant masses. Looking back one may say that it was Gandhi's *tour de force.* Barrington Moore, who describes Indian peasants as "docile", writes that the alliance between the Congress and the peasants was forged and maintained via non-violence; the bourgeoisie became reconciled with peaceful peasant movement.[122] What needs to be noted is that Indian peasants, who, lived in scattered villages, became politicized in the wake of the nationalist movement. The general spirit of defiance of authority generated by the nationalist movement from 1920 onwards and Gandhi's charisma surely promoted the growth of peasant movement almost throughout the country. Once the path of peasant mobilization was taken it was difficult to halt.

The rent paying tenants were drawn in the agrarian movements in a few regions. As the "ryot sabhas" became moribund towards the close of the nineteenth century, the Kisan Sabha grew on the crest of agrarian movements. As an official report described the new trend in Indian politics in 1921:

"In various parts of India the movement for tenants' unions or Kisan Sabhas has become increasingly prominent. In many cases these unions have confined themselves to collective bargaining with local landholders and overlords, and to secure improved conditions of tenure. . . . There has been a tendency, at least in certain parts of India, towards action of a semi-Bolshevik character. This has been considerably increased by the policy of hostility to the government preached by the non-cooperation party. .. there is a considerable increase in the class consciousness of the rustic."[123]

It seems that the Kisan Sabhas often represented an independent power in the countryside; these sabhas sprang up as agrarian movements became intense in a particular region. These Kisan Sabhas surely remained in a rudimentary stage. Nevertheless, the ground was prepared for the formation of the All India Kisan Sabha, a central organization of the peasants, in 1936. As this organization took up the cause of the poor peasants and rent-paying tenants, the nationalist leadership that championed the landlords and rich peasants was faced with the dilemma of choice. The nationalist leadership asserted that the Congress alone represented the kisans and refused to give its blessing to the Kisan Sabha.

The techniques of peasant mobilization evolved by Gandhi — meetings, processions, signature campaign, satyagraha corresponded to the agrarian programme of the Congress that included reduction of rent and revenue, abolition of feudal dues and levies, fixity of tenure and moratorium on debts. At the Lucknow Congress (1936), the demand of the abolition of Zamindari earlier included in the agrarian resolution drafted by Jawaharlal Nehru and P. Tandon had to be dropped, as the right-wing Congress leaders rejected it. Over the years the Congress failed to evolve a radical agrarian programme and became alienated, at least in a few regions, from share-croppers and agricultural labourers who mainly belonged to the Scheduled Tribes, Scheduled Castes and the Muslim community. With the growth of militant peasant struggles the zamindars and talukdars gradually joined the Congress. As time passed, the British raj, alas, lost the support of the landlords on whom it had relied in the fight against the

Congress. This became increasingly evident in the last days of the British rule in India.

Mobilization of Ryots

In the summer of 1917 Gandhi embarked upon the mobilization of ryots in Champaran. In this district, the landlords had leased out their estates to the British planters. The ryots' discontent became intense as the planters enhanced rent under the tinkathia system. As indigo trade rapidly declined in the beginning of the present century, the planters resorted to sharabeshi (rent enhancement). The District Magistrate of Muzaffarpur reported on wholesale execution of Kabulyats from the ryots by "nothing less than an organised system of oppression by the factory servants,"[124] Furthermore, the planters who held thika tenure collected abwabs in addition to rent. Gandhi described the planters as "rajas" and summed up the main grievances of the ryots:

The campaign started in April 1917. Gandhi moved from one village to another collecting evidence of the ryots: a novel method of establishing direct contact with the peasants. As Rajendra Prasad tells us: "The statements of tenants continued to be recorded the whole day. There was such a continuous stream of these tenants that there was not a minute's break between 6.30 a.m. and 6.30 p.m." In June, the Government appointed an enquiry committee with Gandhi as one of its members. On 16 July about 10,000 peasants collected to have "a darshan" of Gandhi at the meeting place of the Committee? Under the Champaran Agrarian Act (1917), tinkathia, which had already become a nuisance, was made illegal; sharabeshi was reduced by 20 per cent in the case of Turkanlia and 26 per cent in the case of other factories. Gandhi agreed to a compromise as he felt that "peasants and planters had still to live together."[125] But the ryots were not keen to pay enhanced rent, and litigation considerably increased.

The Champaran movement received the support of lawyers, moneylenders and rich peasants. It seems that the elite did not want to share feudal power with the planters. As Bayley noted in 1875: "It is the favoured classes, Brahmins and Rajputs, who hold their lands at favourable rates, ..., who hate to see their position usurped by the factory amlah -it is to these classes that indigo is specially hateful."[126] Misra, a modern scholar, writes that factory employees, moneylenders, businessmen and landholders were all ranged against the planters who interfered with "a free and undisturbed transfer of tenants' property into their hands."[127]

But the fact has to be admitted that the planters stubbornly clung to rent enhancement and abwabs; the popular support behind the Champaran movement reflected the ryots' discontent against the indigo system that was crumbling in the early years of the twentieth century.

In the spring of 1918, Gandhi launched the Satyagraha of Patidar ryots of Kaira (Kheda) in Gujarat. In Gujarat, a ryotwari area, the ryots paid revenue to the Government; among these ryots there was a category of substantial landowners whose land was cultivated by tenants. In 1917, there was a failure of Kharif crops due to heavy rains, and the ryots demanded suspension of land revenue. The Government rejected the demand on the ground that the crop was more than 25 per cent of the normal yield. On 22 March 1918, as Gandhi launched the satyagraha, the peasants refused to pay the land tax. The pledge which the peasants had to sign read as follows:

"We the undersigned hereby solemnly declare that we shall not of our accord pay to the Government the full or remaining revenue for the year. We shall let the Government take whatever legal steps it may think fit, and gladly suffer the consequences of our nonpayment. . . . The reason why those who are able to pay still withhold payment is that if they pay up, the poorer ryots may in a panic sell their cattle or incur debts to pay their dues. . ."[128]

The Kaira movement was in full swing from March to June, 1918. Meetings were held throughout the district; 2,337 ryots signed the pledge not to pay land revenue; subscriptions were raised mostly from the Gujarati merchants of Bombay. "As the Government tried to suppress the movement by attaching the ryots' property and imposing fines on defaulters, the peasants began to waver. A section of the educated middle class represented by Vallabhbhai Patel, Mahadev Desai, Indulal Yajnik stood by Gandhi to keep the morale of the peasants. As the sowing season approached in June, the peasants started paying up the dues. The satyagraha was suspended. Wellingdon wrote to Chelmsford that Gandhi and Patel suspended satyagraha when they saw "the game was Up."[129]

The patidars played no mean role in peasant mobilization in Bardoli, a taluk in Gujarat. In 1908, the Patidar Yuvak Mandal was founded which held regular conferences and published *Patel Bandhu* that sought to spread nationalist ideas among the people. In 1927, the Scheduled Tribes constituted 50 per cent of the population in Bardoli, while the Patidars formed 25 per cent.

In 1922, Gandhi personally visited Bardoli and permitted the launching of the movement for non-payment of revenue. Presumably it was intended to mobilize the land-owning peasantry that paid land revenue to the government, the rent-paying tenants were left out. Throughout Bardoli the taluk meetings were held, and an ultimatum to the government was sent. The main issue of the Bardoli satyagraha was non-payment of revenue. According to the system of periodic settlement of land revenue in ryotwari areas, the Bombay Government had ordered an enhancement of 22 per cent, and turned down the proposal of the ryots to pay at the old rates. It was decided at a mass meeting that the ryots would "refuse payment of the revised assessment until the Government is prepared to accept the amount of the old assessment . .. or until the Government appoints an impartial tribunal to settle the whole question of revision by investigation and enquiry on the spot."[130]

As the attachment (japti) officials came to the village, they found the doors closed or locked. The volunteers were provided with drums and conches, and as soon as the officials came near the village the drum or the conch gave the alarm. Although some of the Banias, the most vulnerable section in the taluka, paid revenue, the overwhelming majority of the ryots withheld payment. The Government continued to adopt repressive measures, and seemed to be determined to teach the Congress a lesson. They attached land, crops and cattle of the peasants, and employed pathans to assist the officials. The satyagraha had apparently attained its object. Ghanshyam Shah tells us that it was virtually a movement of the Patidars who managed to draw in the tenants and landless labourers. Dhanagavre writes that the satyagraha hardly brought in any change in the agrarian social structure.

"Government wants to divide you and *shahukar*, but for you your *shahukar* is everything. You should laugh at and consider him a fool if somebody says that you should change your *shahukar*. It is just like asking a *patibrata* (i.e., a dutiful wife) to change her husband. How can you leave a *shahukar* who has helped you in your difficulties?"[131]

Since the rich peasants wanted to improve farming and embark upon commercial agriculture, they needed credit, and did not become a contented and prosperous class, partly because the government and the commercial banks did not offer them adequate credit. Until the end of the British rule they clung to traditional methods of cultivation and clamoured for remunerative prices for cash crops. It is also a fact that the burden of the land tax fell heavily on the landowning peasants in ryotwari areas. From 1929 onwards the rich peasants tended to be increasingly militant as agricultural prices slumped. Few writers have emphasized that there was a downward trend in their income from the sale of their produce between 1929 and 1936. The position of the rich peasants began to change with the rise in prices during the Second World War.

Tenant Struggles

It was in Uttar Pradesh that the struggles of rent-paying tenants flared up in the 1920s and in the 1930s. The situation in Oudh deserves particular notice. After the 1857 rebellion the ruling class showed a tendency to appease the Oudh talukdars who resembled the Bengal zamindars and collected rent from the tenants. In the Oudh Rent Act of 1868, even the twelve years' rule about occupancy right was denied to the tenants. After the Rent Act of 1886 was passed, the landlords often evicted the tenants in order to get *nazarana* from new tenants; eviction was also a device of the talukdars to make it difficult for old tenants to become occupancy tenants. In 1899-1900, non-occupancy tenants formed 82 per cent of all tenants in Oudh.24 Eviction of tenants continued unabated. In Pratapgarh, for instance, 936 notices of eviction were served on the tenants in 1906-7; this figure rose to 2593 in 1919-20. The Deputy Commissioner of Pratapgarh reported in 1920: "Fathers have sold their daughters for *nazarana* money to husbands of advanced years."[132] The tenants knew that failure to pay *nazarana* could lead to their *bedakhil.*

The problem of indebtedness had become acute in the United Provinces. This could be partly related to the enhancement of rent undertaken by the landlords. Whitcombe notes that money lending was "the most profitable area for investment of local capital," partly because the revenue system created "further incentive to borrow." Besides seed and food loans the peasants had to borrow to pay rents, buy cattle or to fulfil social obligations. For grain loans they had to "pay back two or three times the amount of grain originally loaned in order to arrive at its cash value at the time of borrowing."[133] What is significant is that the landlords formed the most important source of rural credit. According to the estimate of the Banking Enquiry Committee of 1929, about 40 per cent of the loans was supplied by the landlords, while moneylenders supplied 28.3 per cent. Since the landlords in eastern U.P. could make an easy fortune in usury, they hardly invested capital in agricultural development. This partly explains why eastern U.P. remained sunk in stagnation while western U.P. showed signs of growth, thanks to the extension of commercial agriculture.27 It was in eastern U.P. that the peasant movement was intense in the 1920s and 1930s. What is remarkable is that peasants became organized, though in a loose manner, in the Kisan Sabha.

In Uttar Pradesh, the nationalists seemed to show a great deal of interest in the agrarian problem. Pandit Madan Mohan Malaviya organized U.P. Kisan Sabha in 1918, which generally represented Rajput tenants and small landlords. In 1919, Jawaharlal Nehru was drawn to the peasant movement directed against "the barons of Oudh." There were *Kisan Sabhas* in the villages, whose leaders worked at the grass roots. Of these leaders the most prominent was Baba Ram Chandra, who achieved remarkable success in organizing the tenants in the Kisan Sabha. In the summer of 1920, the tenants of Pratapgarh rose in struggle under the leadership of Baba Ram Chandra who, dressed like a sannyasi, moved among the peasants and addressed meetings reciting melodious verses from the *Ramayana.* When he was arrested the peasants assembled in the Court compound demanding his release. When he was released the peasants considered it to be, as Nehru noted, "a big triumph", and about 60,000 peasants assembled to see Ram Chandra Maharaj, who was certainly not a Congress stalwart.[134]

In January 1921, the peasant movement rapidly spread from Pratapgarh to Rae Bareli, Fyzabad and Sultanpur. Crops on the *sir* land of talukdars were destroyed; the houses of merchants and moneylenders were raided; talukdars store godowns were destroyed or looted. On 13 January, Lambert noted that the southern portion of Rae Bareli "was in a very disturbed state". On 22 January disturbances broke out in Sehgaon Pachhimagaon village. As the peasants 'turned loose the zamindar's cattle in his sugarcane field" the police promptly intervened; a clash followed and a constable was killed.[135] In early March 1921, agrarian disturbances spread from Fyzabad to the adjoining district of Sultanpur. In one village in this district swaraj was proclaimed and a paralled government set up. There was severe repression. The Independent reported on 6 March. On 18 May, Gandhi wrote in *Young India.* "Whilst we will not hesitate to advise the kisans when the moment comes to suspend payment of taxes to the government. It is not contemplated that at any stage of non-cooperation we would seek to deprive the zamindars of their rent."[136]

In the wake of the Civil Disobedience Movement launched by the Congress in 1930, there was a new wave of tenant struggles in Uttar Pradesh. With a network of Congress Committees and khadi centres at the village level and an army of volunteers recruited mostly from students and the youth, the Congress had a strong base in this province. From 1928 onwards the Congress spread nationalist ideas among the people in towns and villages with the help of journals, pamphlets, sale of khadi, and numerous meetings and processions. After the Lahore Congress, young Congress leaders in the districts seemed to be keen to mobilize the peasants in the movement for independence.[137]

With the onset of the Great Depression in 1929, agricultural prices began to fall. By 1931 agricultural prices fell by 50 per cent, which severely hit not only the poor peasants but also the rich peasants. From 1927 onwards there was a series of bad harvests. In this situation the relation between the landlords and the tenants was of crucial importance. Neale has told us that the number of non-occupancy tenants in Oudh and Agra decreased between 1921 and 1927, thanks to the tenancy legislation; in 1926-27 non-occupancy tenants formed 10.5 per cent of all tenants in Oudh and 4 per cent in Agra. What needs to be noted is that the zamindars in eastern Uttar Pradesh, propped up by the government, continued to enhance rent, collect *nazarana* and evict the tenants. In Bara Banki, for instance, the zamindars undertook, as a local Congressman put it, "forcible realisation of rent, forcible enhancement of rent, illegal eviction of tenants." In many villages the actual rent exacted from the tenants was not shown in the Patwari papers, and rent receipts were seldom given to the tenants.[138]

Kisan Sabha in Bihar

It seems that the UP peasant movement made much impact on Bihar, where the Kisan Sabha was formed in 1920 and became a force in the countryside in the 1930s. As in Uttar Pradesh, so in Bihar, the large estates survived; a large proportion of the peasants worked as tenants on landlords' estates. The landlords often sublet a portion of their land to the under-ryots who paid produce rent (*batai*). Under the batai system the tenants had to pay a large proportion of the produce as rent to the landlords. The Settlement Officer of Palamau reported in 1879 that "when a landlord, in whose villages rents have been hitherto paid in cash, desires to harass or to oust his ryots, he has only to introduce the battaya system, and his object is soon fulfilled."[139] The priests, teachers, doctors and lawyers, who had acquired landed property, showed a tendency to turn over the land to *batai* cultivation. There was also the *danabandi* system (a division of the estimated crop), which the zamindars found profitable as prices rose from 1900 onwards. Over the years land alienation continued unabated, and the dispossessed peasants were often resettled on the land as under-ryots.

In the autumn of 1920 Swami Bidyanand, the leader of the Kisan Sabha in north Bihar, started addressing village meetings. It seems that the leadership of Bihar Congress hardly sought alliance with the Kisan Sabha. When the Congress launched Civil Disobedience Movement in 1930, rent-paying tenants were hardly mobilized, partly because the Congress leaders were themselves small landlords, who reconciled with the non-payment of Chaukidari tax undertaken in Champaran, Saran, Patna, Monghyr and Sahabad districts. When the national movement was in an impasse after the withdrawal of Civil Disobedience in 1934, the horizon began to light up as the Kisan Sabha organized partial struggles of peasants in rural Bihar. In August 1934, the Kisan Sabha held its second provincial conference at Gaya, where the question of zamindari abolition was discussed, although no resolution was adopted. Tht Congress Socialist Party joined the kisan sabha, which was based mainly on the Bhumihars. It seems that the Kisan Sabha concentrated on such issues as reduction of rent and canal tax, fair price for sugarcane, commutation of produce rent into money rent; thana conferences were held in some districts, and cane-growers' strike was organized at the Bihata sugar mills for raising the price of sugarcane which had considerably fallen during the depression.[140]

Agrarian Movements in Bengal

We have already pointed out how agrarian disturbances in 1873-75 brought to the fore the problem of the rent-paying tenants in Bengal. Although the ryots benefited from the Bengal Tenancy Act, 1885, the *bargadars* who paid 50 per cent of the produce as rent to the landlords remained unprotected. It seems that land transfer continued unabated, and the dispossessed peasants were being resettled on the land as *bargadars* in the Bengal districts. The Collector of Dacca reported in 1913: "The increase in *barga* lands and *khas* lands of proprietors and tenure holders is largely due to the indebtedness of the ryot ... many of the landlords. . . gradually acquire holdings, keeping them in their own possession or letting them out on *barga*."[141] The Settlement Officer of

Midnapore wrote in 1917, "far from *bhag* rent showing any tendency to disappear in favour of money rent it seems to be on the increase."[142] In Dinajpur Bell found that "adhi is more than 3 years on kabuliyat, notably when a khai khalasi is made, that is, the mortgagee settles the mortgagor as adhiar."[143] In Jalpaiguri the ryots who lost their holdings during the depression in the 1930s "have been allowed to cultivate the lands as bargadars."[144] The Land Revenue Commission, 1940 reported that 21.1 per cent of land was cultivated by the bargadars.

The poverty of the small peasants and bargadars was the soil on which usury could grow. What we witness in Bengal is the growth of merchant and usurer's capital. Jute, the main commercial crop, was grown by scattered small peasants, who were compelled to raise loans to provide circulating capital on onerous terms of repayment. Although the Bengal Tenancy Act, 1885 improved the condition of the tenants, the zamindars were not anxious to abdicate. Jaykrishna Mukherjee, for instance, embarked upon purchasing estates, made a fortune in moneylending and grain trade, and knew how to deal with recalcitrant tenants. As politics came to the countryside in the wake of the no-tax campaign in 1920, all categories of peasants including the rich peasants simultaneously rose in sporadic struggles in the different districts. Broadly speaking, these struggles were directed against the Midnapore Zamindari Company (a British Company, that held land in Midnapore, Rajshahi and Nadia), and also against Chaukidari tax and settlement operations.

Significantly, the no-tax campaign aroused the expectations of rent-paying tenants who showed signs of launching a rent strike in a few districts. The tenants of the Maharaja of Kasimbazar raised the demand that they would not pay rent if he continued to pay the land revenue. The peasants in Mymensingh, probably influenced by the Khilafat volunteers, not only refused to pay chaukidari tax but said that they would not pay anything to anyone in the world, since they lived in the land of God. In Rajshahi and Dinajpur the Wahabis seemed to be active under the leadership of Abdullah Baki, and trouble between landlords and tenants broke out. In Tipperah the Muslim peasants were ranged against the Hindu landlords and moneylenders, and taxes and rents could not be collected either by the government or the landlords; as armed police moved in to make arrests villages were evacuated. As the movement against chaukidari tax became widespread in Rangpur, it developed into a no-rent movement, and clashes between the police and peasants took place in the most affected subdivision of Nilphamari. Predictably, the tenure-holders and jotedars turned against the movement and the Congress volunteers were found helping the police and inducing the peasants to disperse. Whenever the tenants launched a no-rent movement over the head of the local Congress, repression was let loose on the peasants and the movement petered out. The landed middle class was scared by the growing rural unrest, the like of which was not witnessed during the Swadeshi movement.

Jogindra Chakravarty, a prominent Congress leader of Dinajpur, warned that the middle classes who had their lands cultivated by the bargadars would be ruined if the bargadars were given occupancy right. Surendra Biswas pointed out that the ryot would cease to invest in land purchase if he knew that the bargadar would be given occupancy right. Nalini Rajan Sarkar, a rising politician, supported the landlord's right of salami and pre-emption. The government beat a retreat, and bargadars were not treated as tenants in the Bengal Tenancy Act of 1928. Thanks to the opposition of the Swarajists, the motion of Nurul Haque Chaudhuri, supported by Azizul Huq, that the produce-rent paid by the bargadar should be one-third instead of half was 10st.75 By the Bengal Tenancy Act, 1928 the occupancy holdings were made transferable, subject to the payment of a transfer fee to the landlord; the landlord was given the pre-emptive right to purchase the holding. Commutation of produce-rent into cash rent was abolished.

The Swarajists apparently championed the zamindars and jotedars and let down the rent-paying tenants. From 1929 onwards, as agricultural prices slumped, there was rapid increase in the number of bargadars; "the usurers and petty professional middle class men" invested in land purchase "to buy their way into the rent-receiving class." It was not fortuitous that the Muslims and Namasudras who worked as tenants on landlords' fields were being alienated from the Congress.76 As Broomfield tells us, Islamia Anjumans were engaged in anti-Hindu and anti-Congress propaganda, and caste associations were organizing lower castes. The elite was faced with the problems of "a plural society". While the Congress was in decline ecept in Midnapore, the Workers' and Peasants' Party that had a radical programme and the Krishak Praja Party, a peasant party per excellence, became active in rural Bengal. The Workers' and Peasants' Party came into existence in 1926, in which the Communists and intellectuals like Nazrul Islam, the famous poet, Dr. Naresh Sen Gupta, an eminent lawyer and litterateur, Atul Gupta, also a rising lawyer and litterateur, Hemanta

Sarkar, member of the Legislative Council, played the leading role; the party sought to bring radical ideas into the peasant movement, published *Langal* and *Ganavani*, and organized peasant conferences.

Meanwhile, agrarian disturbances had broken out in several districts. On the one hand, peasant discontent had come to a head with the onset of the depression. On the other hand, the Civil Disobedience movement had generated a spirit of defiance among all sections of the people who had to face limitless repression during Anderson's terrorist rule. The salt satyagraha became a popular movement in Midnapore. The tribal peasants of Midnapore, Manbhum and Singhbhum joined the Congress in large numbers; in Dinajpur district the arrested satyagrahis included Santals and Rajbansis.[145] While the landlords generally succeeded in containing a no-rent movement, they did not fail to turn against the government scheme of voluntary restriction of jute cultivation.

As Rasul tells us, Krishak Samitis were formed in Tipperah, Noakhali and Burdwan in 1933, which tried to mobilize the peasants against the oppression of the landlords. When the Communist Party was declared illegal in 1934, local communist workers continued to work in the Krishak Samitis.[146] By 1936 Krishak Samitis had been formed in Tipperah, Noakhali, Burdwan, Faridpur, Chittagong and Rangpur, in which communists, Congressmen and local Muslim notables were active. From early January, Bengal was in the grip of severe food scarcity, and test relief works had to be undertaken in several districts, notably Murshidabad, Birbhum, Bankura, Burdwan, Hooghly and the 24 Parganas. Elections under the Act of 1935 were in the offing. The police reports indicate that Krishak Samitis which were quiescent became active, particularly in Tipperah and Noakhali. In these districts meetings were held in which "grievances against zamindars and moneylenders" were emphasized, and the demand was raised for the establishment of debt conciliation boards.[147]

Moplah Rebellion

We now come to peasant unrest in South India that did not remain quiet during the nationalist movement. Although there is a great deal of controversy on the nature of the Moplah rebellion in Malabar, it seems that it reflected agrarian discontent; the communal element came to the fore as the frustrated Moplahs were being ruthlessly crushed by the British. We shall briefly review the agrarian conditions in Malabar in order to comprehend why peasant unrest was intense in the 1920s and also in the

1930s. As we shall see, peasant movement actually began to grow in Malabar from 1934 onwards.

Throughout the nineteenth century, a series of Moplah revolts flared up in South Malabar, while the Pulayas, Tiyas and Izhavas remained quiet. Between 1836 and 1856 twenty-two revolts occurred in which the Moplahs often attacked *jenmi* landlords, burning or looting their houses. In 1855 and 1896 several Moplah outbreaks, though of minor importance, were reported in the official documents which invariably recommended stern measures against the "jungle Moplahs." In fact, repression was limitless, and the Moplahs became, as Conrad Wood suggests, increasingly anti-British. And they said, 'there is no room for Mussalmans in the country,' 'we Mussalmans can't abide here,' 'we have had much oppression at the hands of the white folk.'[148]

By 1920 Gandhi had forged unity between the Non-cooperation Movement and Khilafat agitation. Gandhi, Shaukat Ali, Abul Kalam Azad and Hakim Azmal addressed public meetings which were attended by the Moplah peasants. The Moplah rebellion which remained confined to Ernad, Walluvanad and Ponnani taluks in South Malabar, began in August 1921 when the police went to arrest Ali Musaliar and other leaders. As the rumour spread that the army had raided the Mambrath mosque, the Moplahs flocked from different parts of the region to the mosque and clashed with the police. Between August and November there were two major battles between the Moplahs and the armed forces, in which about 600 Moplahs were killed.[149] During the rebellion railway and telegraph lines were cut, post offices, government offices and police stations were raided and burned. Many *jenmi* landlords were attacked and killed. In Ernad and Walluvanad the Moplahs established their raj, issued fatwahs, restricted looting and collected taxes. In the face of severe repression the Moplahs tried to organize guerrilla warfare. At this point, the Moplahs attacked and killed Hindus. Namboodiripad writes that in a region inhabited by about four lakh Hindus only 600 were killed and 2500 converted.[150] Yet the fact is that hundreds of Hindus were killed when the Congress-Khilafat alliance was continuing. The tragedy of the Moplah rebellion lay in the fact that it did not live up to its secular ideals. From 1930 onwards the Moplahs turned gradually to the Muslim League and hardly played any significant role in the peasant movement.

Karshaka Sangham

As we have already pointed out, the kanamdars had been carrying on the campaign for tenancy legislation, which centred on the kanam tenants only. With the onset of the depression the problem of the tenants came to the fore. It was from 1934 onwards that peasant conferences were held, focussing on rent reduction and indebtedness. In February 1934, the Pattambi Peasants' Conference was held, in which the Congress Socialist Party played the leading role. Karshaka Sangham or peasant union was set up in a few villages; meetings and jathas were organized in which demands for exemption of tax on poor peasants, moratorium on debts, introduction of a graded tax were raised. A. V. Kunhambu, K. A. Karaleeyan, A. K. Gopalan, Krishna Pillai were the early leaders of Karshaka Sanghams, which remained in a rudimentary stage and hardly attracted public attention.[151]

The Malabar Tenancy Act of 1929 was designed to safeguard the interests of the Kanamdars who had already become a powerful category, while the tenants who worked on Kanamdars' lands had no security of tenure. The Karshaka Sangham sought to organize all categories of tenants, and particularly the Tiyas, against enhancement of rent, illegal exactions and renewal fees, and extended its base in north Malabar.[152] As years passed these peasant unions tried to draw in the Izhavas who formed a large section of the rural population in Malabar, Cochin and Travancore. The reform movement initiated by Sri Narayan Guru, who was born in an Izhava family near Trivandrum, exerted considerable influence on the Izhavas; the Cochin Izhava Sabha, founded in 1916, fought against social disabilities and demanded free access to public roads, entry into temples, and an equitable share in government service.[153] With rising expectations the Izhavas turned to the Karshaka Sangham which befriended them.

Agrarian Disturbances in Madras

When Malabar was in the throes of the Moplah rebellion, agrarian disturbances occurred in parts of Madras where politics had come to the village in the wake of the nationalist movement. It seems that agrarian disturbances became intense with the onset of the great depression and were often led 'by the rich peasant who had become, as Washbrook tells us, the "local boss". Some of the main features of the agrarian system may be noted in passing. In Madras the ryots with whom the settlement was made always represented "the high-caste elite, *therayalu* or leaders of the village"; the labouring peasants continued to work on the lands of these ryots. As in the zamindari areas intermediaries grew between the ryot and the government. Agriculture was over crowded, and there was a great deal of migration of the Madrasis mainly to Malaya, Burma and Ceylon. With the extension of commercial agriculture the ryot-moneylender became a rising category. The problem of rural credit was acute.

In rural Madras the non-Brahmin Reddis and Kammas formed important agricultural castes. Since the Brahmins enjoyed considerable prestige and authority and were the allies of the ruling Justice Party, the Congress tried to woo the Reddis and Kammas, who entered politics, formed caste association, set up schools and hostels, and agitated for tenancy legislation. There is an element of truth in Elliot's contention that the early peasant movement was based on the support of the Reddis and Kammas, on whom N. G. Ranga relied.[154] What is significant is that Ranga focussed attention on the condition of zamindari ryots and directed his attack on the zamindars. Although Madras was a ryotwari area, a large proportion of the rural area, particularly in the Andhra coastal districts, was under zamindari tenure in 1911, the area under ryotwari was 61.5 million acres, under inam 4.4 million acres, and under zamindari 24.7 million acres.[155]

In the 1920s Guntur was the main centre of the no-tax campaign which was started without Gandhi's sanction and achieved remarkable success in eighteen villages. Passive resistance seemed to be the main form of the no-tax movement which was faced with repression. There was virtually an uprising in Pedanandipad area where Kisan raj was established; the peasants refused to pay taxes or to give any information to the armed forced regarding the direction to village ponds or wells.[156] Guntur became a strong base of the Congress which established links with the Kammas. There was another uprising in the Vizag Agency in Andhra, which flared up in 1922 when the non-cooperation movement was called off. It was an uprising of the Koyas who fought for their traditional rights in the forest and also against forced labour. It seems that the uprising owed much to the work of Seerama Raju, a sanyasi, who came from West Godavari, lived among the Koyas and finally led them in the struggle against the raj.

In 1930s organised peasant movement began to take shape in Madras. On the one hand, the Civil Disobedience Movement stirred the urban middle class that organized no-tax campaign in a few areas, notably Guntur.

On the other hand, the depression hit all categories of peasants and particularly rich peasants who were drawn in peasant struggles. What is noteworthy is that the peasant movement was directed mainly against the zamindars. In 1928, the Andhra Provincial Ryots Association was formed in Guntur which took up such issues as reduction of revenue, agricultural indebtedness, internal social reform. Baker writes that rich peasants were in the forefront of these struggles. The zamindars had agreed to commute rent payments from kind to cash, which were not resented so long as agricultural prices were high. As prices sharply fell from 1931 onwards. The "rich tenants" rose against the zamindars in the early 1930s. Agrarian disturbances occurred in Tirupati and Maniyachi estates in 1931. In Mamandur the tenants resorted to incendiarism in 1933. Throughout Krishna and Godavari deltas meetings and demonstrations were held, in which the demand of withholding revenue payments was discussed.

Tribal Peasants

The revolts of the tribal peasants in different parts of India have already been described. Most frequently, these revolts had millenarian overtones and were quickly suppressed. 'What is remarkable is that the struggles of tribal peasants broke out in the 1920s and also in the 1930s that could be related to the nationalist movement. Broadly speaking, these struggles were directed against the government which had encroached on their rights in the forest. The tribal peasants looked upon the forest as their home which supplied them food, fuel, honey and housing material. With the growth of towns and industries and the rise in population large areas of forests were cleared and brought under cultivation, and tribal peasants were driven away from the forests; the forest officials often charged grazing fee for cattle and prevented the tribal peasants from collecting wood in the forests. In this background the struggle of the tribal peasants flared up in Madras in 1921.

With the coming of the Civil Disobedience Movement, the nationalists in the Central Provinces tried to woo the tribal peasants, and the forest satyagraha, a new experiment in peasant mobilization, was launched in 1930. As in Andhra, the discontent of the tribal peasants against the restrictions on grazing rights, loss of the traditional rights in fuel and fodder, and oppression of the forest officials was expressed in this satyagraha. There was a great deal of response of the tribal peasants, and the satyagraha was faced with repression. Predictably, the tribal peasants did not always remain peaceful. As a Congress report indicates, the Gonds went in a mass to break forest laws and were "provoked by the police "to some acts of violence."

By July 1930, the forest satyagraha had spread to Nagpur and Jubbulpore, and large numbers of women and even children took part in it. As Butler noted, "large bands of Maenads are raging the forests, emotionally cutting grass and wood". The satyagraha reached its peak in August-September, and punitive police was posted in twelve villages. The peasants refused "to give evidence or any help to the Police and Forest Officers". It proved difficult to arrest the tribal peasants who lived in scattered villages; the main form of the movement was the cutting of grass in Government forests. 110 While the local Congress leaders avoided non-payment of revenue and rent, they seemed to concentrate on the tribal peasants who were drawn in the forest satyagraha. Since the main thrust of the movement was directed against Government forests, the landowning peasants and the urban middle class readily gave their blessing to it. In fact, the dominant position of the landowners in the rural economy was not challenged. In 1932 the local Congress again launched the forest satyagraha which faced severe repression and petered out quickly.

The forest satyagraha was also undertaken in Berar, where the leadership came from the Marathis. The movement spread to 106 centres, and 460 volunteers and 225 workers were involved in it; the main forms of the movement included grass cutting, arson, and picketing of fuel, and timber auctions. There was a great deal of response from the tribal peasants, and the movement "spread deep in the countryside". There were clashes between the police and the tribal peasants. By October 1930, the movement was suppressed.[157] Nevertheless, the involvement of the tribal peasants in the nationalist movement was surely a new experiment that achieved a large measure of success. What was important for the future was the extension of the mass base of the Congress in the countryside. As the 1937 elections showed, the Congress had considerable rural support in the Hindi region, which was not eroded over the years.

References

1. Agrarian structure is the sum total of the ways in which each group operates in relation to the other groups (Daniel Thorner: *The Agrarian Prospect in India*, p.8).

2. (i) Dadabhai Naoroji : *Poverty and Un-British Rule in India*, London, 1901; (ii) Romesh Chunder Dutt : *The Economic History of India in the Victorian Age*, Kegan Paul, London, 1905.
3. Agrarian population can be divided into three broad groups: land owners, cultivators and wage labourers. When these functions are combined in one person he is known as peasant.
4. (i) *Report of the Congress Agrarian Reforms Committee*, New Delhi, 1949; (ii) Planning Commission, Govt. of India: *The First Five Year Plan*, New Delhi, 1951, Chapters I and II.
5. S.Kesava Iyenger: *Economic Investigations in the Hyderabad State*, Hyderabad, 1932.
6. A.M. Khusro: *Economic and Social Effects of Jagirdari Abolition and Land Reforms in Hyderabad*, Osmania University Press, Hyderabad, 1958.
7. *Ibid.*
8. Agrarian Reforms Committee (1949) of Hyderabad recommended a good amount of legislation; and consequently the following were enacted by the Government: (i) Hyderabad Tenancy and Agricultural Lands Act, 1950; (ii) Hyderabad Land Revenue Amendment Act, 1952; (iii) Hyderabad Prevention of Victims Ordinance, 1952.
9. *Pyravees* were a kind of brokers for government business and they created unnecessary problems and collected their brokerage money on different occasions from the poor and illiterate peasants.
10. A number of such local disturbances are recorded in the revenue records.
11. (i) B.H. Baden Powell: *Land Revenue and Tenure in British India*, London 1894; (ii) *A Manual of Land Revenue System and Land Tenure in British India*, 1982.
12. Nilmani Mukharji: *The Ryotwari System in Madras*, Calcutta, 1982.
13. *Report of the Zamindari Committee, 1937*, Madras 1939; (ii) W.R.S. Sathianathan: *Report on Agricultural Indebtedness in the Presidency of Madras*, 1935, Para 9.
14. Sundara Raja Iyengar: *Land Tenures in the Madras Presidency*, Madras, 1918.
15. W.R.S. Sathianathan: *op.cit.*, para 9.
16. M. Atchi Reddy: *Tenancy Report 1985*, Chapter 15.
17. A.M. Khusro: *op.cit.*
18. Suresh Rambhai: *Vinoba and his Mission*, Wardha, 1954.
19. P. Sundarayya: *Telangana People's Struggle and its Lessons*, Calcutta, 1972.
20. *Police Action in Hyderabad* (Anonymous, in Telugu), Sriram Book Depot, Hyderabad 1949.

21. *Feather of Handloom Movement* (Anonymous, in Telugu), Hyderabad, 1964.
22. P. Sundarayya: *op.cit.*
23. Such cases are widely reported in the districts of Khammam, Warangal, Karimnagar and Adilabad, where most of the leftist organisations have been active.
24. Planning Commission, Government of India: *Implementation of Land Reforms*, Delhi, 1966, p.22.
25. A.M. Khusro: *op.cit.*
26. Planning Commission, Government of India: *Implementation of Land Reforms*, Delhi, 1966, pp.21-32.
27. A.M. Khusro: *op.cit.*
28. M. Atchi Reddy: 'Labour Relations in Andhra Pradesh Agriculture, 1881-1981', *Indian Journal of Labour Economics, XXVI*: 3, October 1983, pp. 160-187.
29. Planning Commission, (1966), *op.cit.*
30. The lowest district-level yield of rice crop in 1956-57 in the Andhra area was 985 lbs per acre in the Anantapur district, while the highest average yield in the Telangana area was 809 lbs. in the Nizamabad district. Other districts in Telangana averaged even under 700 lbs. per acre. Almost the same is the case with many other crops. See *Season and Crop Report* of *Andhra Pradesh* 1956-57, Bureau of Economics and Statistics, Govt. of Andhra Pradesh, Hyderabad, 1959, pp. 104-116.
31. The only study that brought some of their problems into light was V.V. Sayana: *Sharing and Fixed Tenancy Systems*, The Business Week Press, Madras, 1949.
32. The magazine was producing its 58th volume in 1987. It gave numerous details of the anti-zamindary and the Congress movements in its weekly issues between 1930 and 1947.
33. *Report of the Special Officer on Land Tenures in the Ryotwari Area of the Madras Province*, Govt. of Madras, 1951, Chapter VI, Para 2.
34. F.A. Nicholson: *Report Regarding the Possibility of Introducing Land and Agricultural Banks into the Madras Presidency*, Vol. I, Madras, 1985.
35. *Royal Commission on Agriculture in India, 1927*, Vol. III. Evidence taken in the Madras Presidency.
36. Report of the Special Officer : *op.cit*. Chapter VI, Para 4.
37. V.V. Sayana: *Sharing and Fixed Tenancy Systems*, the Business Week Press, Madras, 1949.
38. V.V. Sayana: *Land Sales, Land Values and Land Transfers*, S. Chand and Company, Delhi, 1952.
39. *Ibid.*, p.54.

40. M. Atchi Reddy: Tenancy Report 1985. Chapter 18.
41. See the Reports of the Land Reform Committees of various States compiled during the 1950s.
42. J. Krishnamurthy: 'Agricultural Labour Force in India: A Note', *Indian Economic and Social History Review,* IX : 3, 327-322. See also Thorner, Alice and Daniel: *The Working Force in India* 1881-1951, Bombay, 1960.
43. M. Atchi Reddy: 'Agrarian Structure of Nellore: Tenants and Tenancy, 1800-1980', Social Scientist, No.166, March 1987, pp.48-76.
44. The sizes at the village level can be worked out from the records kept by the Patwaries and Patels or Karanams and Munsifs, but it is very difficult to extend them to the districts.
45. *Report of the Andhra Land Reforms Committee*, Kurnool, 1955, p.6.
46. M. Atchi Reddy: 'Labour Relations in Andhra Pradesh Agriculture 1881-1981', cited.
47. *Report of the Andhra Land Reforms Committee*, Kurnool, 1955, p.6.
48. *Ibid.*, pp.10-11.
49. *Ibid.*, p.7.
50. B. Sarveswara Rao: *The Economic and Social Effects of Zamindari Abolition in Andhra*, Government of India Press, Delhi, 1963, p.100.
51. Planning Commission: *Implementation of Land Reforms*, Delhi, 1966, p.22.
52. P.C. Reddy: *A.P. Land Reforms Act, 1973: A Handbook*, Prabhat Publications, Nellore, 1975.
53. The word 'operated holding' is used to point to the difference between the actual size of the holding that was under operation and the optimum size for operation which can be indicated by 'operational holding'.
54. M. Atchi Reddy: *Tenancy Report, 1985* Chapter 11.
55. M. Atchi Reddy: "Cooperative joint farming in Nellore District: A Measure of Equity" *Indian Jr. of Agl. Economics, XLI,* Conference Number.
56. D.V. Subba Rao et al.,: "Degradation of Agro-Eco-system – An Exploratory study on Cotton Farming", *Indian Jr. of Agl. Economics,* 1987, 410-415.
57. Kripa Shankar: *Concealed Tenancy and its Implications for equity and Economic Growth*, Concept Publishing House, New Delhi, 1980.
58. *Agricultural Census of Andhra Pradesh 1970-71, 1975-76, 1980-81*, Bureau of Economics and Statistics, Government of Andhra Pradesh.
59. M. Atchi Reddy: *Tenancy Report 1985*, Chapter 3.
60. C.S. Murthy: Influence of Socio-Economic Status on Contractual terms of Tenancy". *Economic & Political Weekly*, XXII, 39, 26 March 1987, pp. A 111-120.

61. M. Atchi Reddy: *Tenancy Report 1985*, Chapter 16.
62. The reasons for such migration are (i) the education of their children, (ii) loss of their status and respect in the village, (iii) other socio-economic changes that affected their interests and (iv) expectation of some employment in the towns.
63. See Hardgrave (1969) for a fascinating account from nineteenth-century Travancore of the maneuvers of the near-Untouchable Nadars, supported by Christian missionaries, between a conservative Hindu authority and a more liberal British resident, in the "breast cloth controversy" (pp.55-70).
64. S.B. Chaudhuri, *Civil Disturbances During the British Rule in India, 1765-1857*, 1955. In this pioneering study Dr. Chaudhuri relates agrarian disturbances to the discontent of the peasants against the landlords and the moneylenders.
65. For millenarian movements see E. Hobsbawm, *Primitive Rebels*, 1974. Hobsbawm describes these movements as "blind and groping", "impractical and utopian", yet the "revolutionary aspirations" of these rebels cannot be denied. Also S. Fuchs, *Rebellious Prophets*, 1965.
66. B.Chaudhuri, Peasant Movements in Bengal, 1850-1900, *Nineteenth Century Studies*, 1973.
67. Calcutta Review, 1856, cited in K. Datta, *The Santal Insurrection of 1855-57*, 1940. Professor Datta pioneered studies in peasant rebellions in India
68. Datta, *op.cit*.
69. *Ibid.*
70. *Ibid.*
71. Singh, *The Dust Storm And The Hanging Mist*, 1966, p. 53.
72. *Ibid.*
73. Deposition of witnesses, *Bengalee*, 21 July 1900, reproduced in Singh, *op.cit.*, Appendix-F.
74. Singh, *op.cit.*, also K. Datta, *History of the Freedom Movement in Bihar*, Vol. I, pp.101-3; N.Kumar, Ranchi District Gazetteer, 1970.
75. Singh, *op.cit.*, Appendix-L.
76. *Ibid.*, pp.186-87; also Ranchi District Gazetteer, pp.73-74.
77. N. Ray Choudhury, *Tribal Uprisings in the Second Half of the Nineteenth Century*, 1978 (unpublished Ph.D. Thesis).
78. *Tripura District Gazetteer*, 1975, p.160.
79. B. Kling, *The Blue Mutiny: Indigo Disturbances in Bengal, 1859-60*, 1966.
80. R. Guha, "Neel Darpan: The Image of a Peasant Revolt in a Libeal Mirror", *The Journal of Peasant Studies*, October 1974.

81. Temple Collection, cited in C. Palit, *Tensions in Bengal Rural Society, 1830-1860,* 1975, p.185.

82. K.K.Sen Gupta, *Pabna Disturbances and The Politics of Rent, 1873-85*, 1974, p. 30.

83. S. Sen, Agrarian Relations in India, 1793-1947, 1979, Ch. 3.

84. R.C. Dutt, "An Apology for the Pabna Rioters", Bengal Magazine, September 1873, Dutt wrote this article under the pseudonym "Archydae".

85. *Ibid.*

86. Sen Gupta, *op.cit.*, pp.50-51.

87. Chaudhuri, *op.cit.*

88. The Bengalee, 5 July 1873.

89. Dutt, *op.cit.*

90. J.C. Bagal, *History of the Indian Association, 1876-1951.*

91. Report of the Deccan Riots Commission, 1875, Vol.I, pp.55-56.

92. *Ibid.*, pp.50-51.

93. *Ibid.*

94. M. Darling, The Punjab Peasant in Prosperity and Debt, 1928, p.208.

95. Curzon's speech in the Legislative Council, see C.H. Philips, The Evolution of India and Pakistan, 1858-1947, pp. 649-50.

96. H. Banerjee, Agrarian Society of The Punjab, 1848-1901, 1976 (unpublished Ph.D. Thesis).

97. N.G. Barrier, "The Punjab Disturbances of 1907", The Punjab; Past and Present, October 1974.

98. S.Sen, *op.cit.*, pp.79-80; also D. Narain, Impact of Price Movements on Areas Under Selected Crops, 1900-1939, 1965.

99. G. Blyn, Agricultural Trends in India, 1891-1947, 1967. There was substantial increase in the proportion of land under improved seed in greater Punjab; waste land and forests were reclaimed and brought under cultivation.

100. This paper was first read at a meeting of the South Asia Colloquium of the Pacific North-west held at the University of Washington on April 23, 1968. The research is based on field-work in Kerala and Madras in the late 1940s and early 1950s, and in Kerala in 1964. Fieldwork in Kerala was made possible by grants of William Wyse and Anthony Wilkin Studentships from the University of Cambridge in 1947-49, and by an Auxiliary Research Award from the Social Science Research Council and a gift from my mother-in-law, Mrs. David W. Aberle, in 1964. The Tanjore research was financed by a British Treasury Studentship. My thanks go to all of these bodies and persons.

101. Hamza Alavi, 'Peasants and Revolution' reproduced above, Eric R. Wolf, 'Peasants and Revolution', a paper read 'Ill the Socialist Scholars' conference, New York, September, 1967; and Andre Gunder Frank, *Capitalism and Underdevelopment in Latin America; Historical Studies of Chile and Brazil,* New York, Monthly Review Press, 1967.

102. For Studies of agrarian relations in the two areas, see Adrian C. Mayer, *Land and Society in Malabar,* Oxford, Oxford University Press, 1952; Thomas W. Shea. 'The Land Tenure Structure in Malabar and its Influence on Capital Formation in Agriculture', unpublished Ph.D. thesis. University of California Press, 1965; Dagfinn Sivertsen, *When Caste Barriers Fall,* London, Allen and Unwin, 1963; Kathleen Gough, 'Caste in a Tanjore Village', in Edmund R. Leach (ed.), *Aspects of Caste in South India, Ceylon and Pakistan,* Cambridge, the University Press, 1962. E.M.S. Namboodiripad, *Kerala Yesterday, Today and Tomorrow,* Calcutta, National Book Agency, 1967, and A.K. Gopalan, *Kerala, Past and Present,* London, Lawrence & Wishart, 1959, provide especially valuable 'inside' views.

103. Mao Tse-tung, 'How to Analyse the Oasses in the Rural Areas', *Selected Works,* New York, International Publishers, 1954, I, pp. 138-40.

104. See Daniel and Alice Thorner, *Land and Labour in India,* New York, Asia Publishing House, 1962, pp. 51-70. The free sale of land and labour came about at different dates in different regions. Kerala had had some wage labour and considerable sale of land before the British conquest of 1972, but they had been restricted by law to particular castes. Land sales appear to have been rare in Tanjore before British rule began in 1799. Under British law, land seems to have been freely marketable in Kerala by about 1830; in Tanjore by 1865. (W. Logan, Malabar, Madras, the Government Press, 1951, Vol. I, p. 582,

F.R. Hemingway, Madras District Gazetteers, Tanjore, Madras, the Government Press, 1906, p. 184. The various kinds of slaves and agricultural serfs were gradually freed between 1812 and 1854.

105. Unfortunately we lack comparative data since we do not know much about revolts or famines among peasants in Tanjore and Kerala before British rule, nor do we know the precise amounts of their real incomes before the nineteenth century. We do know, however, that the population of Malabar District increased from an estimated 465,594 in 1802 to 2,261,000 in 1891 and 4,758,300 in 1951, and that there were severe famines almost every year between 1836 and 1896, especially in the years of the worst revolts. Since I have not found accounts of large-scale evictions and unemployment, of prolonged famines, or of revolts of peasants against their landlords (rather than on their behalf, against other authorities) for pre-British Kerala, I conclude that the upheavals and disasters of the nineteenth century did spring primarily from the introduction of colonial capitalism. It is true, of course, that productivity must have increased in order to support such a

rapidly expanding population, but that fact does not bear on the rate of exploitation of the peasantry. It is also equally true that the eighteenth century saw other kinds of disasters, particularly massive reductions of the population through wars. These wars were themselves, however, largely a result of competition between the European mercantile' powers and between them and the indigenous rulers.

106. A.S. Memon, *Kerala District Gazetteers,* Trivandrum, Government Press, 1962, p. 180.

107. P.C. Joshi, 'Unmasked Parties and Politics', March, 1940, quoted by Gene D. Overstreet and Marshall Windmiller, *Communism in India,* Berkeley andLos Angels, University of California Press, 1959, p. 181.

108. For accounts of these revolts, see Overstreet and Windmiller, *op. cit.*, pp. 276-312 and Alavi, *op. cit.*

109. John F. Muehl was an eye-witness of this revolt, which he describes in Interview With India, New York, John Day, 1950.

110. B.T. Ranadive, 'Struggle for People's Democracy and Socialism-Some Questions of Strategy and Tactics', *Communist, II,* June-July, 1949, p. 71, quoted in Overstreet and Windmiller, *op. cit.*, p. 287.

111. The Tanjore Tenants and Pannayals Protection Ordinance, 1952, which raised the wages of tied labourers and raised the tenant's share of the crop from one-fifth to two-fifths. The Ordinance did not, however, affect the wages of the increasingly large number of day-labourers, nor did it strengthen the claims of tenants who had no written leases.

112. For articles relevant to the Naxalbari revolt and the official Left communist attitude towards it, see *People's Democracy,* Calcutta, Vol. 3, Nos. 23, 24, 25,26,27,28,29, and 30.

113. See 'Notes', *Liberation,* Calcutta, No. 3, January 1968, pp. 95-96; 'Revolutionary Comrades on the March', *Liberation,* No. 4, February 1968, pp. 77-82; 'Rebelltion is Right!' *Liberation.* No. 5, March, 1968, pp. 92-96; and *'Rebellion is Right!' Liberation,* No.6, April 1968, pp. 96-109.

114. Programme of the Communist Party of India, Calcutta, 1964, p. 23.

115. This view is partly influenced by A.G. Frank's analysis of the Brazilian economy (op. cit.) and by his argument that the character of the capitalist metropolitan countries' monopoly of the world capitalist economy is changing from a monopoly ownership of most branches of industry itself to a monopoly of the technology of industry. This gives the metropolitan powers, especially the United States, increasing control over the new industries recently established in underdeveloped regions. My view is also based partly on the observation that in 1964 I found a marked sense of economic, military, and psychological dependence on the United States among almost all members of the Indian bourgeoisie whom I met, in contrast to the views I heard expressed in 1947-53.

116 See Bowani Pathak, 'Character of the Indian Bourgeoisie', *Liberation,* No. 2, December 1967, pp. 76-82. An official Left communist argument against this position is made in 'Is the Indian Big Bourgeoisie Comprador?' *People's Democracy,* Vol. IV, No. 17, April 28,1968, pp. 6-8.

117. *Techno Economic Survey of Kerala,* Trivandrum, the Government Press, 1962, p. 211.

118. *People's Democracy,* Vol. IV, No. 6, February II, 1968, p. 5.

119. Between the Census of 1931 and the Census of 1951 the percentage of Kerala's population dependent on agriculture is reported to have increased from 34.2 per cent to 53.84 per cent. *Techno-Economic Survey of Kerala,* p. 211.

120. Resolution of the Government of India, January 1902. *Gazette of India*, 18 January,1902.

121. N.G. Ranga and Swami Sahajanand Saraswati, *History of Kisan Movement*, All India Kisan Publications, Madras.

122. B. Moore, *Social Origins of Dictatorship and Democracy*, 1967.

123. R. Williams, *India in 1920-21*, 1922.

124. Note of the District Magistrate of Muzaffarpur, cited in K. Datta, *History of the Freedom Movement in Bihar*, Vol. I, pp.183-85.

125. J. Brown, *Gandhi's Rise to Power*, 1915-22, 1972, p.72.

126. General Administration Report, Patna Division, 1875-76, cited in G. Mishra, *Agrarian Problems of a Permanently Settled District of Bihar* : Champaran, 1976, p.411.

127. B.B. Misra, *Select Documents on Mahatma Gandhi's Movement in Champaran*, 1963, p.18.

128. S. Choudhury, *Peasants' and Workers' Movement in India 1905-27*, 1926. pp. 36-37.

129. Brown, *op.cit.*, p.111.

130. M. Desai, *The story of Bardoli*, 1929, p. 53.

131. Dhanagare, and G.C.Shah. Traditional Society and Political Mobilization: The experience of Bardoli Satyagraha, 1920-1928, *Contribution to Indian Sociology*, new series 8, 1974.

132. S. Gopal, *Jawaharlal Nehru: A Biography*, Vol. I, p. 43.

133. E. Whitcombe. *Agrarian Conditions in Northern India, 1860-1900*, 1971, pp.161-65.

134. M.H. Siddiqi, *Agrarian Unrest in North India, 1918-22*, 1978, pp.117-18, p.133.

135. Siddiqi, *op.cit.*, p. 161. Siddiqi writes that it was essentially a tenant agitation.

136. S. Gopal, *op.cit.*, pp. 56-57.

137. Pandey, *op.cit.*, see the section on Congress organization. The members of the P.C.C. who came mostly from lawyers, doctors and teachers apparently represented the urban middle class.

138. Situation in Bara Banki district by K.N. Khare, 2 July 1931, cited in Pandey, *op.cit.*, Appendix-A. The zamindars and local officials were "anti-Congress, anti-Kisan".

139. B. Chaudhuri, Agrarian Relations in Bengal, in N. Sinha, ed. *History of Bengal*, p. 272.

140. K. Datta, *History of the Freedom Movement in Bihar*, Vol. 2, pp. 235-36.

141. Survey and Settlement Report, Dacca, 1910-17, cited in Chaudhuri, The Process of Depeasantization in Bengal and Bihar, *Indian Historical Review*, July 1975.

142. *Settlement Report, Midnapore, 1911-17.*

143. *F.O. Bell Collection, Miscellaneous Papers*, 1931-41. In his tour diary Bell writes on the purchase of land by the jotedars during the depression.

144. Evidence of Jalpaiguri Bar Association, see *Report of Land Revenue Commission*, 1940.

145. T.Sarkar, The First Phase of Civil Disobedience in Bengal, 1930-31, *Indian Historical Review*, July 1977. Sarkar writes that the interest of the Bengal Congress leadership in the rural movement was limited.

146. A. Rasul, *Krishak Sabhar Itihash*, p.51.

147. *Report on the Political Situation in Bengal (confidential)*, January to September, 1936. In some of the meetings local Congressmen and men of "communist persuasions" took prominent part; in Burdwan Dasarathi Ta. in Noakhali Maulavi Muhammad Fazlul were active in the peasant movement: the Proja Saitis held numerous meetings in East Bengal districts which raised the demands of the abolition of zamindari.

148. Conrad Wood. The Moplah Rebellions Between 1800-02 and 1921-22, *Economic and Social History Review*, January-March 1976.

149. R.E. Mulle, *Mapila Muslims of Kerala*, 1976, pp.137-38.

150. K.N. Panikkar, Peasant Revolts in Malabar, A.R. Desai, *op.cit.*, pp.621-22; Dhanagare, *op.cit.*

151. P. Karat, The Peasant Movement in Malabar, 1934-40, *Social Scientist*, September, 1976.

152. P. Radhakrishnan, Peasant Struggles and Land Reforms in Malabar, *Economic and Political Weekly*, December 13, 1980.

153. K. Saradamoni, *Emergence of a Slave Caste*, 1980, p.130, pp.138-40.

154. C.M. Elliot, Caste and Faction Among the Dominant Castes: The Reddis and Kammas of Andhra, Kothari, *op.cit.*, p.152.

155. C.J. Baker, *The Politics of South India, 1920-37*, 1976, p.202.
156. Ranga and Sahajanand, *op.cit.*
157. Baker, *op.cit.*

2

Models and Theories of Indian Untouchability

To be an Untouchable in a rural Indian caste system is to be very low in, and partially excluded from, an elaborately hierarchical social order. The consequences of this lowness and partial exclusion, however, are not those argued in much of the anthropological literature on Untouchability and caste. Untouchables do not necessarily possess distinctively different social and cultural forms as a result of their position in the system. They do not possess a separate subculture. They are not detached or alienated from the "rationalizations" of the system. Untouchables possess and act upon a thickly textured culture whose fundamental definitions and values are identical to those of more global Indian village culture. The "view from the bottom" is based on the same principles and evaluations as the "view from the middle" or the "view from the top." The cultural system of Indian Untouchables does not distinctively question or revalue the dominant social order. Rather, it continuously recreates among Untouchables a microcosm of the larger system.

More formally, the present argument is for fundamental cultural consensus from the top to the bottom of a local caste hierarchy - a consensus very much participated in by the Untouchables. "Consensus" here does not refer to simple and uniform agreement between actors of every rank in their spontaneous statements about caste and its cultural matrix, for no such consensus exists in south Indian villages. It refers, instead, to deeper and often un-articulated identities of cultural construction. The subject of these identities are such matters as the human and non-human units in the world, and the appropriate relations of these units one to another. The present argument for cultural consensus is not meant to rule out the possibility that power plays a role in the maintenance of this consensus. Nor is it meant to rule out the existence of certain types of cultural variation from caste to caste. But the argument is meant to suggest that these variations exist within, and must be interpreted within, a framework of shared definitions and values.

In what follows, cultural consensus will be demonstrated in a number of ways. First, cultural consensus or even identity will be illustrated descriptively, by setting side by side important collective representations of the Untouchables and of higher-caste actors. Second and more interestingly, cultural consensus will be demonstrated by a structural analysis involving the concepts of inclusion and exclusion, and complementarity and replication. Untouchables are defined as persons of a discrete set of low castes, excluded for reason of their extreme collective impurity from particular relations with higher beings (both human and divine). The same Untouchables are included, however, in other relations with these same higher beings. It is then shown that, in contexts in which Untouchables are included, they complement. They play the appropriate low roles necessary to the maintenance of the human and divine order. Complementarity is interpreted as an indicator of cultural consensus, but it is a weak indicator. For the Untouchables might be acting in accord with the definitions and norms of the total system because of the power of the higher castes, not because of strongly internalized agreement with the postulates of the system. The Untouchables might be "role playing."

There is a stronger indicator of cultural consensus in the present analysis, however. Structurally, it is here shown that where the Untouchables are excluded, they replicate. They recreate among themselves the entire set of institutions and of ranked relations from which they have been excluded by the higher castes by reason of their extreme lowness. Replication is a stronger indicator of cultural consensus than complementarity, since it operates within the Untouchable subset of castes, where the power of the higher castes does not directly operate.

In the following ethnographic analysis, this argument and its structural framework will become both more concrete and more complex. Ethnographically, the subject will be investigated in two broad domains: social relations (caste) and relations with the divine (religion). The description will proceed in opposite directions in the two domains. First, social relations will be unpacked, Chinese-box fashion, from large units (village and caste) to smaller units (grade, lineage, and family), to show the progressive unfolding of complementary and replicatory structures among the low castes. Second, the same units will be reassembled, from small to large, in a description of the ritual relations between Untouchables and the deities of person, family, and territory. The structural vocabulary will become somewhat more involved as the analysis proceeds, and it will eventually include such terms as isomorphic transformation, code-switching, conflation, differentiation, many-to-one mappings and one-to-many mappings. But the general argument will remain the same throughout: for a pervasive cultural consensus between the Untouchables and the higher castes of Endavur.

The argument for a pervasive culture of caste among those whom the caste system appears to benefit least—the Untouchables—is in clear opposition to a set of disjunctive approaches to Indian Untouchability, approaches that argue that the essence of being an Untouchable is seeing the system in a different way. These disjunctive approaches in turn reflect quite different approaches to culture, to caste, and to comparative social inequality. "Consensus," in particular, is a fighting word in contemporary sociology, with a whole range of functionalist connotations often set in simplistic opposition to those of a more Marxian "conflict" perspective. Before we begin specific analysis of the present material, therefore, let us review in more detail these disjunctive approaches to Indian Untouchability and the theories of caste and social stratification to which they contribute—as well as the general and comparative framework to which the present approach to Untouchability is intended to contribute.

Early Images of Indian Untouchability

Perhaps the earliest and simplest Western image of Untouchability is embodied in the term "outcaste." In this view, to be an Untouchable is to be beyond the reach of Hindu culture and society, to be almost cultureless. Thus the Abbe Dubois, a remarkable French missionary with first-hand knowledge of village India between 1792 and 1823, contrasts the Untouchable "Pariahs" with those higher-caste Hindus on whom the system has had its beneficent moral effect: "We can picture what would become of the Hindus if they were not kept within the bounds of duty by the rules and penalties of caste, by looking at the position of the Pariahs, or outcastes of India, who, checked by no moral restraints, abandon themselves to their natural propensities." Dubois accomplished his proto ethnographic goals in south India in the immediately pre-British period by acting as Brahmin like as possible, and his Brahminocentric view of the

Pariahs includes a catalog of their "natural propensities" that includes drunkenness, shamelessness, brutality, truthlessness, uncleanliness, disgusting food practices, and an absolute lack of personal honour (Dubois 1959 [1815]: 29, 54-55). The word "Pariah," which derives from the Tamil name for the caste to be described in the following pages *(Paraiyan)*, has accordingly moved into the English language as a synonym for the socially ostracized and the morally depraved.

The early outcaste image, as it is articulated by Dubois, implies a major disjunction between the higher "caste Hindus" and the lowermost Untouchables, or outcastes. The very terms express the disjunction. The main body of the Hindu population "has caste," and is regulated by its social and cultural conventions, while the Paraiyans are outside the system and its restraints, and are thus in the grip of their distinctly reprehensible natures.[1] The Paraiyans, Dubois continues, both deserve and accept their low and asocial state. "The idea that he was born to be in subjection to the other castes is so ingrained in his mind that it never occurs to the Pariah to think that his fate is anything but irrevocable. Nothing will ever persuade him that men are all made of the same clay".

Implicit in this last statement of Dubois', however, is a contrary early image of Indian Untouchability, a simple consensus model. If Untouchables accept their status, they believe in the legitimacy of the system. If they further possess their own caste organization, they also act in accordance with the system. Dubois knew very well that Paraiyans and other low groups had caste organization, but he failed to draw out the implications of the fact. However, another Western observer of the same period did. Dr. Frances Buchanan, who surveyed newly acquired territories in Mysore for the British in 1799, describes the Untouchable Madiga as follows: "[The Madiga] are divided into small tribes of ten or twelve houses, and intermarry with the daughters of these houses only, in order to be certain of the purity of their race; of which they seem to be as fond, as those castes that are esteemed infinitely superior in rank" (Buchanan 1807: 640). Buchanan thus sees the Madiga as acting in the same way as higher castes, and in terms of the same values-concern with the "purity" of their group.

These two views of Untouchables and caste, the outcaste image and the simple consensus image, dominated Western thinking through the British period. Often they were held simultaneously and inconsistently by the same observer, but they could be brought together. Rev. Stephen Fuchs, accomplishes this in a descriptive monograph on the Untouchable Balahis of Madhya Pradesh, by interpreting Balahi culture as consistent with the culture of the higher castes, but as entirely imitative: "[The Balahis'] social customs and conventions are not their own invention, but are copied after the pattern of other castes. Their moral laws and the regulations of public life are not based on high moral ideas, but mainly on fear of public opinion. . . . The rites and ceremonies. . . are each and all imitations of the rich ceremonial of their Hindu environment. Their religious ideas are no less confused. . . than those of the other castes in the [region]." (Fuchs 1950: 434). Balahi culture may thus be in agreement with higher-caste culture, but this represents a weak, copied consensus. To be an Untouchable is not to be excluded from the culture of caste, but it is to possess this culture in a thinner and less convincing form.

Contemporary anthropological perspectives on the situation of Untouchables in caste represent both continuations of and reactions to these earlier Western views. Three sets of approaches can be distinguished in the literature since 1950. The first is a continuation of the "outcaste image": the cultural and social forms of Untouchables are determined by their being at some remove from a single high Brahminic culture. The second set, which are usually stated more explicitly, can be termed "models of diversity": Untouchables are the carriers of differentially valued alternate traditions, which have historically archaic or ethnically distinct roots, or which somehow express the distinct needs and experiences of those at the bottom. The third set of analytic frames is, like the first, a continuation of an older view, and can be termed "models of unity." Several of these models have been argued for the caste system in its higher reaches, but the model of unity has never been extensively argued in the contemporary anthropological literature on Untouchables. It is a form of this model that will be applied in the present work, one that states, most simply, that there is nothing distinctive about Untouchables culturally or socially, other than their placement at the bottom of a consensually defined hierarchical system. Let us look at the disjunctive models and the models of unity in more detail.

Outcaste Images

A modern example of an outcaste image can be found in Kathleen Gough's analysis of the Untouchable Pallans of South India. Unlike Dubois, and like most modern ethnographers of Indian Untouchables,

Gough is empathetically biased in favor of the low castes and against what she sees as the hierarchical, etiquette-bound high castes. If Dubois viewed the "nature" of the Paraiyans as uncivilized and degraded, Gough reverses the evaluation, and sets up tacit oppositions between the inhibiting "culture" of the Brahmins and the freer "nature" of the Untouchables. She discerns in the Pallans a looser, more psychologically healthy, approach to life. In their relation to sexuality and aggression, for example, the Pallans are said to be less restricted than the Brahmins: "The expression of aggression toward elders and peers [among the Pallans] is not strictly inhibited [as it is among the Brahmins]. . . . Similarly, the lower castes do not favor ascetic control of sexuality in marital relationships. . . The ascetic control of sexuality for its own sake does not increase a man's spiritual strength" (Gough 1956: 847).

The cultural dimension of Gough's approach is "certain moral values deriving from the Sanskrit religious tradition, of which [the Brahmins] are the main carriers" (1956: 826). Since the Pallans are among the lowest castes, farthest spatially and socially from the Brahmins, they are of all the castes in the village most free of the restraints of this Sanskritic culture. As with her psychology, most of Gough's cultural typifications of the low castes are framed in opposition to negatively loaded Brahminic traits: "The low castes place much less emphasis than do Brahmins on otherworldliness and on the fate of the soul after death. Engaged in the practical business of earning a living through manual labour, the low castes care more for health and prosperity in this life" (Gough 1956: 846).

Gough's positive restatement of the outcaste image is stated psychologically, but it is set within a broader materialist analysis. A closely related example of the modern outcaste image is found in the work of Joan Mencher and Gerald Berreman. This image is similarly materialistic, but it frames the cultural component differently. Here, Untouchables are seen to have demystified caste and its accompanying ideology. They view the caste system in an objective and cuiture free way for what it really is a system of oppression. Thus Joan Mencher feels that Paraiyans in south India have a more "explicitly materialistic" view of the system and their place in it than do those at the top, and that "those at the bottom of the hierarchy have less need to rationalize its inequities" (Mencher 1974: 476). The term "rationalize" expresses a particular view of culture held widely in the anthropological literature on Untouchability: that the culture of caste is a mask for what is in fact occurring in the sociomaterial world. It is a form of false consciousness. Since this consciousness serves only the interests of the high castes, the oppressors in the system, it is accordingly weak or absent among the low castes. What form of consciousness is present among the low castes is not, however discussed systematically in Mencher's work.

Gerald Berreman applies the same image in a comment on the consciousness of rural Untouchables in a Himalayan village in north India. In a short critique of Louis Dumont's structural theory of caste, Berreman claims that when he presented his version of the Dumontian model to rural Untouchables, "they laughed, and one of them said, 'you have been talking with Brahmins" (1971: 16-23). Like Mencher, Berreman maintains that Untouchables in some way reject a high-caste model of the system, but he does not tell us what alternate model of the system is held and enacted among them. None, perhaps. In their realistic view of the system, Berreman seems to tell us, the lowest castes are uninterested in rationalizations and ideology. Untouchables act in accordance with the system because they are forced to so act, but they cannot be forced to believe.

Berreman's interpretation of Indian Untouchables is part of an explicit defense of the "caste school of race" in American sociology (found in the work of W. Lloyd Warner, John Dollard, Gunnar Myrdal, and others). In its original form, this school constructed a comparative analogy between the racial system of the American south in the 1930s and 1940s and the Indian caste system. In both systems, there are said to be two or more rigidly ranked groups between which individual mobility is impossible. Membership in each group is permanent and defined at birth (or "birth ascribed"); each group is endogamous; and each system is maintained by prohibitions on inter-group contacts, especially on sexual ones between males of the low groups and females of the high groups. Ultimately, each system is maintained by the power of the high groups-by coercion rather than by consensus.

The black sociologist Oliver Cox criticized this equation of caste and race at length in 1948, before the postwar ethnographic data on the Indian caste system became available in the United States. His critique contrasted the simple consensus model of caste given above with American race as it was known first-hand from the monographic studies of the sociologists. Cox's theoretical point is that race is a highly specific and historically recent phenomenon, tied as ideology and practice to Western capitalism and imperialism. Caste, on the other hand, Cox views as a social system adapted to a non-capitalist economy. Cox's comparative point is that race in the American South violates the dominant egalitarian ideology of the society in which it occurs, while caste operates within a homogeneous set of non-egalitarian values, which are equally accepted by its superordinate and subordinate groups. "[Caste] carries in itself no basic antagonisms" (Cox 1948: 502).

Berreman's position on Untouchables is a return to the functionalist comparisons of the caste school of race, adding to them insights from the more detailed anthropological fieldwork on caste carried out in the 1950s in India. Berreman points out that the power of high Indian castes does have a role in maintaining the caste system, and that caste is rife with manipulation and conflict. Thus it does not differ from race in terms of these sociological abstractions. To show further that Untouchables are no more in agreement with the dominant ideology of caste than are Southern blacks with the dominant ideology of race (and that Southern whites are as undefensively hierarchical as Indian Brahmins) is once again to bring race and caste together as sociological equivalents (see Berreman 1960, 1972b).

The modern outcaste image of Indian Untouchables has another comparative affinity, though this one is less explicit. It is with Oscar Lewis's "culture of poverty" hypothesis for the urban poor in Western societies. In Lewis's restatement of the concept, the culture of poverty is a thin one- "the poverty of culture is one of the crucial aspects of the culture of poverty" (1970: 78). This thinness is a consequence of the purely rational adaptation of the urban poor to the situation in which they find themselves. The poor in capitalistic societies have less reason than the middle class to act in terms of middle-class values, since these values do not payoff for them. Nor do the urban poor have an alternate tradition or system of meaning available to them, other than the weakly structured and negatively defined "culture of poverty." Likewise, Untouchables in India do not accept high-caste culture because this culture has no rationalizing value for them. The Untouchables' alternatives vary according to the image. For Dubois, Untouchables are in a state of unbridled license, while for Gough, they are in a state of psychologically healthy removal from an obsessive high-caste culture. For Mencher and Berreman, they are the sceptics and demystifiers of caste-perhaps even its existentialists and protorevolutionaries.

Models of Diversity

The second set of contemporary anthropological approaches to Untouchables and caste argues for essential cultural diversity, and is itself an exceedingly diverse set. Like the outcaste images, the models of diversity are disjunctive; they stress contrasts between Untouchables and the higher castes. Unlike the outcaste images, however, they do not state these contrasts in terms of culture versus lack of culture. Rather, they view Untouchables as the bearers of alternate social and cultural systems, or of variants of the dominant system particularly adapted to the needs and experiences of those at the very bottom of the system. These needs and experiences vary according to the particular model. Their analytic cruxes include historical, communicative, psychological, economic, and political determinants. Each particular model of diversity tends to be tighter analytically than the outcaste images. Each generally makes a clear statement about the nature of the Untouchable subsystem, and about the mechanisms that have produced this subsystem. Taken as a whole, however, the predictions for "difference at the bottom" of all of these models of diversity form a rather heterogeneous set.

Consider, for example, Bernard Cohn's analysis of the Untouchable Camars of north India. Cohn sees the Camars as differing from the high castes for the same reason that Gough's Pallans differ from the Brahmins: for reason of the social and spatial separation between Untouchables and higher castes. Because Untouchables cannot hear the Vedas, or be served by Brahmins, or enter high-caste temples, they suffer from a kind of communications block. The result of this block, however, is not a form of culturelessness, but the retention of a historically prior pre-Aryan little tradition. Unlike the great tradition of the higher castes and of the Brahmins in particular, the little tradition of the Camars contains a "pre-Aryan and non-Brahmanic" religion, which emphasizes the propitiation of goddesses of disease, and the use of mediums and exorcists (Cohn 1955: 58). Cohn has to qualify these disjunctive contrasts considerably, however: "It is almost impossible to sort out those traits which are Sanskritic and those which are non-Sanskritic . . . and . . . what is idiosyncratic to the Camars as a group and what is a common body of ritual and belief held by other low castes and high castes as well" (Cohn 1954: 175). Given this qualification, then, Cohn's analysis amounts to a set of tentatively specified contrasts within an unanalyzed framework of cultural continuities.

Cohn's sub-cultural dichotomies, however, form only the baseline for his treatment of social change. For the Camars have in the last fifty years attempted to Sanskritize, to raise their status by adopting symbols of higher status in their local hierarchy. In doing so, they have abandoned many of the features of their distinctive little tradition, and have adopted the dominant Thakur's traditional caste code, which includes a non-beef diet, a tighter joint family, and more "Brahmanic" ritual practices. Therefore, although the Camars may have possessed a somewhat distinctive culture of their own in the base-line period, it is not a culture that they distinctively valued in any way, for they were quite willing to abandon it in an effort to raise their status.

A second model of diversity is found in Pauline Kolenda's treatment of karma doctrine among a caste of Untouchable Sweepers in north India, and turns on a psychological argument. Of the models of diversity that we are considering here, Kolenda's is the most minimal and the most carefully stated. Kolenda begins her analysis by demonstrating that the basic themes in the Sweepers' religion are common not only to higher-caste religion but to themes found in the ancient Sanskritic texts. She then deals with a single disjunction — with the question of how the Sweepers deal with one unpleasant implication of the linked doctrines of karma, dharma, and transmigration. According to these doctrines, which the Sweepers understand in abstract form, one's caste status in a given birth is the result of the total score of one's good or bad karma ("action" in accord with one's dharma, "duty," as defined in a given caste) in past lives. If the Untouchable Sweepers were to apply the karmaic explanation to their present low status, they would be admitting that they deserved such a status – that they had been unusually wicked in past rebirths. This admission, according to Kolenda, would cause them "religious anxiety." Why it would do so is not entirely clear. The hidden psychological assumption seems to be that no one wants to accept bottommost status in a ranked system, or that no one wants to accept the idea that they deserve so low a status.

For a third model of diversity for Untouchables in caste, we must turn once again to Kathleen Gough. Though Gough's explicit analysis of culture and Untouchability amounts to an example of the outcaste image, her clearly formulated analysis of the material determinants of Pallan social organization also makes major predictions for evaluative and normative differences between the high and low castes. Gough's analysis can thus be seen in another light as a model of diversity, in which cultural differences are generated by political and economic variables.

Gough's explanation of Pallan social organization begins with the highly asymmetric political and economic relationship between the dominant Brahmins and the Untouchable Pallan labourers of the village. Traditionally, not only did the Brahmins have direct authority over their Pallan labourers, but they held most of the land in the village. As the result of the Pallans' lack of land and movable property, says Gough, there are no material bases for ranked differences within the Pallan caste. The internal social organization of the Pallans is therefore characterized by "lack of privacy. . . fanatical emphasis on equality, and the extreme control of the street over individual affairs." "The street" here refers to Pallan political organization. The Pallan caste is divided into four streets, each with its own assembly and its own headman, and these assemblies affect the individual Pallan "at the slightest sign of individual nonconformity or in the smallest crisis of family life." And the tightness of this political organization is a consequence of two factors: the need to present a solid front to the Brahmins, who hold an entire Pallan street collectively responsible for an offense committed by any member; and the weakness of an alternate internal authority system, the family (Gough 1960a: 43-44).

The weakness of the family Gough again attributes to the Pallans' relationship to the land. She posits a direct relationship between landholding and the depth of the patrilineage: "the *Aadi-Draavidas* [the Pallans] do not own land. . . [and] their patrilineal group is therefore very shallow." As agricultural labourers, Pallan women are independent wage-earners, as are sons from early adolescence. Thus, an economic base of the husband and father's authority is missing-the common working of a common piece of land. This factor then feeds back as "equality" within the kin group: "rank is underplayed in the low caste kinship system and great stress is placed on the equivalence and solidarity of peers" (Gough 1956: 845-46).

Starting with a material factor and a political factor, then the relation of the Pallans to the land and the relation of the Pallans to the Brahmins-Gough derives a distinctive social and cultural subsystem at the bottom of a local caste hierarchy. The solidarity and egalitarianism of the Pallans are said to be in particularly strong contrast to comparable patterns in the Brahmin caste, for the Brahmins have no internal caste organization, and they predicate every social relationship on rank. Gough sums up these contrasts in a personal statement about the ethos of Pallan life: "Pallans show an almost fanatical passion for equality within their caste group. In fact, I found the equal and comradely style of life in the Pallan street a great relief from the obsessive ritualism, hierarchy, and envy in the Brahmin street. . . . [The Palians] react to their poverty (of which they are well aware) with a combination of anger, resignation, wryness and humor" (Gough 1973: 232, 233-34). Gough does not, it should be noted, include in her analysis a consideration of the relations between subunits of the Pallan caste, the "streets." Nor does she discuss the relations between this caste of Pallans, the Devandra Pallans by subcaste, and another Pallan subcaste (the Tekkatti Pallans) that lives separately in the same village.

Miller's evidence for the contours of this entirely disjunctive cultural system among the Mahars is mostly formal and decontextualized, however. He cites oral tradition and the written statements of politicized Mahar groups, but gives no detailed information on the baseline for Mahar change, on social organization, on behavior, or on how their "escape from the system" is in fact working out.[2]

What are we to make of all these models of diversity, other than that they reflect a very real empirical diversity in India, which became apparent after the first round of anthropological fieldwork in the 1950s? One way to sort them out is to note that two, Kolenda's and Gough's, are non-historical. These two make synchronic predictions about necessary differences between the high and low castes in a traditional village hierarchy. The other two models of diversity, Cohn's and Miller's, are stated as models of change. As such, both could be basically accurate at different points in time. See, for example, Owen Lynch's study of Untouchables in a north India city, where a particular caste of leatherworkers has pursued a strategy of Sanskritization in the early part of the century (more successfully than Cohn's Camars), and then switched over to a mixed strategy including an anticaste ideology (with less cultural reconstruction than Miller's Mahars) (Lynch 1969). We will reserve these empirical critiques for later.

For now, let us consider the theoretical implications of these models of diversity, particularly their approaches to culture, to caste, and to comparative social stratification. To begin with, the models of diversity as a whole assume a different theory of culture than do the outcaste images. Outcaste images imply that culture (or the culture of caste, at any rate) is only a manipulative rationalization, and that culture-free perception and action are to some degree possible. In the outcaste image, some cultures can be more realistic than others, some can be thinner than others. Models of diversity make no such assumption. For this set of approaches, all the varying cultures of caste are equally thick and equally relativistic. The culture of a given caste varies with its position in the system, but none of these cultures is necessarily truer than any other. Models of diversity attempt to explain the determinants of cultural difference from caste to caste, not to determine the objectivity of these differences as judgments of a system of oppression.

Despite a different underlying treatment of culture, however, models of diversity can have the same implications for general theories of social inequality as outcaste images. For both, approaches to Indian Untouchables are disjunctive. To the extent that models of diversity analyze only difference and ignore cultural continuities between castes, they can then be taken to imply that power and oppression alone account for caste stratification. Models of diversity then differ from the outcaste images only in that the latter imply that Untouchables have some awareness of their own oppression, while the former contain no such implication.

To see how these equations between cultural disjunction and power are made, consider a recent typological article by Berreman, in which the analogy between caste and race is extended several steps further, to include ethnic stratification and even class as comparable sociological phenomena.

There is one other reason for the degree to which disjunctive models outcaste images and models of diversity—have dominated analyses of Indian Untouchability. This reason is both pragmatic and perceptual. Ethnography that discovers something new is rewarding, while the overt payoff may seem minimal in an extended study that concludes that the only surprise is that there is no surprise, that there is nothing new culturally. The degree of commonality and cultural sharing between Untouchables and higher castes may seem self-evident and trivial to any Indianist with field experience; why run through a tedious litany of all the resemblances? The alternative, however, is to reify part cultures as if they were whole cultures, and to lose sight of systematic interconnections between the parts. Charles Valentine has made a similar criticism of the culture of poverty studies which, he notes, generally start with some statement that the culture of the poor in complex Western societies is really a "subculture." These studies then go on, he says, to describe the subcultures of the poor as if they were self-contained wholes, emphasizing distinctiveness and failing to weigh continuities with the larger culture. Valentine calls of a countervailing attempt to "discern what cultural features are shared by different but related subsystems, and how subcultures are articulated with universals in the total system" (Valentine 1968: 115). It should be clear by now that we are here making a similar call with respect to the cultural system of Indian Untouchables.

Models of Unity

There are two important models of unity among the contemporary approaches to India, the structural model of Louis Dumont and the "ethnosociological" model of McKim Marriott, Ronald Inden, and Ralph Nicholas. Unlike the disjunctive approaches above, both of these models are fundamentally concerned with "ideology" or culture; neither treats culture in caste as an epiphenomenon of something more sociologically universal (such as stratification, power, or oppression). Both models state that there is a consistent set of underlying principles that structure Indian cultural conceptions that these principles are found universally within India, but that they are also unique to India. Both models contain principles of diversity, but in each model diversity is either "encompassed by," or generated from, a more basic unity. And both models assume agreement on the basic cultural principles as profound among Indian Untouchables as among anyone else in the caste system.[3]

The framework for the following ethnographic analysis is inspired by Dumont's structural model of Indian society. The ethno-sociological approach, however, and its particular application to Indian folk religion by Susan Wadley (Wadley 1975), are also conceptually useful in attempts to grasp the indigenous cultural categories of the Endavur Untouchables.

What, then, is Dumont's structural approach to Indian society, and what are its implications for "being an Untouchable?" To begin somewhat simplistically, Dumont does not see caste as an inexplicably "unequal" system that requires an explanation because of the way in which it violates the more fundamentally egalitarian "nature" of man. Rather, Dumont reverses the comparative question, and suggests that it is Western egalitarian ideology that is the social-scientific puzzle, and that rank or hierarchy is more transhumanly comprehensible: "man does not only think, he acts. . . . To adopt a value is to introduce hierarchy, and a certain consensus of values, a certain hierarchy of ideas, things and people, is indispensable to social life. . . . In relation to these more or less necessary requirements of social life, the idea of equality, even if it is thought superior, is artificial" (Dumont 1970: 54-55). Caste represents the institutionalisation of hierarchical values, the most elaborate known working out of a set of values that we in the West have been systematically denying for the last three hundred years. To understand fully this egalitarian effort in the West, Dumont says, we must confront its polar opposite in India, hierarchy.

In his comparative epistemology, Dumont differs radically from Berreman and from other conflict theorists and functionalists. For Dumont, to compare is not to search for abstract, ahistorical essences common to caste, race, and ethnic stratification, and to dismiss ideological specificities as unimportant detail. To compare is to construct a structural analysis of each ideological and social formation, and then to confront these fully and specifically analyzed formations with one another (see Barnett, Fruzzetti, and Ostor 1976: 627-28). The purpose of the confrontation is dialectically to improve the understanding of each structure. Thus a provisional understanding of caste as a total ideological and social formation might contribute to a better understanding of race, and further insights about race similarly analysed might be dialectically fedback to a more adequate understanding of caste.

At present, Dumont's comparative analyses contain a suspicious number of simple logical oppositions, but they are nevertheless interesting.[4] For example, on caste and race, Dumont returns to Cox, but not to Cox's materialism. Caste, Dumont says, is a homogeneous moral system that values hierarchy and does not isolate and value the individual as the "measure of all things." Racism, on the other hand, is ideologically linked to egalitarianism, individualism, and to the Western denial of hierarchy. According to Dumont, in denying hierarchy in the social realm as a legitimate innate quality of the relations between humans, Western ideology must resituate it in a rigorously differentiated natural realm as racism, referred exclusively to natural difference (see Dumont 1960; Dumont 1970: 35-55).

Thus in Dumont's approach, Indian Untouchables are not the abstract sociological equivalent of racially subordinate groups in Western society. What, then, are Indian Untouchables, and how do they fit into the specific ideological and social formation? To begin indirectly, there is in Dumont's conception of Indian hierarchy an unstated implication about the "view from the bottom." For if, in India, hierarchy can be apprehended as a positive value, it must therefore be satisfying for actors throughout the system, even for those at the bottom. Either that, or power must suddenly intrude somewhere in the system, to hold down a set of people who have made a cognitive break from these hierarchical values. Dumont's position assumes the first possibility, and denies the second. There is a further possible implication of Dumont's argument for a positive view of hierarchy: that it represents an unmodified return to the old "simple consensus model" of caste, in which caste is seen as a system almost idyllically free of strife and conflict. Such is the implication that Berreman in particular draws from Dumont (see Berreman 1971: 18-19). Dumont, however, explicitly denies this particular implication of hierarchy, and points out that hierarchy in fact generates conflict. "India . . . emphasizes [hierarchy] to the point that situations tending to equality are unstable and conflict is called for to solve them by the establishment of a gradation. This might well be the basic reason why dispute is so endemic in India: however developed it might be, the system has not succeeded in establishing a perfect gradation of the whole of social life" (Dumont 1957b: 18). Therefore hierarchy, like "consensus" above, is not a term intended to deny the existence of dispute, but rather to frame the matters that are appropriately the subject of dispute. Dumont sees most disputes about rank in caste as disputes about one's legitimate position in a ranked system, not about the legitimacy of the ranked system itself. And this is as true for Untouchables as it is for higher-caste actors.

Dumont is more specific about the relation of Untouchables to the Indian social order, however. In his holistic conception of caste, hierarchy is expressed in an Indian cultural code of relative purity and impurity, in a continuously graded status order whose extremes are the Brahmin at the top — the most pure of men—and the Untouchable at the bottom—the least pure of men. Brahmin and Untouchable are conceptually opposed in a number of ways that contribute to their archetypal purity and impurity, according to Dumont. The Brahmin lives in the centre of the village, and is a "god on earth," while the Untouchable lives outside the village and is apparently excluded from religious life. The murder of a Brahmin is as heinous a crime as the murder of a cow, while the Untouchable is the scavenger and the eater of dead cows. The Brahmin purifies himself in order to approach the gods, and thus mediates between man and god. The Untouchable makes personal purity possible by removing the strongest sources of organic impurity, and the Untouchable mediates between man and the maleficent "demons." For Dumont, however, this opposition of

Brahmin and Untouchable is also a complementarity—the completion of a "whole" by two equally necessary but unequally ranked parts. "The impurity of the Untouchable is conceptually inseparable from the purity of the Brahmin." Since "the execution of impure tasks by some is necessary to the maintenance of purity for others. . . society is a totality made up of two unequal but complementary parts" (Dumont 1970: 92, 93).

What this means for Untouchables is fairly simple. If we follow Dumont's logic through, rank defined in unambiguous terms of relative purity and impurity should be as clear among Untouchables as it is among the highest castes. Diversity and dissension should be sought instead among the middle-ranking castes in the system.

The middle castes are not the subject here, nor is Dumont's "encompassment" theory central to the interpretative problems that we are raising for the Untouchables of Endavur.[5] More important for the present purpose is the general idea of a pervasive and continuous social hierarchy marked by relative purity and impurity. More specifically important is the possibility that Untouchables might define their own internal social organization as consistently in these terms as do the higher castes, and that they might be as pervasively "rank-conscious" as the higher castes. These simple ideas we will be testing with the data which follow.

The structural model that follows is also based on Dumont, though it is considerably more formal in its present statement. In his analysis of the lineage cults of the Pramalai Kallar of south India, Dumont in effect shows that orthodox cultural structures are replicated among a low and territorially isolated dominant caste. The Kallars divide the "divine" into two categories, Dumont says: high, pure gods who receive only vegetarian offerings, and lower, less pure gods who receive bloody sacrifice. This dichotomy of the divine is isomorphic with a basic human dichotomy: that between the pure but powerless Brahmins and the impure but dominant Kallars. By worshipping among themselves a divine world so organized, Dumont suggests, the Kallars admit to their own status inferiority vis-à-vis the Brahmins, and reaffirm the holistic interdependence between high and low god, between Brahmin and Kallar. The Kallar also state and rank the dichotomy according to orthodox cultural principles, relative purity and impurity (here expressed by the type of offerings to the respective gods) (see Dumont 1957a; 415-19; Dumont 1959). This model of structural isomorphism and of structural replication will be formalized and elaborated in what follows, to make a similar argument for a deep sharing of cultural codes among a group of Untouchables.

As for "ethnosociology" and its use here, this approach, whose purpose is to describe the "pervasive indigenous assumptions" (Marriott 1974: 1) behind social action in India, is a model of unity even more radical than Dumont's. A linguistic analogy might give a sense of its relevance to the issue of Untouchables and Indian culture. Ethnosociology is presently endeavoring to construct a model of Indian cultural assumptions so basic that it can be compared to the categories of a language grammar. To suggest that low-ranking actors who act in terms of a culture so analyzed might also "reject" its categorical assumptions is then logically equivalent to suggesting that some speakers of a given language might similarly reject its grammar. Neither, of course, is possible. The principles are too deep; they are the very stuff of thought and of action.[6]

Ethnosociology accordingly makes no specific predictions about Untouchables; it simply assumes them to be sharers in a deep cultural grammar common to everyone in Hindu village India. Nor does ethnosociology in its present formulations (Marriott and Inden 1973; Marriott and Inden 1974; Marriott 1974; Inden and Nicholas 1972; Inden 1975) have much to say about social or cultural comparison, other than an essentially negative comparative point that exogenous models of society, drawn from Western social experience, are unilluminating when applied to Indian social reality. As a relativistic view from within, ethnosociology can be taken as antithetical to Dumont's structuralism. But as a model of unity, with a distinct, more carefully cultural focus, it can also be taken as complementary to Dumont's approach, and we shall so take it here. Ethnosociology is currently generating some useful propositions about indigenously defined units of action, and about the semantics of the relations between these units. It is becoming increasingly clear, for example, that "purity impurity" is too simplistic and too misleading a gloss of the relation between high and low-caste actors, that the indigenous definition of rank also contains ideas about auspiciousness, power (as it is culturally understood), and control. Similarly, the concept of a "transaction," which in its initial statement was a type of raw behavior (Marriott 1968), has recently been rethought in cognitive terms (Marriott 1974), and as such constitutes a more precise and specific tool for decoding the meaning of a given caste's status and identity than does anything found in Dumont. Finally ethnosociology is considerably revising our perhaps ethnocentric ideas about the relations between humans and gods in Indian culture (Wadley 1975).

Ethnosociology thus provides us with more precise approximations of certain Indian cultural conceptions than does Dumont's approach. Where it does, we will adopt its insights. Ethnosociology is, however, at present less explicit about the total structure of the Indian social order than is Dumont's model. It has virtually nothing to say about the relation between culture and behavior. And its suggestions for trans societal comparison are neither as explicit nor as interesting as Dumont's. For this reason, the Dumontian structural model of caste and Untouchables will very much "encompass" ethnosociology in the following ethnographic analysis.

References

1. The term "outcaste" or "outcast" has two different referents relevant to the present discussion. If a person violates his caste's code for conduct, he can be temporarily or permanently "outcast" for the offense. He is then without any caste at all, and must either seek readmission into the caste of his birth, or be admitted to a much lower caste, or lead an asocial existence. Since the ancient *dharmasastras* account for the origins of many low castes in a single mythic act of outcasting (usually for an improper mixed marriage), and since persons expelled from higher castes are occasionally incorporated by Untouchable castes (usually when their offense is a sexual alliance with a person of that Untouchable caste), some early Western explanations of caste assumed that all Indian Untouchables were historically derived from individual higher-caste outcasts and their descendants. When these low castes were then labelled "outcastes," the assumption stole in that there was no caste organization among them. This second assumption is emphatically incorrect. To keep the two referents of the terms straight, it is convenient to define "outcast" as an individual expelled from his caste, and "outcaste" as a largely deceptive synonym for the partially excluded lowest castes.

2. For a more detailed and sophisticated treatment of a low group that is manipulating the "great civilization" in a politically self-conscious way. see Martin Orans' *The Santal: A Tribe in Search of a Great Tradition* (Detroit: Wayne State University Press, 1965). I am not considering Orans' analysis here because of the additional complexities introduced into the argument by the Santals' recent tribal background. There is yet another model of diversity relevant to just this variable, however: the idea that the present Untouchable groups in India, or some of them at any rate, are the historical precipitate of ethnically and culturally distinct tribal entities that have been Hinduized and introduced to the "bottom rung" of local caste hierarchies. Such is the thrust of Irawati Karve's "agglomerative" interpretation of caste. though

Karve does not actually argue that Untouchables are more likely than higher castes to bear the markers of their former tribal backgrounds (see Karve, 1961). Nor am I aware of any other anthropologist who has tried to sustain this kind of argument of tribal diversity for any of the major contemporary Untouchable castes of India.

3. There are profound differences between the two approaches as well, though they are not central here. For a pro-Dumontian gloss *nor* the disagreements, see Barnett, Fruzzetti, and Ostor, 1976. See also Marriott 1969, Dumont 1971, and Marriott and Inden 1974.
4. Dumont has pushed his comparison of *homo hierarchicus* and *homo aequalis* considerably further in Dumont 1977. We are not considering this elaborated comparison here.
5. An empirical problem is that transactional and opinion analyses of caste-rank orders do not show any greater indeterminancy in the middle ranges than at the extremes of caste (see Marriott 1968). For some interpretative and theoretical problems, see Marriott 1969.
6. In one article, Marriott does generate a diverse set of transactional strategies from the fundamentally unitary ethnosociological model. Without going into the technicalities of his argument, let us only note that this approach to diversity—like Dumont's, but for very different reasons—also predicts most of its diversity in the middle ranges of local caste hierarchies. Here also, Brahmins and Untouchables are more like one another than they are like the middle castes, for both are restricted to "asymmetric" strategies (see Marriott 1974: 23-24).

3
Review of Literature

Agricultural activity in Andhra Pradesh has produced a unique social institution known as Paleru[1] system or contract annual/biannual basis for a fixed amount of remuneration in lieu of the service rendered by the farm servant.

There are no written rules or regulations for the appointment of a farm labourer or paleru. Everything goes by convention, custom and unwritten way, it is a word of agreement between the employer (farm lord) and the employee (Paleru). The system of Paleru has come down from generation to generation without any friction whatsoever Paleru has become a synonym for the Scheduled Caste people, the institution of Paleru is as old as the Jamindari system. Large tracts of land when brought under the plough by a single owner it became necessary for the employment of farm labourers or farm servant on a fixed payment for a fixed time.

Agriculture and Animal husbandry go hand in glove. As such, the farm servant or paleru was also to look after the cattle in spare time and looking after the household duties of the landlord's family during non-agricultural seasons. Thus the paleru system has become very much essential for the landlords who used the services of Paleru and his family in many respects, as a most faithful servant in the farm, as a cowherd and a domestic servant.

The palerus and their family being untouchables, uneducated and having no choice for other profession,[2] completely depended upon the landlords for their survival.

The advent of the British along with their Christian propagation brought about a tremendous change in the lives of farm contract servants. Starting of schools, providing boarding and houses for the children, free medical and educational facilities brought about a great change in the lives of these farm servants. Earlier they used to follow all the dictations of their landlords and used to vote to those whomever their landlord supports.[3] The Palerus have no individuality or voice to say anything against their landlords. With the coming of the British and Christian conversions the Palerus began to come out slowly from the clutches of the landlords.

There was a great demand for aqua-products in foreign countries. The Andhra coast being rich for the production of aqua products 90 per cent of the paddy growing areas have been converted into fish ponds. Demand for agriculture labour decreased. Many farm servants migrated to urban areas in search of livelihood. At the same time, there were very good opportunities for employment in the Gulf countries even for uneducated and unskilled people as domestic servant.[4]

The profitable employment in the Gulf countries made the paleru families very rich and wealthy. Once they felt proud to be called palerus of some farmlords but today they have become landlords by the Gulf employment.

Thus, the institution of paleru whose origin is not known has become a grand victim of untouchability and all other social evils in the area. The present study focusses on the functioning of paleru system with special reference to the Scheduled Caste communities of West Godavari district.

1. Introducing the Problem

The Paleru system is one of the offsprings of rigid caste system. Though all Sudras are labelled as serving communities, according to tradition, the *atisudras* or those people who have been below the Sudras in social scale became the target of highly specialised victims of untouchability. In fact, these people have to choose the profession of tenure contracts as palerus accepting all hard and fast rules imposed by the landlords. In fact, the institution of *Paleru* has become a part and parcel of untouchability. Palerus were synonymous with Malas or untouchables.

Their agreement was one sided. The Paleru has no voice to bargain his services. From one generation to another they were forced to lead the condenced economic and social life without any choice or option for another profession.

The atrocities committed on the palerus and their families continued as long as they were not exposed to any type of education.

The socio-economic and cultural life of the Paleru communities in the pre-independence period was worse than slavery. They led the life of a traditional slave.[5]

No law came to their rescue. Nobody supported their cause until the coming of the Christian missionaries who gave them education and a new way of life along with Christianity. Thus, the problem of the *Palerus* is one of the social evils of the area which had deep roots in the local traditional way of life.

The present study focusses on the gradual but unconscious development of the *Paleru* system anchored in the economic and social traits obtainable in the caste ridden Hindu society. The study further focusses on the genesis of social change incumbent on the Christian Missionary institutions which brought about awareness among the lower echlons of the society and educated them as per the need of the hour. Reflections are made as to how the paleru people can rid of their economic and social bondage. Suggestions are made to uplift the Paleru community through alleviation programmes.

Need for the Present Study

The history, tradition and culture of the untouchables, popularly known as Scheduled Caste are as old as the brahminical traditions in India. Being noteworthy of any significance, the activities and sacrifices done by the Scheduled Caste people through the ages have not been recorded as a part of the study. With the coming of the British, an indological research gave birth to several interesting facts recorded about the original inhabitants of India. Translation of social histories and anthrosociological studies have been undertaken, the information gathered from the original Sanskrit works of India amply supplemented the gap of social history in India. Growing interest in the indological studies particularly towards the Dalit histories and problems necessiated by political pressures brought to light many facts from the hidden history of the Dalits in India. Studies on the natives, particularly the forgotten tribes and the untouchables, can be traced back to the beginnings of this century. Several social movements hastend the process of making crucial enquiries into the caste and present problem of Dalits.

Poets, writers, journalists, photographers, social reformers and myrids of other people brought to light many aspects of Dalit way of life. Today untouchables raised their voice and fought restlessly for their survival, social justice and economic status. The following works would throw some light on the problems and prospects of the Scheduled Caste people in India.

Significant studies on the Malas are very few. A brief account of the origin of Mala is presented by some ethnographers like Edgar Thurston (1909) and G.S. Ghurye (1961) who have given description of the culture of Mala. In fact they have written the monographs on the basis of census records and official documents.

Thurston (1909) mentions in his book *Castes and Tribes in South India* that the Malas are considered to be servants of upper castes for whom they act as caste messengers on the occasion of marriage and funerals. L.S.S. O'Malley (1932) in his book, Indian Caste Customs (1932) mentions the origin of untouchables. The untouchables are commonly referred to as "the depressed classes" and are sometimes called the "out castes" or "out caste Hindus" as distinguished from other higher castes which are referred to as caste Hindus. George W.Brigg's book *The Chamars* (1920) contains the cultural account of the Chamars of Uttar Pradesh.

Sachchidananda (1977) in his book *The Harijan Elite* has tried to analyse their status, mobility and role in transformation, Sunanda Patwardan (1973) in her book entitled *Change among India's Harijans* studies the major group of Harijans in the state of Maharashtra. This study reveals that some of the major Harijans in Maharashtra give two broad trends - positional and structural.

The depressed classes in India - an enquiry into their conditions and suggestions for their uplift (1977) is one of the compilations of several articles written by various reformers and academicians with an introductory note given by Rajendra Singh Vatsa. It deals with their origin, who are socially ostracised, economically exploited and politically deprived.

L.P. Vidyarthi and N. Mishra (1977) in their book *Harijan Today* deal with the sociological, economic, political, religious and cultural analysis of the Harijans from the two (Maghahi and tribal zones) of the four culture-linguistic zones of Bihar. Mumtaz Ali Khan (1980) in his book *Scheduled Castes and their Status in India* studies about the Scheduled Castes in Bangalore district.

Michael Maffatt (1979) in his book *An Untouchable Community in South India* makes a detailed study of the untouchables in the village of Endeavour of Tamil Nadu.

B.S. Murthy (1971) has also contributed a lot on Harijans in his book called *Depressed and Oppressed.* He himself being a Harijan has narrated the problems of his fellowmen. Dr. Ambedkar's (1946) three books, *Who were the Sudras? The Untouchables* and *What Congress and Gandhi have done to the untouchables* are well recognised and often quoted. Through these books, he stressed social and religious systems of untouchability and the political safeguards of the Harijans of recent origin.

Sri A.Aiyappan (1966) in his book, *Social Revolution in Kerala Village* and K.C. Alexander (1966) in his book, *A Study of the Changing Patterns of Behaviour*, the Pulaya Untouchable of Kerala have reported certain changes among Irva and Pulaya of Kerala. Both these groups have experienced rapid change and have gained in social status through education.

Sri R.R. Trivedi (1976) in his book entitled Scheduled Caste *Women Studies in Exploitation with a Special Reference to Superstition, Ignorance and Poverty* deals with the Exploitation of the Scheduled Caste women for immoral traffic in human flesh. The study was undertaken in three regions, Bijapur district in Karnataka, Raipur in Madhya Pradesh and Uttar Kashi in Uttar Pradesh.

Mrs. C.Parvathamma (1968) in her book *Scheduled Castes and Tribes a Social Economic Survey* gives some account of frustration prevalent among the Scheduled Castes in the post-independent India.

J. Michael Mahar (1972) has studied about untouchables in his famous book, 'The Untouchables in Contemporary India'. He dealt with the role of the untouchables in rural community, religious reforms, government efforts to abolish untouchability and the social and psychological response to the change of status.

Kamble (1982) in his book, 'The Scheduled Caste', observes that in addition to constitutional safeguards and several legislative measures to abolish untouchability and bring them at par with other sections of Indian society by providing educational facilities and reservations in political educational, occupational spheres which constitute the biggest core of welfare schemes for the scheduled castes.

G.Viswanatham and K.Narasimha Reddy (1985) have made explorative attempt to find out the determinants of educational achievement among Scheduled Castes in their book *Scheduled Castes : A Study in Educational Achievements*. Most specifically they have examined whether or not there are class-wise variations among them with respect to educational achievement. Their research study is based on the assumption that the Scheduled Castes are no longer homogeneous community and that there are perceptive differences among them with respect to class status and power, parental attitude and its perception as a valuable channel of upward social mobility, availability of tradition of education and the existing of education oriented sub-culture.

D.Venkateswarlu (1990) makes a different study about the conflicts between the Harijans and upper castes. In his book, Harijan-Upper caste Conflicts. he observed that there is a new level of awareness and consciousness among them that has not only enhanced their aspirations and ambitions but also made them assertive. This is not tolerated by the socially and economically dominant caste Hindus. There a situation of conflict develops when the Harijans wish to realise their aspirations or assert their rights which the dominant among caste Hindus do not concede.

Jaatiya Prabodhamu

Written by Sri Yeluri Appala Swamy from Rangoon in 1939 highlights the need for the awakening of the Scheduled Castes who have been suppressed by the higher castes in respect of economic, social and cultural spheres at their lives. The author has witnessed several atrocities when he came from Burma to his native district, i.e.,West Godavari. He was surprised to see atrocities being committed on the untouchables. He laments on the deplorable conditions of his people who were once the rulers of this country. He awakens his people to renounce the religion which does not treat them as human beings, also advises them to rise in revolt against the archaic way of life. This work, though very small in volume but highlights the mega problem of the untouchables, caused by the higher caste people.

Sri Boya Bhimanna's first published writings, around 1936, described the inhuman conditions of village life, 'highlighting the need for establishing a socialistic patterns of society'. Then *Paaleru* ('A Farm Boy') published in 1940 showed Dalit village struggles and suffering at the hands of landlord and unenlightened father; the way out, it depicted, as town based education and service in the bureaucracy. Kooli Raju, written in 1941 and published in 1947, described the agricultural labour movement in the villages, but had its resolution when a Dalit woman is elected as government head. Finally, Raaga Vasishtam (1940), described the marriage of Vasishta and Arundati, emphasizing a 'strong casteless nation' and arguing that 'Harijans and Aryans' make a harmonious blend of the society. These writings depict the rural base of caste-class conflicts, but they show a Hindu incorporationism and a middle-class reformist solution. This also seems to have been accompanied by an anti-Muslim orientation.

On the other hand, the militancy of lower class Dalits was increasingly being expressed in communist agricultural labour organizing, in active struggles so patently lacking in the resolutions of the Adi-Andhra conferences. Many young Dalits joined the movement from the early 1940's, including Guntur Bapanaiah, Prasad Rao, M. Sriramulu, Koneru Ranga Rao, R.A. Kotayya, Kandhi Kaithaya, Nagabhushanam (of East Godavari), K. Mohan Rao (East Godavari) and M. Svarnavamanaya. Guntur Bapanaiah became general secretary of Agricultural Labour Union (ALU) and K. Surya Prakash Rao became its president from 1941 to 1943. Even the strong anti-Ambedkar stance of the communists aroused tensions, Surya Prakash Rao, for example, reports that his final alienation from the party came in 1944 when a resolution of ALU described the Muslim League as a political party, but called the Scheduled Caste federation a 'Communal Organization'. He opposed this and circulated a dissenting note emphasizing the economic and social degradation of Dalits and the need for unity of the toiling masses, arguing finally that social upliftment was even more important than economic upliftment.

Malapalli ('Mala Quarters' or 'Mala Village')

The famous reformer Unnava Lakshminarayana, describes the social and economic effects of commercialization in the delta and the responses of Dalits to this. Agricultural labourers are depicted as realizing the manipulative potential of the new wage system in eroding real wages' use of coercion, preventing cattle from grazing on private lands, beatings of Dalits and the eviction of poor peasants from their lands are shown, along with a major crisis of traditional cultural values. As Hargopal summarizes.

The main reason presented for the absence of class consciousness in the hegemony of the Hindu world-view conditioning the consciousness of the Harijans. This prevents them from revolting. This theme is presented through one character who finds several philosophical explanations for their degenerating living conditions. His elder son......... opts for the Gandhian model of resistance which broadly fits the Hindu Philosophy of

Action. He joins the 'Panchama' movement launched by the Scheduled Castes and attempts to organise his caste people. But the landlord who smacks the potential of the movement violently kills him. This act gets absorbed by the peace loving nature of these groups coupled with the manipulations by the ruling elite and the intervention of the state. This indicates not only the structural constraints in which the poor Harijans were locked but the cobweb of consciousness which permitted them little concerted and organized action.

Harijan Nayakudu (Harijan Leader)

Written by N.G. Ranga, the famous Parliamentarian published in 1933 reflected the ideological position of this peasant leader. The hero is a 'Harijan' social reformer who agitates on various issues, opposing the violence against and abuse of Dalits, organizing inter-caste marriages, establishing schools, fighting for entry into temples and use of public wells. Dalits are depicted as allying with peasant kammas in contrast with the kamma landlords who do not soil their hands.

Hargopal, as a Marxist critiques the reformist (integrationist) consciousness depicted in the Dalits falling prey to theme of class harmony and change of heart, in accepting their status as Hindus. But what even the Marxist did not recognise (and it is striking that even in 1980s and 1990s Marixsts throughout India continued to refer to Dalits as '*Harijans*'), is that in 1920s and 1930s militant Dalits were throughly rejecting both the Panchama and Harijan identity and were organising themselve as Adi Andhras.

2. Statement of the Problem

The institution of Paleru is one of the menial systems that prevailed in India with different names, being constituted from the members of the Scheduled Caste. Population who were once, even now in some parts of the country are considered as untouchables. This institution of Paleru has come into existence on account of agricultural needs but in course of time Paleru became a part and parcel of the landlords family activities. The Paleru became half farm and half domestic servant. Once Paleru meant a co-plougher but latter it denoted a domestic servant as well. Once the activities of paleru are purely confined to agriculture and its allied branch the dairy which again associated with cattle rearing and breeding.

The activities of the farm servant closely reached to the activities of domestic servant thus a patron-client relations developed between the landlord and the paleru. This proved a bilateral system in which the landlord benefitted by making use of the liberty, freedom and other civil rights of the palerus. Palerus lost everything and began to act as dependents for anything and everything, they could not send their children for schools, they could not borrow even at a low interest from others, they could not cast their vote at their own choice. They could not go to the Court of Law against the cognisable atrocities committed on them. The best of the things they produced were given to the landlord and the left over of the landlords family accepted as items of feast. Thus the paleru system paved the way for the social, economic, political and ethical degradation of these scheduled caste people who served as contract paleru from one generation to another.

This problem of servitude, social and economic indebtedness, much variation in the standard of living of the palerus is the crux of the problem of the study. The present study is concerned with the identification of various circumstances, causes that led to the creation of tools of oppression that stood in the way of the progress and development of the palerus of the West Godavari district. It is possible to find out the other forces that work which have helped for the non-functioning of the paleru institution in the area under study.

The results of the study would help to solve similar problems concerned with similar institution elsewhere. By this it is also possible for the government and the non-governmental agencies to find out ways and means for problems to solve and progress to achieve.

3. Objectives of the Present Study

Official list of Scheduled Castes of Andhra Pradesh contain as many as 59 in number. All of them one way or other enjoy the lowest social economic, political and cultural position outside the pale of Hinduism. They are Hindus as part of Hindu society but enjoyed a second grade citizenship in their own country. Being part and parcel of the society, their interaction with their fellow upper caste people in the spheres of social, economic, political and culture is inevitable. In the context of rituals and social gatherings the Scheduled Caste people are subjected to the concept of pollution. This stamped system of untouchability forced the incumbants to become victims in all spheres of social progress. In order to find out a way to bring the Scheduled Caste people on par with other communities solutions are yet to be found out. To find out solutions, studies on these people from different viewpoints are very much in need. Keeping in view the above points. The following specific objectives have been drawn for the present study.

The present study is concerned with the problems of farm servant system in respect of its origin, relevance and survival.

Secondly, the study examines the impact of the Paleru institution, on social, economical, political, educational and cultural spheres of the Scheduled Caste farm servant families of Andhra Pradesh in general and in the area in particular.

4. Importance of the Study

Research studies undertaken on the West Godavari district in the sphere of agriculture and agricultural labour are of no doubt of a much valuable nature. Many studies have covered - crop pattern, wages, labour migrations etc., but never focussed any attention on the tied up farm labour otherwise known as the palerus, very much prominent in the area since times immemorial. Palerus, a separated agricultural contract employee, who was governed by no government rules played an important role in the socio-economic, political and religious spheres of the village life. The paleru was less than a partner and more than a domestic servant. The contract of appointment and removal of paleru is not guided by any written rules of the government; they are simply based on convention tradition, oral agreement.[6] The remuneration or wages of a term is also not based on any established government rule which can be questioned in the court of law, thus a social institution purely rural based agricultural contract job has survived for a long time simply on the belief, custom, convention of the villagers and the final judgement given by the village elders.

Due to the absence of written documents for the tenure of palerus and also due to the illiteracy among the palerus many of the personal accounts pertaining to financial matters were entered by the creditor without the knowledge of the borrower (Paleru). Due to illiteracy, the borrower accounts could not be settled and much injustice was done as they were socially backward and economically poor. The palerus could not raise their voice for freedom and simply led their life just above the water level satisfying themselves with the meagre earnings which gave them hand to mouth existence. Such problems confronting the paleru communities certainly deserve the attention of the researcher.

Studies pertaining to the social, economic, political and cultural aspects and also the tools of suppression and discrimination used on this people would help us to make a theoretical frame work of the study. The real information required through interview schedule method in the area would give tangible information pertaining to their problems. The information so gathered and tabulated in the cases could be analysed. The cases so analysed would help to find out solutions for the problems identified.

Practical implications of the study would help to solve the problems of the palerus and the abominable and meaningless, outdated institution like the palerus.

Secondly, the study would trace the origin and development of various atrocities and injustices done to them in the social, economic, political and cultural spheres. The study further examines the degree of resistance given and the type of fight the palerus made against their suppressors for social justice. The struggle made by the palerus against economic, social and political oppressions to come out of traditional bondages would serve as a model for similar communities to solve their problems. Thus, the present study would serve practically a great social purpose.

References

1. It is a system of appointing farm servant by landlords prevalent in different parts of Andhra Pradesh with different names.
2. There is no choice for the Scheduled Caste man to pursue a profession which is profitable for him. Tradition made his life inelastic.
3. Farm servants have no freedom to caste their adult franchise according to their choice even today.
4. According to the survey in the field 60 per cent of the paleru families went to Gulf countries, i.e., Dubai, Abu Dubai, Muskat, Iran, Iraq, Kuwait etc., to work as helpers, massons, electricians, domestic servants and housemaids.

5. Even today in certain parts of Andhra Pradesh (Rayalaseema) the farm servant is known as *Kattubanisa* or tied up slave.
6. All rules and regulations pertaining to the appointment and termination, pay payment and penality of a farm servant are finally settled, in case of default on the Rachabanda/village platform where the elders of the village convene a meeting with pedda mala or the elder man of the Scheduled Caste council.

4

The Setting: West Godavari District—A Profile

The West Godavari district has been the granary of Andhra Pradesh for it produced abundant quantity of paddy, thanks to the work done by the great genious,[1] Sir Aurthor Cotton, a British Engineer who planned the future of Agriculture in Godavari districts by constructing an anicut at Dhavaleswaram (East Godavari District) on the river Godavari and subsequently a well planned network of irrigation and drainage canals has been added to the anicut system. This was a great mega engineering skill which lasted without any trouble for a century, by satisfying the needs of drinking and irrigation requirements and (water) preventing floods by its deep drainage canals. Because of this great work drought, famine, disease and pestilence have ran away from the Godavari districts eversince.[2]

1. Profile of the Area : The West Godavari District

The district has an area of 7,742 sq.kms. which accounts for 2.79 per cent of the total area of the state. It occupies 19th place in respect of area in the state. The district at the time of study was administered through three revenue divisions viz., Eluru, Kovvuru and Narsapuram. According to the amended act of the local self-government, the district has eight municipalities viz., Eluru, Tanuku, Bhimavaram, Palakollu, Tadepalli-gudem, Narsapuram, Nidadavolu and Kovvuru. The District which contained 14 taluks in the earlier system was converted into 46 mandals with a total number of 839 villages.

(a) Land form and topography

(b) The Rivers

(c) Climate

(d) Rainfall

(e) Forests

(f) People and settlemenis.

(a) Land form and topography

The West Godavari area presents an interesting topography. The north western and western parts of the district are abound in hill country characterised by the southern extensions of the 'eastern hills' forming part of the Eastern ghats. The adjacent area extending due east and south-east is characterised by sub-montane plains with occasional erruptions of isolated hills. Further east, boardering the coastline is the deltaic zone characterised by the alluvial sediments brought down by the Godavari and consolidated times ago. Along the coastal strip there are sand bars occasionally holding waters as inland pools and lakes — the best example however, is the lake Kolleru, a fresh water lake formed by the sand bars and strand lines close to the coast. The terrain of the West Godavari shows a gradual incline to south, south-east as can be observed from the tributary system, the trunk channel of the Godavari and the main distributaries which flow due south-east.

(b) The Rivers

Godavari is the important river flowing in this district. This river[3] borders the entire eastern boundary of the district. At Vijjeswaram, the river breaks into Rivers of Andhra Pradesh (1989).two branches namely, the Gautami, Godavari (eastern branch) and Vasistha Godavari (Western branch) and flows towards the south of the district before falling into the Bay of Bengal near Antarvedi. The other minor rivers which feed the irrigation tanks in upland areas are Tammileru, Yerrakalva, Byneru, Kovvada Kalva, Juleru, Rallamadugu and Gunderu. The Kolleru lake is an extensive shallow depression occupying an area of 67359 Kms. created by a gradual rise in the level of the country. On either side by alluvial deposits from the Godavari and the Krishna canals. This lake receives a large volume of drainage water of the surrounding deltaic country. It has an outlet to the sea through Upputeru.

(c) Climate

The climatic conditions of the district are more or less of the extreme type. During the summer the district is very hot and it is chilly during the winter. As the district adjoins the Bay of Bengal in the Southern parts, the sea breeze to some extent renders the climate moderate and tolerable in the southern portions. The hilly areas of Polavaram are however, comparatively cooler than the plains during winter and likewise, severe in summer.

(d) Rainfall

The annual rainfall in the district is 1,081.7 mm (42.59").[4] The district gets rain both during the South West and post-monsoon seasons (June to September) which constitutes about 67 per cent of the annual rainfall, while the retreating monsoon season accounts for about 23 per cent. July is the rainest month.

(e) Forests

The forests in West Godavari district are confined to the hill ranges, hills and plains in the northern half of the district. The floristic composition shows considerable variation starting from the rich and well stocked forests occurring in the Agencies to various types of deciduous forests occurring in the scattered hills and hill ranges all over the upland areas and denuded forests in the plains which tend towards thorny scrubs. The principal species in the Agency are *Terminalia tomentosa* (Nallamaddi), *Pterocarpus marsupium* (Yegi), *Xylia xylocarpa* (Velutury), *Lagerstroemia parviflora* (Chennangi), *Chloroxylon swietenia* (Billudu); *Anogeissus latifolia* (Chirumanu) others. Species like *Lannea grandis* (Gumpena), *Cleistanthus collinus* (Kodsha), *Albizzia amara* (Narling), *Strychnos Nuxvomica* (Mushti) are prevalent. Memecylon and Mimusops are predominant species in the evergreen scrub forests in Nallajerla.[5]

(f) People and Settlements

All the villages of the area have separate settlements for Malas and Madigas. These settlements are called *Pallis*.[6] These *Pallis* are delinked from the main villages. They have their own wells, pumpsets and temples to worship. Majority of the houses are thatched. Only very few are found to be pakka houses. Also most of them are agricultural labourers living on the meagre income with little savings. On the whole, their socio-economic conditions are extremely poor and wretched.

2. Rise in the Standard of Living

Sir Aurthur Cotton's work produced tremendous welcoming results in the Krishna-Godavari deltas. People of these areas began to achieve better standards of life when compared to the people of the contiguous districts such as Visakhapatnam, Vijayanagaram in the north, Guntur, Prakash and Nellore in the south. People in search for work migrated from the above districts to Godavari district as there was no work for their survival in their districts. These districts continued to enjoy the fruits of draught and famine, disease and pestilance. Agriculture in these districts was dependent upon the natural rains. Agriculture here was a gambling in the hands of monsoons. The situation in Godavari districts, was however different from the rest of the districts. Network of canals provided timely water for irrigation and successful agricultural operations were prevalent in Godavari districts. The land owners and the farmers, agricultural labour were sure of the yield of the crop but for the natural calamities like cyclones and floods of the river.[7] Across the Godavari and its tributaries, the environment was quite congenial. Godavari districts provided employment for agricultural labour even on a continuous basis — what was called then the paleru system of contract labour annual or biannual basis was arranged.

3. Population of the West Godavari District

The population in the West Godavari district comprised of Brahmins, Kshatriyas locally known as *Rajulu*, Vaisyas or Komatlu, Vyaparulu, Sudras comprising Kapus (cultivators), Kammas, Reddies, Velamas, Gowdas or toddy tappers, Yadavas or Gollas, Pallekarus or fishermen, Salaes or weavers and the Ati Sudras or the traditional untouchables, the Madigas and Malas who come under the Scheduled Caste finally, Koya, Boya, Kondadora, Yerukala and Yanadi who come under the Scheduled Tribes.

The present study is concerned with Scheduled Caste Mala palerus of West Godavari district. Among the 59 Scheduled Castes in the state, four castes are spread throughout the state. They are Chalvadi, Chamar, Madiga and Mala. Among these four, Madiga and Mala are fairly larger in number and are present almost in every village. They can be considered as the typical representatives of the Dalits (or) Harijans of Andhra Pradesh.

Between the Malas and Madigas, there is a constant conflict over their respective status in relation to other though both are untouchables to the caste Hindus. But the caste Hindus seem to grant the Malas higher status rather than to the Madigas. Subba Reddy[8] has listed certain activities which are exclusively assigned to the Mala and Madiga castes. These are:[9] (1) the office of the village servant and this entitles manual assistance to the village officers, i.e., the Karanam and the Munsif; (2)

disposal or the dead cattle; (3) digging of graves and the two important tasks of capturing sacrificial animal and cutting its neck during the festivals of the village goddess. These duties in certain districts fall to the Mala and elsewhere to the Madiga and there is no fixed rule.

The term 'Harijana' was not the invention of Mahatma Gandhi as supposed by majority of the people in India and abroad. It was Nursingh Mehta, according to B.S.Murthy, the term "Harijans" (meaning children of God), so called by a Gujarati saint-poet Narasingh Mehta in the 19th century and popularised by Mahatma Gandhi in this century, refers to the people of all the untouchable castes in the country.[10]

Both the Malas and Madigas work as agricultural labourers, Malas provide additional hands whenever required by the non-brahman higher castes, for example, carrying a Reddy landlords luggage from a nearby bus-stop to the village or the other way.

Madigas are traditionally leather workers. They tan the skin of dead animals and make leather articles like foot-wear, large leather bags for lifting water from low levels, bell-belts for cattle to decorate oxen, leather genes, saddles and demmi goggles for horses to the villagers, for which they are paid in cash or kind. They are also carrion-disposers and during the festival occasions like marriage and ceremonies in honour of the village deity they serve as drum-beaters and sacrificers of the sacrificial animals. The Scheduled Castes in the districts are divided into 59 castes.

List of Scheduled Castes in Andhra Pradesh

1. Adi Andhra
2. Adi Dravida
3. Anamuk
4. Arya Mala
5. Arundhatiya
6. Arwamala
7. Bariki
8. Beda Jangam, Budajangam
9. Bindla
10. Byagara
11. Bavoori
12. Chachati
13. Chalavadi
14. Chamar, Mochi, Muchi
15. Chambhar
16. Chandala
17. Dakkal, Dokkalurer
18. Dandari
19. Dhor
20. Dom, Dobara, Paidi, Pana
21. Ellamalwar, Yellmala Wandlu
22. Ghari, Rellichachandi
23. Godagali
24. Godari

25. Gosangi
26. Holeya
27. Holeya Dasari
28. Jaggali
29. Jumburulu
30. Kolupulvandlu
55. Relli
56. Samagara
57. Samban
58. Sapr
59. Sindhollu, Chindollu
31. Madari Kuruva
32. Madiga
33. Madiga Dasu, Mashteen
34. Mahar
35. Mala
36. Mala Dasari
37. Mala Dasu
38. Mala Hannai
39. Mala Jangam
40. Mala Masti
41. Mala Sale, Nekkani
42. Mala Sanyasi
43. Mang
44. Mang Garodi
45. Manne
46. Mashti
47. Matangi
48. Mehtar
49. Mitha Ayyawar
50. Murdala
51. Raky, Roti, Thoti
52. Pambade, Pambanda
53. Pamidi
54. Panchama, Pariah

Source: Census of India 1981 series 2, Andhra Pradesh District Census Handbook, West Godavari District, Parts—XIII-A & B.

Malas Sub-divisions and Exogamous Septs

(a) Reddi Bhumi

Avuka, Marsh
Kalika, Collyrium
Bandi, cart
Naththalu, snails
Bommala, dolls
Paida, money or gold
Bejjam, holes
Pilli, cat
Dakku, fear
Rayi, stone
Dhidla,platform or black-door
Samudra, ocean
Dhomagnal or mosquito
Silam, good conduct
Gera, street
Thand, bottom of a ship
Kaila, measuring grain in thrushing-floor

(b) Pokunati

Allam, ginger Mailari,
Dara, stream of water
Gadi, cart
Gone, sack
Gurram, horse
Maggam, loom
Washerman
Parvatha, mountain
Pindi, flour-powder
Pasala, cow
Thummala, Sneezing

(c) Sarindla

Boori, a kind of cake
Ballem, spear
Bomidi, a fish
Challa, buttermilk
Chintala, tamarind
Duddu, money
Gali, wind
Karna, ear
Kaki, crow
Mudi, knot
Maddili, drum
Malle, Jasmine
Putta, anthill
Pamula, snake
Pidgi, handful
Semmati, hammer
Uyyala, see-saw

(d) Daindla

Dasari, priest
Doddi, court or backyard
Gonji, Glycosmis pentaphylla
Kommala, horns
Marri, Ficus bengalensis
Pala, milk
Powaku, tobacco
Thumma, Acacia arabica

The following legend professes to account for the existence of the three divisions. When Virabahuvu went to the rescue of Harischandra, he promised Kali that if she granted him success, he would sacrifice to her his wives, of whom he had three. Accordingly, after his conquest of Vishvamithrudu, he returned and called his wives that he might take them to the temple in order to fulfill his vow. The wives got some linking of what was in store for them and one of them took refuge in the house of Reddi Bhumula, another ran away to the eastern country (Pakanati), while the third, though recently confined and still in her dirty (Muriki) cloth, determined to abide by the wish of her husband.

She was therefore sacrificed to Kali, but the goddess, seeing her devotion, restored her to life and promised to remain forever her helper.

The reason given for the change in the method of wearing the cloth is that, after the incident described above took place, the women of the Murukunati section, in order to express their disapproval of the two unfaithful wives, began to wear their cloths on the opposite, viz., the left shoulder. In marriages, however, whatever the *paita* (the end of the saree covering over the breast and finally kept on right or left shoulder) of the bride, she must wear the cloth over the right shoulder.

"The Reddi Bhumulu and Pakanativaru say that the reason they wear the cloth over the right shoulder is that they are descendants of the gods. According to a legend, the goddess Parvati, visit on a journey with her Lord Parameswarudu, discarded one of her unclean *(maila)* cloths, from which was born a little boy. This boy was engaged as a cattle-herd in the house of Parameshwarudu. Parvati received strict injunctions from her Lord that she should no account allow the little Mala to taste cream. One day however, the boy discovered some cream which had been scraped from the inside of the pot sticking to a wall. He tasted it and found it good. Indeed, so good was it that he came to the conclusion that the udder from which it came must be even better still. So one day in order to test his theory, he killed the cow. Then came Parameswarudu in great anger, and asked him what he had done and to his credit be it said, the boy told the truth.

Then Parameshwarudu cursed the lad and all his descendants and said that from henceforth cattle should be the meat of the Malas[11] - the unclean.

References

1. Rudhraiah Chowdary, G. Delta Silpi, p.10.
2. Manual of Godavari District. p.50.
3. Rivers of Andhra Pradesh (1989).
4. Statistical Supplement to Part II of Andhra Pradesh Gazette, Hyderabad. dated 15-1-1991 monthly and annual rainfall table, p.21.
5. Andhra Pradesh District Gazetteers, West Godavari District.
6. *Palli* is a settlement of the untouchables. It is so called because of the Buddhist and Jain affiliation. Buddhists and Jains were excommunicated by Hindus and they were forced to live outside the main settlement. Thus the *Pallis* became separate settlements of untouchables.
7. Rivers of Andhra Pradesh, p.16.

8. N.S. Reddy, 'Community Conflict among the Depressed Castes of Andhra , *Man in India* 30, pp.8-9.

9. Committee on the revision of lists of Scheduled Castes and Scheduled Tribes, 1967.

10. B.S. Murthy, *Depressed and Oppressed*, 1971, p.45.

11. Thurston, E. *Castes and Tribes of Southern India*, Delhi, Vol. II, 1975, pp.346-7.

5

Research Methodology

In order to fulfil the objectives of the present study a systematic research design has been drawn out, the required data for the study was collected through primary and secondary sources, research tools such as interview schedule and participant observations were used to collect primary source. Official records and other published materials are used as secondary source. Data pertaining to primary source was collected through the use of purposive sampling method.[1]

The Mala paleru's are unevenly distributed throughout the West Godavari district since all agricultural operations are located in the rural areas and the Scheduled Caste palerus make their living in the rural areas and 80 per cent of the scheduled caste population live in the rural areas. The researcher has selected purposively 20 mandals out of the 46 mandals of the West Godavari district.[2] Two Scheduled Caste villages from each mandal were taken for collecting samples for the study, the 20 mandals selected are:

(1) Achanta (Thillapudi, Agarrru),

(2) Gopalapuram (Nandigudem, Thallapudi),

(3) Bhimavaram (Andaluru, Goraganamudi),

(4) Undi (Ai-Bhimavaram, Bondada),

(5) Penugonda (Kakiluru, Juttiga),

(6) Tanuku (Moyyeru, Rapaka),

(7) Palakollu (Penumanchili, Kodamanchili)

(8) Narsapur (Chittavaram, Saripalli)

(9) Attili (Pekeru, Unikili)

(10) Denduluru (Kaikaram, Gudigunta)

(11) Kovvuru (Munipalli, Nandamuru)

(12) Chagallu (Pasivedala, Dommeru)

(13) Pentapadu (Krishnaipalem, Racherla)

(14) Polavaram (Puchikapadu, Dondapudi)

(15) Penumantra (Ogidi, Vaduru)

(16) Yelamanchili (Uttada, Kaza)

(17) Mogalturu (Perupalem, Thunduru)

(18) Palakoderu (Mogallu, Vendra)

(19) Veeravasaram (Bethapudi, Thokalapudi)

(20) Poduru (Mulaparru, Ballipadu)

A sample of 800 Mala farm servants (Paleru) were considered for the present study by filling interview schedule from all the 40 villages from 20 respondents from each village. The sample consists of 740 male Palerus and 60 female Palerus. Of the females palerus 38 of them are widows and the rest are unmarried women who have no parents. The distribution of sample in the 20 Mandals and 40 villages of West Godavari district is shown in Table -1.

The respondents have been divided into six groups on the basis of their age. The sample shows that a majority of the respondents are between 25-33 age group. They are neither too young nor too old and their total number is 166 whose percentage is 20.75 (Table 2). The Respondents were interviewed at their own houses through an elaborate interview schedule in simple vernacular language, i.e., Telugu spoken by the Respondents. The schedule contains straight questions pertaining to the social, economic, political, educational and cultural spheres. The schedule was also designed to elicit information pertaining to their awareness of constitutional provisions and the actual use of government's welfare measures meant for them.

Besides these schedules, the method of participant observation was employed in order to check the inaccuracies that have crept in the interviewed data.

The data collected through the above two methods were carefully assembled, tabulated and analysed. Finally the simple percentage calculation method was employed throughout.

Table 1
Distribution of Sample

Sl. No.	*Name of the Mandal*	*Name of the Village*	*No. of Respondents*	*Total*
1	Achanta	(a) Thillapudi	20	40
		(b) Agarru	20	
2	Gopalapuram	(a) Nandigudem	20	40
		(b) Thallapudi	20	
3	Bhimavaram	(a) Andaluru	20	40
		(b) Goraganamudi	20	
4	Undi	(a) Ai-Bhimavaram	20	40
		(b) Bondada	20	
5	Penugonda	(a) Kakileru	20	40
		(b) Juttiga	20	
6	Tanuku	(a) Moyyeru	20	40
		(b) Rapaka	20	
7	Palakollu	(a) Pènumanchili	20	40
		(b) Kodamanchili	20	
8	Narsapur	(a) Chittavaram	20	40
		(b) Saripalle	20	
9	Attili	(a) Pekeru	20	40
		(b) Unikili	20	
10	Denduluru	(a) Kaikaram	20	40
		(b) Gudigunta	20	
11	Kovvuru	(a) Munipalli	20	40
		(b) Nandamuru	20	
12	Chagallu	(a) Pasivedala	20	40
		(b) Dommeru	20	
13	Pentapadu	(a) Krishnaipalem	20	40
		(b) Racherla	20	
14	Polavaam	(a) Puchikapadu	20	40
		(b) Dondapudi	20	
15	Penumantra	(a) Ogidi	20	40
		(b) Vaduru	20	
16	Elamanchili	(a) Utada	20	40
		(b) Kaza	20	
17	Mogalturu	(a) Perupalem	20	40
		(b) Thunduru	20	
18	Palakoderu	(a) Mogallu	20	40
		(b) Vendra	20	
19	Veeravasaram	(a) Bethapudi	20	40
		(b) Thokalapudi	20	
20	Poduru	(a) Mulaparru	20	40
		(b) Ballipadu	20	

Table 2

Age Composition of the Paleru Respondents (Farm Contract Servants)

	Age	*Number of Respondents*	*Percentage*
(1)	7 – 15	142	17.75
(2)	16 – 24	156	19.50
(3)	25 – 33	166	20.75
(4)	34 – 42	134	16.75
(5)	43 – 51	106	13.25
(6)	52 – 60	96	12.00
	Total	**800**	**100.00**

Area of the Study

1. The Physical Aspects

The district of West Godavari was carved out of the old Godavari district and as the western delta of the river Godavari lies in this district. it was appropriately named West Godavari. The Headquarters of the district is located at Eluru. It is bounded on the north by Khammam district, on the south by Krishna district and Bay of Bengal, on the east by river Godavari and on the west by Krishna district. The West Godavari is located between the northern latitudes of 16°15' and 17°30' and the eastern longitudes of 80°50' and 81°55'. It occupies an area of 7,742 sq.kms. and has a population of 2,873,958 persons as per the census count.

2. Important Statistics

Table 3

Comparative Figures of the State and District

Description	*Male Female*	*Andhra Pradesh State*	*West Godavari District*
Total Population	Persons	53,549,673	2,873.958
	Males	27,108.922	1,443.651
	Females	26,440,751	1,430.307
Rural	Persons	41,062,097	2,277.084
	Males	20,697,627	1,143.034
	Females	20,364,470	1,134.050
Urban	Persons	12,487.576	596.874
	Males	6.411,295	300.617
	Females	6,076.281	296.257

(Contd.)

Description	*Male / Female*	*Andhra Pradesh State*	*West Godavari District*
Decennial Population growth Rate 1971-81		23.10	21.04
Geographical Area Sq.Kms)		275,068	7,742
Density of Population (per Sq.Km)		195	371
Sex-Ratio (Number of Females per 1,000 males)		975	991
Literacy Rate	Persons	29.94	37.64
	Males	39.26	43.58
	Females	20.39	31.59
Percentage of Urban Popu-lation to total population		23.32	20.77
Percentage to total population			
(i) Main workers	Persons	42.26	41.20
	Males	57.12	58.63
	Females	27.01	23.61
(ii) Marginal workers	Persons	3.50	2.07
	Males	0.56	0.41
	Females	6.53	3.75
(iii) Non-workers	Persons	54.24	56.73
	Males	42.32	40.96
	Females	66.46	72.64
BREAK-UP OF MAIN WORKERS PERCENTAGE AMONG MAIN WORKERS			
(i) Cultivators	Persons	32.74	21.60
	Males	36.86	27.72
	Females	23.79	6.26
(ii) Agricultural labourers	Persons	36.79	49.64
	Males	26.51	38.52
	Females	59.07	77.51
(iii) Household Industry	Persons	4.70	3.54
	Males	4.50	3.52
	Females	5.14	3.59
(iv) Other workers	Persons	25.77	25.22
	Males	32.13	30.24
	Females	12.00	12.64

(Contd.)

Description	Male / Female	Andhra Pradesh State	West Godavari District
Percentage of Scheduled	Persons	14.87	16.15
Castes population to	Males	14.90	16.28
Total population	Females	14.84	16.02
Percentage of Scheduled	Persons	5.93	2.82
Tribes population to	Males	5.97	2.31
Total population	Females	5.89	2.32
Number of occupied Residential houses		10,422,448	561,117
Number of villages	Persons	29.281	879
	Males	27.379	839
	Females	1.902	40
Number of Towns		252	11

References

1. Purposive sampling is one in which the sample units are selected with definite purpose in view.
2. The West Godavari district has created on 15th April 1925. This district contain fourteen Taluqs and named after the geographical region as West Godavari after the river Godavari. As per the local self government reform of the Telugudesam Government from 25-5-1985, all the Taluqs of Andhra Pradesh are converted into mandals and a mandal revenue officer has been placed in charge of it, in view of the Tahsildar of the Taluq. All the fourteen Taluqs were converted into 46 mandals.

6

The Paleru System

1. Introduction

Indian society is based on the strong bedrock of rigid caste system. Varnasrama-dharmas has been its breath and the four-fold caste system consisted of large number of people at its lowest rung the sudras. Below the sudras were the outcastes known by the name, the atisudras. They have also been called as untouchables. They were never allowed into the main stream of the upper caste society. They lived by following meanest of the mean professions living outside the main settlements. Tradition and custom made them recognised as untouchables. As they were many in number they also participated in the agricultural operations such as ploughing, plantation, harvesting and looking after the domestic cattle cleaning the premises of the landlords, being submissive to the tradition. Being illiterate these untouchables were forced to serve their masters from generation to generation. This type of untouchable labourers attached to farm landlords from generation to generation is known locally as the palerus. The palerus are tradition bound farm contract servants. The palerus are known by different names in different parts of Andhra Pradesh. The institution of paleru has become proverbially a self slave. That is why in Rayalaseema, the western part of Andhra Pradesh, the palerus are known as *Kattubanisa* or self bound slave. In southern districts of Andhra Pradesh, the palerus are known as *Pallegadu* or those who are given part of the agricultural produce in lieu of their service.

The word paleru literally means co-plougher though the landlord had an extensive land he could not plough and put under agricultural operations himself. Agricultural operations are no doubt seasonal for ploughing, preparation of seed beds, transplantation, irrigation, weeding, manuring, harvesting, storing of the grain etc., require regular employment of agriculture labour. As all agricultural operations commence at the same time for all landed people it is not possible to secure the required labour for attending the agricultural operations. Moreover occurrence of natural, untimely or sudden havocks such as cyclones, floods, heavy rains etc., demand timely completion of the required operations. An artificial scarcity[1] of labour is often felt. The number of agriculture labour of a region, however would be the same and as such those landlords who can pay more wages can only afford completing agricultural operations well in time. Other farmers are marginalised by virtue of land holdings, have to wait and start or complete their agricultural operations for the availability of the workers.

2. Regular Agriculture Labour

In order to ensure the supply of agriculture labour one has to take necessary measures for the regular supply of agriculture labour. Past experience made the rich farmers to take necessary steps and arrangements for the supply of agriculture labour as and when the occasion demands. Several temporary and also permanent methods have been designed to procure agricultural labour. Agriculture labour has to be kept in abeyance for future needs. Of such methods mention may be made of Vatandari, Nemani, Paleru etc. systems.

The method of ensuring agriculture labour for temporary purpose Vatandari method is employed. In the Vatandari system, labour or coolies attending agricultural operations are arranged on a fixed wage system for a specific period of time. The landlord would select a group of workers or a few families of workers to attend his specific work. For this purpose, he promises them for employment of seasonal work in his farm. As there is a guarantee of work in a particular period with fixed wages such coolies will not accept any work outside even though there is a hike in the wage rate and extra facilities. Thus committed workers are secured by the landlords, the workers who attend for landlords assignment regularly for a period is known as the Vatan system.

The Vatan labours have an advantage of approaching the landlord as and when some financial assistance was required. In turn, the landlord earns the goodwill of the vatan labourer and gets their support in political issues and in settlement of local issues one way or the other. The vatan agricultural labour, though work during certain seasons for the zamindar, continue to support the landlords and mostly the relations were cordial.

3. Nemani System

There is a customary system prevalent for acquiring the agricultural labour for the village officials, i.e., the Karanam and the Munsiff and sometimes the landlord. This is known as Nemani custom. Village officials, the Karanam and Munsiff, are very important for any information pertaining to the land records, revenue and assessment of taxes and revenue. Through the villagers have to correspond with the mandal and district officials and thereon, the village Sarpanch and the local landlords also play a vital role in the life of the villagers. As the Government acts through these officials, people feel it necessary to do certain services unasked to them. All the lands of the Munsif, the Karanam, the Sarpanch and the local landlords are ploughed, transplantation, weeding, harvesting etc., were done by the members of the agricultural labourers free of cost. For all occasions of agricultural seasons simply the workers of the village take a date for attending the agricultural work of the Karanam, the Munsif, the Sarpanch and the landlord and all of them go at one time and complete the work. The agriculture labour take their own tools and these officials provide them with sumptuous meals in the noon as a mark of their hospitality. Without any comment or murmer the agriculture labour render their services. The Nemani system may be traced back to the *Vetti* system by which the lower class people were forced to render their service. The Nemani system may be described as a refined form of *Vetti.*

4. Paleru System

Apart from attending to the agriculture works, the landlords required somehow workers to look after their daily and animal husbandry and horticultural works. These works can be attended by Nemani and Vatandari workers. In order to ensure regular attendance of, farm labour, people belonging to Scheduled Caste are employed by the landlords.

5. Employing Palerus : Reasons

There are very many reasons for employing scheduled caste people as palerus. First they were socially degraded and as such they are highly submissive and proverbially faithful to their village. They have no ritualistic priorities and as such no sentiments and no excuses for attending any type of low work. They have also no revolutionary attitude towards their masters; they were committed and faithful and stick to the work assigned by their masters. They are also prepared to sacrifice for the welfare of their master even accepting the covert judgements pronounced on their master and their relatives and prepared to undergo imprisonment on behalf of their masters and their kith and kin. Several incidents noticed during the survey reveal that farm servants belonging to scheduled caste community have gone to the court for taking the risk of accepting the crime on them, only to save the honour of their masters who have actually committed crime. Being vulnerable, economically poor, the scheduled caste paleru accepted any type of force without any argument or bargain.

Scheduled Caste people are by nature grateful and they always prefer to repay their gratitude not only through service but even by sacrifice also. These qualities substantiate the preference given to them by the landlords when they were taken into service.

6. Paleru Culture

Landlords used to take into their service agriculture labour basing on the need of a farm. As has been stated earlier, apart from the daily wage system, labour is also taken as "coolie". The labourer is engaged for a day, where the wages for that day are given. In this system, the landlord has no obligation with the coolies, at the same time, the coolie has no further obligation or responsibility after the work spot is left. In *Vatan, Dakala, Nemani* systems also the responsibility seizes and there is no commitment on either side. In the paleru system, however, agriculture labour are sought on some sort of convictional commitment arranged with regard to the type of tenure and mode of payment along with other conditions for attending to several works of the landlord.

The Palerus of the present study come from the Mala community, the right hand untouchables of Andhra Pradesh in general, the West Godavari in particular.

The food and drink and attire of the Mala Palerus were quiet distinct from the rest of the other communities in general and their own fellow untouchables in particular.

They are non-vegetarians by custom and tradition. Edgar Thurston[2] observed that they eat meat of cattle, pork, goat, sheep and all kinds of birds and fish. The past thirty years, as has been observed by Thurston, they were eating all the non-vegetarian food. The Malas[3] claim superiority over the other dominant untouchables, i.e., the Madigas who were traditional leather workers and butchers of cattle. As they eat the meat of dead cattle and attend to tanning work, they ought to stay much far away from the Malawadas. The Malas never accept food or water from the Madigas for this reason. They do not even make any inter-caste marriage with the Madigas.

Due to the acculturation process, the Malas began to copy certain manners of the upper caste people to raise their social status. Most of them stopped going to beef and pork stalls openly. Earlier, serving pork in wedding and other ceremonies, was considered very high in their community dinners. If pork is not served in the wedding feast, people used to underestimate the economic condition of the wedding parties.

Pork and arrack and toddy if served, the function is supposed to be a grand one. Drinking of toddy (the juice collected from toddy tree is very intoxicating). *Sara* or spirit made out of jaggery and ammonia was a staple drink of these people. Liquor made out *Kallu* was served to very responsible persons. It was also known by the local name *Chiguru*.

Today these people feel it very low and uncultured to speak of pork in wedding dinners. Pork is replaced by chicken and meat. All other pudding is replaced by chicken *biriyani* or mutton *pulav*. Instead of *Sara* and *Kallu*, hot drinks are also served by economically sound people of this community.

Most of the people who have been benefited by the Gulf employment brought superior crockery and use them lavishly while offering dinners and feasts. A type of western way of life has been developed by these people.

Types of Houses of the Palerus

The residential settlements of Scheduled Castes are kept not only separate but aloof from the main residential quarters of upper castes. The Scheduled Castes people were neither permitted to live in palatial buildings nor allowed to construct pucca or permanent buildings. As they were socially backward and economically poor they could not afford staying in good houses. Of the 800 respondents 640 have thatched houses, who constitute 80 per cent, one hundred twenty families live in tiled roofed houses who constitute 15 per cent. Forty families have concrete houses constituting 5 per cent. Thus we see that a majority of scheduled castes population reside in thatched house only.

Types of Houses of the Palerus

S.No.	*Type of House*	*No. of householders*	*Percentage*
1	Thatched houses	640	80%
2	Tiled roofs	120	15%
3	Concrete slab roofs	40	5%
	Total	**800**	**100%**

Electrified and Non-Electrified Households

The Electrified and Non-electrified types of houses of the scheduled caste palerus are shown in the table, as per the information furnished in the table it is evident that a majority of the houses are non-electrified. Out of the 640 thatched houses 480 (60%) are non-electrified and 160 (25%) are electrified, of the total 120 (100%) tiled houses are electrified. Out of the total 40 (100%) concrete houses all are electrified. By this is evident out of the total 800 houses, 80% are thatched houses, 15% are tiled houses and 5% are concrete houses. It is evident by this only 20% are having some sort of permanent houses where as 80% are living under thatched roofs.

Electrified and Non Electrified Households

S. No.	*Type of House*	*Non-Electrified*	*Electrified*	*Percentage Total*
1.	Thatched Houses	480 (60%)	160 (25%)	640 (80%)
2.	Tiled roofs	--	120 (100%)	120 (15%)
3.	Concrete slab roofs	--	40 (100%)	40 (5%)
	TOTAL	**480 (60%)**	**320 (40%)**	**800 (100%)**

Marital Payment among Palerus

The Scheduled Castes (Malas) have their own type of marriage system. Bride is purchased by payment of some amount known as *Voli or* bride price. Bride is always treated subordinate to her husband as she is purchased by her husband or in-laws. Bride price is however is replaced by dowry or the price paid to the husband. Bridegrooms are being purchased even by Scheduled Castes people. Of the 800 respondents as many as 750 were taking dowry in their marriages of their sons, which constituted 93.75%. Ten people are still following the old traditional *voli* system; which constitute 1.25 per cent. Forty respondents said that they are neither taking or giving dowry or *voli* in their marriages. They constitute five percentage of the total respondents. They are being influenced by Marxist principles and love or intercaste marriages.

Marital Payment among Palerus

Type of Payment	*No. of Respondents*	*Percentage*
Dowry	750	93.75
Voli (Bride price)	10	1.25
Dowry or Voli not given	40	5.00
Total	**800**	**100.00**

Literacy among the Paleru Respondents

Traditionally Scheduled Castes people are not allowed to pursue any education, schools, tanks and temples and roads of the upper caste people but due to social legislation made by the British and Indian Government, the scheduled caste were also admitted into the educational institutions run by government. As a result, we can see some small percentage of literacy representing the scheduled caste community, Interview schedule served to 800 scheduled caste people furnish the following literary representation. Among the males 658 have been exposed to any type of literacy. While 82 persons were exposed to primary education constituting 11.08% among the 60 females 54 were never exposed to any type of education (90%) and six were exposed to primary education (10%). It is clear from the evidence furnished in the table 89% of the respondents were illiterates and 11% were exposed to primary education.

Literacy Among the Paleru Respondents

Sex	*Illiteracy*	*Primary Education*	*Secondary Education*	*Pre-University*	*University*	*Technical/ Vocational Education*	*Total*
Male	658 (88.92%)	82 (11.08%)	--	--	--	--	740
Female	54 (90%)	6 (10%)	--	--	--	--	60
Total	**712 (89%)**	**88 (11%)**	--	--	--	--	**800 (100%)**

Literacy among the Children of Palerus

As per the details furnished in the table. There are altogether 1246 children of which 944 are males and 302 are females. The age of the

Literacy among the Children of Paleru

Sex	*Illite-racy*	*Primary Education*	*Secondary Education*	*Pre Uni-versity*	*Degree*	*Post-Graduate*	*Profess-ional/ Technical*	*Total*
Male	464 (49.15%)	180 (19.07%)	140 (14.83%)	106 (11.23%)	45 (4.77%)	9 (0.95%)	--	944
Female	96 (31.79%)	108 (35.76%)	90 (29.80%)	5 (1.65%)	3 (1.00%)	--	--	302
Total	**560 (44.94%)**	**288 (23.11%)**	**230 (18.50%)**	**111 (8.90%)**	**48 (3.85%)**	**9 (0.70%)**	**--**	**1246 (100%)**

children of Scheduled Caste respondents range from 6 to 30 years. Of the 944 males 464 (49.15%) are illiterate, 180 (19.07%) have primary education, 140 (14.83%) secondary education, 106 (11.23%) in the University education 45 (4.77%) persons in the degree 9 (0.95%) persons Post-Graduates. Of the 302 female children 96 (31.79%) were illiterates, 108 (35.76%) got primary education, 90 (29.80%) secondary education, 5 (1.65%) persons got pre-University education, 3 (10%) persons got degree education.

Table -A

Electrified and Non-Electrified Households of the Palerus

Sl. No.	*Type of Houses*	*No. of Non-Electrified*	*Electrified*	*Total*
1.	Thatched	784 (100.00)	--	784
2.	Tiled roofs	--	16 (100.00)	16
3.	Concrete slab roofs	--	--	--
	Total	**784 (98.00)**	**16 (2.00)**	**800 (100.00)**

Table -B

Electrified and Non-Electrified Households of the Palerus ((1997)

Sl. No.	*Type of Houses*	*No. of Non-Electrified*	*Electrified*	*Total*
1.	Thatched	9 (15.00)	51 (85.00)	60
2.	Tiled roofs	--	345 (100.00)	345
3.	Concreteslab roofs	--	395 (100.00)	395
	Total	**9 (1.12)**	**791 (98.88)**	**800 (100.00)**

Of the many status symbols of an individual, nature of type of house in which one resides would certainly indicate his/her status. A low thatched house with an oil lamp and no furniture would show the poverty of the resident. A pucca concrete house or a palace with good furniture with electricity and T.V. antenna and telephone connection would give an entirely different idea of the status of the inmates

The information furnished in the Table A shows that out of 800 respondents of the interviewed as many as 784 persons live only in thatched houses. They constitute 98% while only 16 persons come from tiled houses constituting 2%.

This shows the poor economic conditions of the respondents. They were leading their lives just at the grass-root levels.

The Table B furnishes the following information. Of the 800 respondents, 1.12% live in non-electrified thatched houses 98.88% people live in concrete slab roofed electrified house.

Within a period, three decades a lot of change by the way of progress or development is seen in the housing pattern of the Paleru community in the area under study.

Table-A

Type of Cultivation of Lands

Sl.No.	Type of cultivation lands	Area in Hectares	Percentage
1.	Paddy	39,000	
2.	Garden	10,000	
3.	Tanks and Ponds	4,000	
	Total	**53,000**	**100**

Table-B

Types of Culivation of Lands 1997

Sl.No.	Type of cultivation lands	Area in Hectares	Percentage
1.	Paddy	13.250	25.00
2.	Garden	5,300	10.00
3.	Aqua-cultivation	34,450	65.00
	Total	**53,000**	**100.00**

The area under investigation in the West Godavari was very much rich in alluvial soil, which was used for paddy and sugarcane growing. The wetland constituted more than dry or garden land. It formed 70% of the total land.

The eastern part of West Godavari being on the east coast of the Bay of Bengal was found suitable for growing of fish, prawns and crabs, which have a lot of demand in countries like Japan, Hong Kong, China and other countries. As a result, most of the fertile paddy and sugarcane growing fields were excavated into fish ponds. Out of the 53,000 hectares of cultivable land in the District, 34,450 hectares of land was converted into fish ponds. This constituted 65% of total land which was earlier under paddy cultivation. Only 25% of land was under paddy and the remaining 10% under garden land.

This was a major development through aquaculture in the area under study. This being an export oriented one secured more profits to the fish pond owners in spite of the frequent floods and cyclones that occur in the region.

One hectare of land through agriculture, one owner used to get 8 quintals of paddy from the Raiyat as rent for the land per crop. There are two crops in a calendar year known as Rabi and Kharif. For two crops, the owner of one hectare land would get Rs.7,000/- per year.

Whereas if a hectare fish pond is given for rent, the owner would get between Rs.25,000 to 35,000 basing on the proximity of the fish pond to the sea or main road. Thus, there is a lot of difference in the income on agriculture land and fish ponds. Those people who depended upon agriculture as Palerus and Coolies fell out of work due to the rapid spread of aquaculture. They have shifted to some other work, i.e., either migrating to urban centres or securing jobs in Gulf countries.

Table A

Land Owning and Landless Palerus

Sl.No.		*Land owning*	*Landless*	*Total*
1.	Frequency	240	560	800
2.	Percentage	30.00	70.00	100.00

Of the eight hundred Paleru respondents, as many as 560 (70%) were landless persons, while 240 (30%) were land owning. This shows that there was a lot of poverty among the Paleru community. As such, all of them were directly depended upon agricultural labour or contract labour for their livelihood.

Table B

Land Owning and Landless Palerus (1997)

Sl.No.		*Land owning*	*Landless*	*Total*
1.	Frequency	680	120	800
2.	Percentage	85.00	15.00	100.00

According to the information furnished in the Table B, as many as 680 (85%) persons have acquired landed property; while 120 (15%) were not having any type of agricultural land.

The information provided in the Table A and the information of the Table B would show that a lot of economic development took place over 30 years of time. As long as they were farm servants they could not grow further.

Table A

Land Possessed by Paleru Respondents

Sl. No.	*Type of possession*	*No. of Respondents*	*Percentage*
1	Inherited	80	10.00
2	Purchased	20	2.50
3	Allotted by Government	500	62.50
4	Inherited + Purchased	200	25.00
	Total	**800**	**100.00**

The Table A shows that 80 respondents (10%) possessed land by inheritance. Twenty respondents (2.5%) acquired land by purchasing. Five hundred respondents (62.5%) got land by the allotment of Government. Two hundred respondents (25.00%) acquired land through inheritance and purchase.

The information furnished by A and B tables shows that the Paleru families are better off when compared to their economic position thirty years before. Earlier people sold away their lands; while the present respondents acquired land, which shows their acquired economic status.

Table B

Land Possessed by Paleru Respondents

Sl.No	*Type of possession*	*No. of Respondents*	*Percentage*
1.	Inherited	80	10.00
2.	Purchased	400	50.00
3.	Allotted by Government	200	25.00
4.	Inherited + Purchased	120	15.00
	Total	**800**	**100.00**

Of the 800 respondents of the Paleru families, 80 respondents (10%) possessed inherited lands; four hundred (50%) acquired land by purchasing; two hundred respondents acquired lands by the allotment of

Government (25%). One hundred twenty respondents (15%) acquired land either by inheritance and by purchase.

Table A

Marital Payment among Palerus

Sl. No.	*Type of payments*	*No. of Respondents*	*Percentage*
1.	Oli (Bride price)	600	75.00
2.	Dowry	40	5.00
3.	Oli or Dowry Not given	160	20.00
	Total	**800**	**100.00**

Table B

Marital Payment Among Palerus (1997)

Sl. No.	*Type of payments*	*No. of Respondents*	*Percentage*
1.	Dowry	610	76.25
2.	Oli (Bride Price)	--	--
3.	Dowry or Oli not given	190	23.75
	Total	**800**	**100.00**

Originally the Malas follow a traditional type of marriage. The Malas purchase the bride at a price known as *Voli*. The marriage is celebrated at the house of the bride-groom.

But recent times the system of purchasing a bride at price has changed due to the socio-economic change brought about in the area under study. Dowry is a practice followed in the affluent Hindu families. Malas who lived outside the Pale of the Hindu society were new to the system of dowry earlier. Now the Malas who have denounced the traditional Paleru system began to earn more by the pursuit of other income earning jobs. As such, they have copied the Hindu dowry system.

Out of the 800 respondents of the Table A, 75% celebrated their marriages with *Voli* or bride price; 5% demanded with dowry and 20% without *Voli* or dowry.

After thirty years the situation appeared in different way 76.25% of the respondents performed their marriage with dowry while 23.75% without any dowry.

Table A

Types of Atrocities Committed on Palerus and Their Family Members

S No.			Respondents	Percentage
1.	Arson	1%	80	10%
2.	Rape; Molestation	2%	160	20%
3.	Murder (or) Ryots	2%	160	20%
4.	Manipulation	1.5%	120	15%
5.	Creation of Obstacles:			
	(a) Sociological	1.5%	120	15%
	(b) Religious	0.5%	40	5%
	(c) Political	1.0%	80	10%
	(d) Cultural	0.5%	40	5%
	Total		**800**	**100.00%**

Table B

Types of Atrocities Committed on Palerus and Their Family Members (1997)

S. No.		Respondents	Percentage
1.	Arson	80	10%
2.	Rape; Molestation	160	20%
3.	Murder (or) Ryots	160	20%
4.	Manipulation	120	15%
5.	Creation of Obstacles:		
	(a) Sociological	120	15%
	(b) Religious	40	5%
	(c) Political	80	10%
	(d) Cultural	40	5%
	Total	**800**	**100.00%**

Palerus who belonged to the lowest strata of the caste system enjoyed no status in any aspect of the general society. Being victims of untouchability, they could not enjoy the principle of social justice or even freedom. As they have been forced to undertake the menial professions of scavenging and removal of dead bodies etc. they could not raise their voice even atrocities were committed on them.

Being servants of farmlords, they were forced to depend upon the landlords and other elder members of upper castes. Atroicities committed on them were never taken seriously. There were no people who could take up their case and plead for justice.

A survey conducted on the Paleru family reveals that during the past three decades, there occurred many a number of atrocities on them. Earlier, such cases were not reported and even if brought to light they were taken in a lighter view. The village councils used to warn and a nominal fine was declared and the amount of penalty was taken away by the Mala-caste council and the victim was not taken into account. Such amounts were spent for kula-drinks, i.e., the elders used to spent for their drink of liquor.

The information furnished in the Table B through the field interview scheduled shows that 160 persons (20%) became victims of rape or molestation, another 20% were put to murder or killed in Royats. 15% became victims of manipulations while 1% of the total 800 cases was put to arson or fire.

The information furnished in the Table B shows that the rate of atrociteies committed on the Palerus and their families has increased.

According to the information furnished in the Table B of 1997, 583 males of the total 800 respondents 25.73% were illiterates 60.03% primary education, 6.86% secondary education, 3.43% pre-University, 3.1% University education and 0.85% were exposed to technical education.

Of the 217 female respondents 86.18% were not exposed to any type of education, 6.91% had primary education, 3.69% secondary education, 1.84% pre-University, 0.92 University education and 0.46% acquired technical education.

Thus it is clear from the table that there is an increase of growth in field of education during the past three decades Scheduled Caste Palerus could educate their children better than before.

Rate of literacy in a particular society or a community would show the cultural level and social mobility. Literacy rate would tell the index of the intellectual growth also. It also serves as a parameter for its awareness of the daily happenings in the current world.

The Palerus who belonged to the Mala scheduled castes were not exposed to any type of education earlier due to various social, religious restrictions clamped on them by tradition. The number of respondents of the area under study have been interviewed at two levels with a gap of three decades.

Table A shows that 85.72% males were illiterates, 8.57% were exposed to primary education and 5.81% had only secondary education, of the females 95% were illiterates and 5% were exposed to primary education.

Table A

Literacy among the Palerus

Sex	*Illiterate*	*Primary Education*	*Secondary Education*	*Pre-University*	*Technical/ Vocational Education*	*Total*
Male	600 (85.72)	60 (8.57)	40 (5.81)	--	--	700
Female	95 (95.00)	5 (5.00)	--	--	--	100
Total	**695 (86.88)**	**65 (8.12)**	**40 (5.00)**	--	--	**800 (100%)**

Table B

Literacy among the Palerus Families (1997)

Sex	*Illiteracy*	*Primary Education*	*Secondary Education*	*Pre-University*	*University*	*Technical/ Vocational Education*	*Total*
Male	150 (25.73)	350 (60.03)	40 (6.86)	20 (3.43)	18 (3.10)	5 (0.85)	583
Female	187 (86.18)	15 (6.91)	8 (3.69)	4 (1.84)	2 (0.92)	1 (0.46)	217
Total	**337 (42.13)**	**365 (45.62)**	**48 (6.00)**	**24 (3.00)**	**20 (2.50)**	**6 (0.75)**	**800 (100.00)**

Table A

Household Furniture of the Paleru Respondents

S. No.	*Description of the household furniture*	*No. of households*	*Per-centage*
1.	No furniture	780	97.5
2.	Stools/Cots	20	2.5
3.	Chairs/Tables/Cots	—	—
4.	Chairs/Tables/Almirahs	—	—
5.	Chairs/Almirahs/Sofas etc.	—	—
	Total	**800**	**100.0**

Three decades back, the Paleru families possessed almost no furniture. Of the 800 respondents as many as 780 Palerus (97.5%) have no furniture at all. Socially the Palerus enjoyed no social status. They were economically poor. They were not allowed to make use of any furniture. They cannot even sit on their own cots or low level-foot stools before the other caste people. As such, these people never felt the need or necessity of keeping any furniture in their households.

Table B

Household Furniture of the Paleru Respondents (1997)

S. No.	*Description of the household furniture*	*No. of households*	*Per-centage*
1.	No furniture	–	–
2.	Stools/Cots	80	10.00
3.	Chairs/Tables/Cots	480	60.00
4.	Chairs/Tables/Almirahs	160	20.00
5.	Chairs/Almirahs/Sofas etc.	80	10.00
	Total	**800**	**100.0**

Furniture used in the households would indicate the financial soundness and economic conditions of a householder. The amount of earning in form of income would adequately illustrate ones capacity to spend on luxury items of furniture.

The Paleru families three decades back by virtue of their low social status and poor economic conditions could own a little or no furniture. Whereas due to the various favourable conditions available in the area under study began to acquire furniture in their pucca households.

Thirty years back, Paleru households mostly contain low stools known as (*Peeta*) and small under sized bamboo cots with short legs and were over with hand made *gogu* fiber ropely. They never used an blankets or bed sheets on them. The cots were used as stools by inverting the position. Gunny bags mostly served as bedsheets and old clothing lied into a *moota* used as pillow.

The following table would show by 1997 there are no households who have no furniture at all. Eighty respondents (10%) possessed stools/chairs/cots. Four hundred eighty (60%) Chairs/Tables/Cots. One hundred sixty respondents (20%) have Chairs/Tables/Almirahs/Cots. Eight have easy chairs/Tables/Almirahs/Sofas/Tea poys etc. This would show their economic status.

Household Furniture

The first survey pertaining to the life of these people three decades earlier revealed that they have a very primitive type of furniture like *Peeta* (low stool), a cot woven with hand spun coir (*nulaka*). This type of household furniture was only used by some paleru families.

Three decades of passage of time made them capable of making use of the most coveted high class furniture made of costly rose-wood, teak-wood, leave alone the use of iron grills, making use of costly paints for their rich buildings. Easy-chairs, rocking chairs, double cots, tables, cup-boards, T.V. and V.C.R. stands. Dining tables and well furnished drawing rooms are the most fastest developments in the area.

From use of hay to the use of gas cylinder

These people were making use of firewood, dry leaves of coconut trees and hay for cooking their food and other things. They have done away with the use of such materials at their (*poyya*) or hearth. Minimum use of kerosene stoves and maximum use of gas stoves is the order of the clay.

Castor earthen lamps once used for lighting of their thatched hut are now replaced by kerosene lamps and electric lights.

From no-sandals to motor cycles

As the paleru belong to a low social status, they were not allowed to wear any kind of footwear and umbrella, either in the *Uru* (the residential area of the upper caste people) or allowed to sit on their cots in their *Wada* (locality of untouchables) when other upper caste people happen to pass nearby.

Wearing of different types of sandles, boots and chappals by these people are seen today. Even upper caste people now a days come to these people to get some foreign articles as gifts. Even some of the upper caste people accept or purchase even used foreign goods, sarees, petty coats, nighties, gowns, briefs, wrist watches, any other fancy items because they are brought from foreign country. Anything foreign is acceptable canned food, tins of beef, fish etc., are also purchased from them. They think that beef is eaten by foreigners, that is why they are strong and healthy. They feel it great to eat tinned beef.

Taguvu or settlement of disputes arising between the paleru and his farmlord is often settled by the elder Kapus, sometimes headed by the Village Revenue Officer, Karanam and the Peddamalas or the elder members of Mala communities. Not always the relations between the farmlord and his contract servant paleru go smoothly due to various ruptures, the attendance and sometimes due to the hasty and hardy temperament of both the parties. Due to village politics and party factions, misunderstandings also creep in between the farm servant and his master. Sometimes theft of articles, agricultural produce, dearth of farm cattle etc., would cause for settlement of service tenure of the Paleru. When the landlord behaved without any justice towards the Paleru, some unhappy things also happen to the assets of the landlords, such as poisoning of the milch cattle and bulls and bullocks, burning of heaped paddy (*Kuppa*), Granaries (*Gadhae & Puri*), poisoning of fish tanks etc. Such unhappy things if caught red-handedly where in the palerus or the allied groups happen to participate, the cases are brought to the notice of the village elders for settling the *taguvu* or dispute. Whatever the village elders decide about the issue, that would be final.

Social and sentimental incidents that occur between the members of the landlords family and the Paleru are indeed very dangerous. Illegal and ceremonial incidents that occurred among these two, i.e., landlord and paleru's family were never digested smoothly. Mostly parties prepared for an instant justice. This justice was done mostly through a murder or an arson. Many of the Palerus when caught in such extramarital activities, the members of the landlord either murdered or beaten them to death or burnt alive. Whereas in the case of a landlord or his relatives involving in an illegal contact with members of paleru families, judgement went in a different way.

Compensation by way of some monetary payment in the form of *tappu* or penalty was levied on the culprit of this a nominal fraction has been given to victims family and the lions share part of it was spent on drink and pork by the Mala elders. Thus a crime committed on the Malas ended in a caste banquet at the cost of the other party. The nature of the village politics is indeed very strange. They erupt like a volcano and subsided immediately by mutual agreements between the landlord and his paleru family. Malas are revangelist people, they are soft and very happy to forget any atrocities committed on them if a small ex-gratia is announced towards them.

Jeetam, Battem and Mamoolu

Jeetam (Pay), *Battem* (allowance) and *Mamoolu* (customary perks). The palerus who are commissioned for a period for attending certain specific work were paid in kind in the beginning in terms of *bastas* of paddy. Each *basta* (bag) weighing 75 kgs. of paddy of the new crop only. Old paddy (*patavadlu*) are given when a delivery takes place in the house of the paleru, it is believed that new rice should not be worked for a women who has given birth to a child upto a period of six months. The palerus feel proud of such facility of getting old paddy from the farmers. They pay of the paleru mostly depended upon the age and the physical fitness. A boy paleru of ten years of age, when commissioned new used to get five bags of paddy per annum, a pair of new clothes and three full meals a day. Generally, such palerus who are below the age of fifteen used to stay in the house of landlord mostly using the cattle shed as his bedroom. They also used to attend the service of the landlord round the clock.

As such palerus used to stay with the landlord round the clock, they used to feel as a part and parcel of the Jamindaru's family, sometimes the landlord used to commission a few palerus on the service. The youngest of such farm servant is known as Chinna paleru or young servant, the eldest of them is called Pedda paleru or elderly servant. The pedda paleru used to get more jeetam than the rest of the paleru. Sometimes they get 25 bags of paddy, 2 pairs of cotton clothes and a couple of cotton towels per year. Apart from this, the old clothing of the farmers family are also given to the palerus and their wifes.

Religion

The paleru's originally being untouchables were not taken into consideration and allowed to mingle with people in the mainstream. Though they were sons of the soil, they were not allowed to worship the deities of the land. For all practical purposes they are Hindus and Indians but coming to the devotional aspect the Malas were denied of temple entry and restricted to the use of public institutions like roads, tanks and temples and educational institutions. As they were not directly allowed to worship the principle deities, they began to satisfy their religious needs by worshipping minor and folk deities popularly known as the *grama devatas*. Each scheduled caste village is endowed with a couple of village deities, one female, the other a male popularly known as 'Pothuraju', another popular deity of the village of the Scheduled Caste is the boundary goddess known as 'Poleramma'. These minor and inferior village deities have been worshipped by the low class people. All these village deities are non-vegetarian by character and animals and birds are sacrificed to them. The village deities are not worshipped regularly but seasonal festivals known as *jataras* are conducted in order to satisfy them. The untouchables, as worshippers of these minor deities, play a vital role in conducting *jataras* and offering sacrifice of animals and birds.

Advent of Christianity

From the beginning, these people were not allowed to enter into mainstream of religious life of the country. Jains and Buddhists admitted them into their religion in course of time. On account of the advent of Islam forceful conversions have been made into Islam. Most of the untouchables joined the Islam.

During the 16th century, foreigners came to India with their religion converted as many people as they can into Christianity. The Christian missionaries gave many facilities to the converts. They have attended to the religious needs of the people by constructing churches for worship opened schools and hospitals. Free Boarding schools are opened for the converts. Education and learning, training and employment by the missionaries brought about a metamorphic change in the lives of untouchables. Western education given by the Christians to the native untouchables provided an opportunity to them to come out from the clutches of servitude, slavery, economic indebtedness and political oppressions.

Western Education given by the Christian missionaries in fact helped the down-trodden to stand on their feet to earn their livelihood. The paleru institution of the scheduled caste community began to disappear acquiring slowly the western way of life brought by the Christian education and training. Scheduled Caste people who were once very proud to call as palerus are now treating it as an abuse. The term paleru is no more in use apart from Christian education, the tremendous changes brought into the field of agriculture and the advent of aquaculture in the district of West

Godavari, no more could accommodate the surplus agriculture labour and permanent paleru staff on their lands. Rapid urbanisation and lucrative job opportunities in the Gulf countries for the people in the coast, in particular, made them rich. They preferred highly rewarding Gulf jobs than a low paid, low class jobs like palerus. Even uneducated, unskilled women or men could get highly paid jobs in the Gulf countries.

The palerus once who lived a meagre and poor life could become rich and lead luxurious lifes on account of the non-acceptance of the traditional contract sarvituble like paleru. The change of profession from traditional one to the modern highly fetching one made them rich and earned them high social status.

The improved economic status of this people made them almost equal with their fellow beings or other communities. Wealthy untouchable Christians began to move freely among the other high caste people. Education coupled with economic status in the Christian background could annihilate the element of untouchability among the Scheduled Caste communities in the area under study.

The Paleru families are originally worshippers of the village deities. Being untouchables, they were not allowed to worship major Hindu deities like Siva, Vishnu etc. Due to the legislations made by the Government for temple entry for Harijans, most of the temples are thrown open to untouchables also. In spite of the relaxation many Palerus do not dare to enter the temples in the village.

Table A

Types of Deities Worshiped by Palerus

Sl.No.	*Name of the Tutelary Deities*	*No. of families*	*Percentage*
1.	Venkateswara of Tirupathi		
2.	Venkateswara of Dwaraka Tirumala		
3.	Narasimha swamy of Antarwedi		
4.	Rama Satyanarayana of Annavaram		
5.	Appanna of Simhachalam		
6.	Kanakadurga of Vijayawada		
7.	Peddintlamma of Kolleru	520	65.00
8.	Gogulamma of Saaripalle		
9.	Subbarayudu of Likitapudi		
10.	Desalamma of Agarru		
11.	Veeramma Perantalu of Chinameeram		
12.	Mutyalamma of Mogalturu		
13.	Mary matha of Gowripatnam	280	35.00
14.	Christian Churches Every villages		
	Total	**800**	**100.00**

According to the information gathered through the field work and interview schedule, 65% of the sample worship the major or minor Hindu deities and 35% attend Christian Churches.

Table B

Types of Deities Worshiped by Palerus (1997)

Sl.No.	*Name of the Tutelary Deities*	*No. of families*	*Percentage*
1.	Venkateswara of Tirupathi		
2.	Venkateswara of Dwaraka Tirumala		
3.	Narasimha swamy of Antarwedi		
4.	Rama Satyanarayana of Annavaram		
5.	Appanna of Simhachalam		
6.	Kanakadurga of Vijayawada		
7.	Peddintlamma of Kolleru	200	25.00
8.	Gogulamma of Saripalle		
9.	Subbarayudu of Likitapudi		
10.	Desalamma of Agarru		
11.	Veeramma Perantalu of Chinameeram		
12.	Mutyalamma of Mogalturu		
13.	Mary matha of Gowripatnam	600	75.00
14.	Christian Churches Every villages		
	Total	**800**	**100.00**

There is a tremendous increase in beliefs of the downtrodden people particularly the Paleru families. Earlier 65% of the Palerus used to worship Hindu deities whereas after a gap of 30 years, 75% of the Paleru families have become Christians the remaining 25% somehow began to follow the earlier form of worship.

The option for Christianity is due to the fact that, the facilities in the fields of education, medical and housing provided by the Christian Missionaries. The Church and the Missionaries never asked anything from the converts when they offer any help to them.

Whereas the government agencies or officers demanded a fraction of the assistance as bribe. Therefore downtrodden people prefer to bank on the Christian Missionaries than the Government where it is very difficult to get an assistance without bribery.

7. Caste Council of the Mala Palerus

The important council of the traditional Indian villages is the caste council. The study noticed the existence of traditional caste council among

Malas in rural areas of West Godavari District. It is a parallel institution of Panchayat Raj, a democratic institution at the lowest level. It plays an important role in the daily activities of Malas. Though statutory Panchayats, which are entrusted with all the authority including maintenance of justice, law and order issues have come into existence, the caste councils are still operating.

The caste council is a powerful decision-making body acting as a legislative, executive and judicial body. It is a deciding factor in solving intra and inter-caste conflicts. Each member first identifies himself with the caste before with the family. It forges unity among the members of Mala caste. The council sits periodically and passes either collectively or individually sanctions against a group or an individual who violates the caste code. It controls the affairs of the community. It takes care of the problem of maintaining law and order within the local community. Though *kula Panchayat* literally means 'Caste Meeting' (Kula=caste, Panchayat=meeting) in practice all the adult members of *Mala wada* participate in its deliberations.

The Malas 'Caste Council' consists of four recognised traditional leaders, the Headman (*Pina Pedda*), the Messenger (*Salvadhi*), the eldest Ryot (*Pedda Kapu*) and the Priest (*Pujari*). All these elder persons are nominated from the dominant surname (*Intiperu*) only who are the original settlers in the village. This has been the traditional practice. In addition to these traditional leaders the elders of the caste also join the meeting and they form the ex-officio members of the caste council and their opinions and views are also given due consideration while passing judgements on any matter of importance. As per the data collected from the 20 Mandals of West Godavari District, the caste council commands good respect, honour and admiration from their own caste members. All the caste members respect the council. They have unfailing loyality towards the caste council. Without the presence of these traditional leaders the council cannot meet and pass resolutions. They discuss and settle and solve the secular issues like property disputes, collection of subscription and other disputes of secular and religious nature. The decision of the council is binding on all the Malas of the villages irrespective of their surnames.

Headman (*Pina Pedda*)

It is a hereditary post. He is the ritual Head of the village. He is the eldest man of the village. He being the oldest man of the village is treated with utmost respect, reverence and admiration. He officiates in all the communal rituals of the village. He also exercises his power like fixing up the dates for the village rituals, functions and ceremonies. He settles quarrels and conflicts. In all cases, however, he consults other village elder persons and gives due consideration and weight to their opinions. If due to sickness or old age or for any other reason he is unable to carry out the affairs of the caste council, his eldest son or an elderly agent will act on his behalf. Though this office is a hereditary one, the individual qualities of the person go a long way to make his role effective. He should be able to take a decision individually and indiscriminately without harming the members' interests.

Chalvadi or messenger

The caste council of the Malas consist of another hereditary post known as Chalvadi. The Chalvadi takes the responsibility of conveying message of the council, of the families, the members of the community. Chalvadi is taken from the seniormost family and it is always held by a male senior member. This post is not given to female. Being hereditary by nature the post is filled by male succession. He informs his caste members about such matters as he is asked to convey, for example, he notifies the date for the council meetings etc. He may also be asked to bring a person before the caste council. Chalvadi is subordinate to *pina pedda*. The former carries the latter's orders. But it is wrong to assume him to be a servant of the community. His specific role is to act as a liaison between the caste council and the community. Like others he also plays an active role during discussions in a meeting.

Pedda Kapu or Eldest Ryot

The eldest (seniormost) male member of the topmost agricultural family of the village holds this position. He is just like *pina pedda*. However, he is a subordinate of *Pina Pedda*. Like *Pina Pedda,* it is also a hereditary post. At the time of meeting during discussions he also plays an active role. In matters of importance *Pina Pedda* always consults *Pedda Kapu* and seeks his suggestions, guidance and moral support and assistance for making a final decision.

Priest (*Pujari*)

The post of a *Pujari* is not hereditary. Any man from the village can act as a priest. He will be selected and nominated by the caste council in consultations with the village elders. His role is to see the welfare of the temple. As a priest he helps village rituals and festivals. He plays an active role in discussions at Council's meeting.

Meeting of the Caste Council

For taking decisions, the caste council meets, discusses and takes consensus decisions on various issues. The date, time and place of meeting, the agenda and other particulars regarding meeting are intimated in advance to the members of the council through *Salvadhi*. Public also participate in the discussions. The meeting of the council usually takes place in the middle of the village which is often called as 'Rachcha Banda', 'the central platform'.

Some of the important functions of the caste council may be mentioned below:

1. The council deals with all matters concerning their caste within its jurisdictions.
2. Settles the marriage as well as birth and death rites.
3. Decides matters regarding family disputes.
4. Prevents or controls the boys and girls from establishing pre-marital relationship in the same surname.
5. Settles matters regarding inter-caste disputes.
6. Decides matters regarding theft and elopement.

Decision Making

The traditional Mala caste council at the local level is a powerful decision-making body. The *Pina Pedda* has all powers to take and implement matters pertaining to the caste members. All the issues which involve the community will be represented to the Caste Council. The Council members assist *Pina Pedda* in the decision making process. The *Pina Pedda* however is all powerful in taking the final decision. But usually the *Pina Pedda* consults his other members and takes appropriate decisions. In the following instances we may examine as to how the caste council plays a crucial role in the community affairs of Malas.

With regard to marriage, in the traditional Indian villages inter-caste marriage are not permitted. Marriage within the caste that too within sub-caste are socially proved and accepted. The cases of inter-caste marriages are referred to the council. For instance, if a Pokanati Mala man married a woman belonging to Reddybhumula Mala it is immediately referred to the caste council. The *Pina Pedda* with the powers bestowed on him conducts an enquiry and later awards punishment to the couple (spouse) who have taken to inter-subcaste marriage. The usual punishment is to ex-communicate them from the main social life. They are socially boycotted in the sense that they are prohibited from taking water from the common well, from participating in community festivals and functions and from entering the houses of local caste families and so on. They are not supposed to have any connection or relationship with their caste people or even with the entire village community whatever the circumstances may be.

The role of *Pina Pedda* in performing marriages in the village may be stressed upon. He plays an active role in the male selection, in the transactions between the parties and fixing the date of marriage and so on. He along with his caste council members attends the marriages and blesses the newly wedded couple.

Apart from marriage, the role of caste council in the life cycle ceremonies such as birth and death ceremonies is significant. The caste councils are highly religious oriented. For example, at the time of the birth of a new child in the village, they look into several aspects pertaining to it. In this context *pina pedda* plays an important role. He is expected to be informed whether the new child was born in auspicious time or not. Several religious sanctions are observed after the birth of a child in order to ensure the well being of the village community.

At the time of death, all the caste members visit the family of the deceased and convey their personal condolences to the bereaved members. The *Pina Pedda* also participates to help the family members of the deceased.

In respect of its judicial jurisdiction's, usually the two litigant parties should totally abide by the rules and regulations as stipulated by the caste council. The cases which are not to be resolved by the caste council and where the parties do not agree to the caste council's mediatory efforts are referred to the village Panchayat. The *Pina Pedda* takes the initiative of bringing the revenue officials to the village and amicably solves the problems. Nevertheless, majority of the cases are settled at the caste council level. This shows that *Pina Pedda* is the supreme authority in solving problems. However, as mentioned earlier, the council members also extend their full cooperation and support to the *Pina Pedda*.

The council is also empowered to punish the culprits. The punishment usually is in the form of fines. These sorts of decisions are taken on the spot and the culprits are expected to pay the fines (amount) at once. Sometimes the council extends time for paying fines.

With regard to the political activities, the council has absolute control and voice over the members. It selects and nominates candidates for the members in respect of protecting and safeguarding the community's identity and interests and for social and economic justice.

Summing up, the caste council of Malas is purely traditional. It consists of elders as members who manage the community's affairs. It is meant to maintain self-identity and self-interests. Thus it is evident from the aforementioned facts that the council plays a pivotal role in the matters pertaining to birth, marriage, death and other social and political aspects of the social structure.

References

1. Elasticity of demand for agriculture labour resulted in hike in wages those landlords who have more farm servants could face this problem with the family members of the farm servants and their relatives. The rest have to pay a heavy penalty to complete their harvests.
2. Thurston, E. *Castes and Tribes of Southern India*, Vol. IV.
3. *Ibid*., p. 330.

7

Socio-economic and Cultural Profile of the Sample

The socio-economic and cultural profile of the Scheduled Caste farm labour in Andhra Pradesh in general and West Godavari district in particular is very interesting to note. The contract farm labourer known by different names in different regions. In Northern districts of Andhra Pradesh (Telangana), the Scheduled Caste farm labour is known as "Kamathagadu", in the western districts he is (Rayalaseema) "Kattugadu", and in the Eastern districts he is known as Paleru, Paleru originally meant partner who ploughed the land along with the landlord but in course of time, when the plough was taken up by the Scheduled Caste people its position has been reduced to that of the farm servant, without respect. Today 'Paleru' means a traditional bonded labourer attached to a landlords family for stipulated period or from generation to generation.

Palerus enjoy no social status for they come from the lowest social order namely the Scheduled Caste and Schedule Tribe. They had their own traditional way of socio-economic, cultural duties and obligations. The farm contract labour, particularly the Scheduled Caste Palerus were traditional families. They have their own way of restricted life very much self imposed by the traditional heritage. They are a particular breed of sturdy race of strength, valour and heroic nature, but they have become a weak and senial, submissive and obedient on account of the traditional injunctions, rules and regulations thrusted upon them. Their way of conduct, life style, and activities of different fields have already been fixed by tradition. Birth in a particular family in India would determine, social, religious and economic movements of an individual. The Scheduled Caste farm labour are of an untouchable stock, Indian society being traditional employed all traditional restrictions upon the untouchables.

Until recently the Scheduled Caste people never dreamt of going to school and it was believed by them and justified by others that the untouchables have no right to study. Rapid growth in the agriculture, particularly research and mechanisation, coupled with industrialisation gave a lot of impetus and scope for the Scheduled Caste people to think of choosing a better alternative way of life by pursing or choosing other than contract farm labour.

1. Endless Contract, Endless Debts

The landlords used to keep the farm labourer or contract labourer from generation to generation by advancing petty loans with compound interest. The family of paleru's solely depended upon the farmlord for financial economic and political support. The paleru and his family members faithfully rendered their services to the landlords, farm and their family. These type of labour tenures continued from generation to generation uninteruptedly. The Paleru families enjoyed protection and security under the umbrella of the landlord. The members of paleru family mostly attended to different services of the landlords-farm and household duties for which they were given the excess food left in the kitchen, the old fashioned clothes discarded by the members of landlord families, some fringe benefits like firewood, paddy, green grass, hay, a few coconuts etc., and cokes and tiffins on festival occasions. This type of natural system worked in a smooth manner for a long time.

However such healthy, smooth, cultural bondage could not continue in a healthy manner. Village politics and personal likes and dislikes sometimes created unhealthy rivalry situation leading to rape, murder and arson. This happened on either side. The paleru system as long as it worked goes very good. It gave wealth and health to the landlords protection, security, continuous employment to the paleru and his family. It was a system very good for slave and master, it is much different from that of the slavery in America, the slave is sold himself but the paleru contracted his labour skills for a stipulated period.

2. Stunted Growth and Stereotyped Life

The paleru and their families could not free from debt made from three or four generations back. The debt was growing ahead of the birth of a successor. A new born male child is destined to repay the loan taken by his great grandfather from the age of 6 to 7 years onwards. The new born young paleru has to join the farm happily and serve the rest of the life until his son takes the responsibility of repaying the endless growing debt. Thus the farm labour could not free themselves even though there is a profitable way of life available to him either in village or outside. If at all he escapes at the mid of the night from the service the next morning his wife and other members of family are subjected to coersion and ill-treatment by the members of the farm family. This is supported by the elders of the village. During elections also these people have no voice and choices of their own. They have to vote to the landlords supporter, they have no party, no liberty in casting franchise.

3. Familiarity Leading to Immoral Traffic

Through, closeness and proximity of generations contract service created an atmosphere of social environment among the members of farm-lord and the palerus. Untouchability is a potential weapon which is strictly followed mostly in the villages. It is very interesting to note in the household of the landlord, the family members of the paleru move closely with the members of landlord and in turn the landlords' attitude to the palerus family is somewhat lenient and cordial. Though they belong to two opposite sections by virtue of their caste, communities and faith, there is an element of attraction and commonness what may be called "our" or "own". The landlord feels the paleru and his family are his "own" property and at the same time the paleru and his family members feel that the landlord is exclusively theirs. This ownness has created mutual trust and belief when the paleru is in trouble. The landlord comes to his rescue at times of need and when the landlord is in trouble, the paleru and his family go to the extent of any sacrifice. In the field work it is reported on several occasions the paleru's went to jail on behalf of the landlord, their sons, brothers-in-law etc.

4. Illegal Sexual Contacts

The paleru system has its own defects Paleru used to spend most of the time in the fields and landlords used to visit the house of palerus on the way to the fields. He used to exploit such situations and began to maintain extra marital relations with the kith and kin of the paleru's. This is one side of the story the paleru's being strong and healthy with muscles of manhood were an attraction to the fair sex of the landlords family. Several landlord families used to keep illegal contacts with the young palerus as their husbands are away most of the time. Village whispers and murmurs the stories of these illegal contacts. Most of the people know it but they never dare to speak it out. Songs of the harvests and sometimes folklores contain such stories with different names. People know the real story but they speak with some other unanimous names.

5. Employment Outside Country

Lucrative highly paid jobs outside the country particularly Gulf countries attracted the unskilled untouchable labourers. The wifes of the palerus are sent abroad by the farmlords financial assistance. When the wife returns back after two years he has to repay the debt along with some costly presentations. Thus lured by the presentations, the landlord used to lend money to paleru's wife sometimes in order to keep away the wifes of the palerus. Interested landladies used to lend money secretely to the wifes so that they may go away to other countries. This system indirectly helped to a great extent from the indebtedness of Paleru to the farmlord. Mostly of them left the paleru tenures which was not only insulting but less lucrative and economically not profitable. Today the term paleru is not allowed be addressed to farm servants. If somebody happened to call anybody as paleru he would get offended. It is almost an insult to be called as paleru.

6. Mechanisation and Industrialisation

With Indian independence and various schemes, plans and projects launched by the Government of India, the native of rural life has been changed, thereby effecting the economic, social and cultural life of the people. The standard of living of the people living at the grass root level bettered on account of employment in fields other than agriculture and its allied fields. People began to move from rural to urban areas in search of employment.

7. Dearth of Farm Labour

As people are vacating rural areas in search of jobs outside there is no agricultural labour in the villages. Demand for labour increased, wages rose to skies and price of agricultural commodities also rose. Farm labourers began to send their children to schools rather than to daily wages. Agricultural operations mostly depended on mechanisation, tractors, power tillers, thrushing machines, sprayers, weeding machines. Ploughing through bullocks is no more an economic agricultural operation.Cattle are maintained either for milk or meat. Growing demand for food is met by another revolution known as the 'blue revolution' or growing of fish. The first phase of five year plans are devoted for agriculture and industries, major irrigation projects etc. This subsequently led to the evolution of blue revolution supplement to green revolution. Most of the fields (paddy) on the east-west of the Godavari district have been converted into fish ponds and prawn, crab and ponds. Large scale tanks have emerged and pressure on agriculture is reduced. The number of agriculture labour required for agricultural operation for unit of land is comparatively high where tilling, transplanting, weeding, spraying, harvesting operations are involved at the same time. There is no guarantee of the produce on account of floods, cyclones etc., and thereby landlords shifted from traditional agricultural system to the modern blue revolution which requires only the initial investment of excavation (digging) of tanks, latter on a few people can manage the entire show. This is highly profitable on account of the high quality of prawns, crabs harvested in the ponds of the district which has a lot of demand through foreign exports.

8. Advent of Aquaculture and Migration of Agricultural Labour

Agricultural activity does not cover the entire year, as such people who depend upon farm-labour for their survival would be thrown out of work for many months. In order to cover this unemployment season Government of India designed certain plans to provide work for the rural unemployed labour.

According to this scheme, at least one hundred days work is to be provided to the unemployed rural labour. Funds were provided to meet this scheme. Administrative infrastructural frameworks have been provided to implement this scheme. Laying of roads, digging of drainage, irrigation canals, tanks are to be undertaken with the rural labour force only. This was the original idea in the scheme. This scheme however is misutilised and the fruits of the scheme are not reaching those for whom it is originally meant. Excavation of tanks, irrigation canals and drainages are given to contractors who employ proclainers to undertake such huge works. Labour force from rural areas is not all employed for this purpose, however to fulfil the technical objection they claim the bill by presenting muster rolls with thumb impressions to prove as if the work was undertaken by the unemployed agricultural rural labour for atleast one hundred days. Thus most of the irrigation works undertaken in the Godavari, Krishna districts are done with the proclainer only. As a result agriculture labour residing in these district were threatened with unemployment and therapy they were forced to migrate to distant districts such as Guntur, Prakasam and Nellore in search of work.

It is surprising to note that the Godavari district, supposed to be the granary of Andhra Pradesh provided continuous work and even attracted enormous agricultural labour from Guntur, Nellore and Prakasam districts earlier is unable to provide employment even to its local agricultural labour. This is due to the fact that 90% of the land in Godavari districts which was under the plough earlier is now converted into aquaculture tanks. Agriculture is a labour oriented system while aquaculture does not require that much of labour, half a dozen labourers can look after the work of one hundred acres of fish ponds. Therefore labour oriented agriculture in the coastal districts is being replaced by aquaculture where that much labour is not necessary.

The East coast is very much favourable for aquaculture and the inland is not suitable for such activity due to the network of irrigation canal connected with Nagarjunasagar and other minor projects. Agricultural activities are being improved in the arid area in Palnadu and other areas where agriculture was a rainfed system earlier.

9. Migration of Labour from East to West

For the past forty years agricultural labour used to move from West to East that is from Nellore, Prakasam, Guntur towards Krishna, West and East Godavari districts in search of agriculture labour. During the transplantation and harvesting season much labour used to migrate from Western to Eastern coast. Apart from paddy crop operation in the first crop, people used to come to secure work in the second crop season also to dry crop work, i.e., Blackgram, Redgram, Groundnut and also cutting and crushing of sugarcane. Thus the increasing demand for aquaculture and backed by the increasing foreign exports of aqua products such as prawns, crabs and fish, gave a death blow to the agricultural wage earners. Many people with the threat of unemployment caused by aquaculture migrated to urban centres in search of work. The enormous migration of rural labour to urban centres created more slums adding more insanitation to the already existing one.

10. When Tradition Changes

Hither to it was believed that the untouchables are born slaves in the service of the upper caste. The untouchable should die, that is be all and end of the life. Untouchability, discrimination, uppression, suppression, social injustice all could not be eliminated through law. But it is proved in the Godavari District that a new economic system a change in the way of life, style of life, acculturation by the influence of new technology can certainly bring about metamorphic change in any social order. Social system may be defined as the change of economic system.

Fifty years ago paleru's are untouchables and used to sit at the lowest step of the landlords bungalow while the landlord used to sit on the chair on the varrandah of his house. The new economic order made the system altogether different, the cart is brought before the horse. It is reported in the field work that one K.Ceenugadu an untouchable, never cared by the villagers, appeared suddenly from the Gulf countries purchased immediately 60 acres of land, a lowry and other things, constructed a big house on the side of the road. He used to sit on a chair with costly cigarette and *Hindu* newspaper in his hand. He learned to read in the Gulf countries. Many caste Hindus who were also land owners used to come to him early morning and used to sit on the steps of his house looking at him to hear the news from the English newspaper.

Srinivasa Rao *garu, Ayyagaru* which meant respectable terms in Telugu language are being used. They never felt ashamed to sit at his feet and sip tea offered by him. Now and then he used to offer a broken stool to one of the big farmers to sit, the offer never was availed by the caste Hindus and they preferred to sit on the steps and go away without any murmur. Moreover they used to praise him loudly for offering tea and other advices. Thus the economic status of Sinugadu made him socially acceptable untouchable. The new economic system operating in the Godavari district starting from Arthur Cotton to the present time made the people wealthier, healthier and wiser, leading a life of ease and happiness. Tradition dies on account of another death blow made by Christianity and evangelical and accliciastical propaganda made by machinery in Godavari district. Varnacular schools, free boarding were provided to Christian boys and girls in the Godavari district. The traditional caste system, the uppressive, suppressive attitude and the discriminative treatment made by the caste Hindus compelled the untouchables to convert themselves to Christianity. Once the untouchables used to hide the caste and they used to tell Christians when asked, but people today adding proudly and openly, the name of the caste such as Mala, Madiga and Adi Andhra, thanks to the work done by the missionaries for educating and awakening the untouchables and others infusing in them the element of liberty, equality and fraternity, through English education. Thus Godavari district became the Kerala of Andhra Pradesh. It is observed in the field work that villages like Agartipalem, Saripalli etc., have become cent per cent literate of Godavari district. Today all Scheduled Caste people are being educated and not even one is left without education.

Malas have social organisation of their own, the caste council known as Sangam which serves as the highest authority connected with birth and death of every Mala. Peddamala is the chief of the Malas of the village. It is a traditional position and it is inherited from a family on male succession. The Peddamala and his family, as they exercise enjoyable position, i.e., *primus interperus* among the community, are expected to lead a clean, exemplary and decent life.

There are other members in the council such as the priest 'Mala Dasari' who looks after all the rituals and ceremonies of the Scheduled Caste Malas. He maintains his own panchangam, scribed on palm leaves and visits the families as and when they are in distress or likely to perform ceremonies of joined sorrow. All the members of the Mala community respect the Mala Dasari and reward him by paying grain and vegetables towards his service. During the harvest seasons the Dasari is also paid some grain and millet. The Mala Dasari maintains separate ritual status and feels as if he is the Brahmin of the Malas. As such, he does not accept cooked food or cakes from Malas, however he takes the sacrificed cock or hen and all the rice, jaggery, coconuts and some coins as *katnam*. Challavadi is the runner of the sangam and he takes all the news to the required place and reports to the same to the Peddamala back. *Kondegadu* is another special messenger who spreads the news of ceremonies, Jataras and other festivals connected with the village deities worshipped by the Malas. The Sangam of the Scheduled Caste Malas is the highest judicial body which meets on occasions when cases are reported. At the centre of the Mala settlements where a vedic or a high platform is erected, the Peddamala and his associates sit on the platform while the accused and the victims present their *Sakshyams*/evidences in support of this case, some times factual evidence is taken into account, sometimes, *sakunams* or soarcery, and sometimes trail by ordial is taken into account to find out the culprit. Walking on burning charcoal, lifting chains from boiled oil, lifting redhot crowbars etc., are sometimes conducted to find out the culprits.

Rice and beetle leafs are served to the gathering and they were asked to spit after chewing, the spittle is examined by the Peddamala one by one and the spittle which contains no salive was confirmed to be the culprit. Punishment and fines ultimately excommunications are some of the methods of judgement for adultary, theft, arson, cattle lifting etc. Fines were levied on the culprits and the amount so collected is used for community dinner which consists of pork and toddy. Such money is, however, not spent on any welfare activities of the community. If the culprits fail to pay the fine and abide by the rituals of the Sangam, they are declared excommunicted by the way of not serving water and fire, not talking to them, not inviting them to any functions on either side.

11. Christianity and Western Education

Scheduled Caste Malas particularly the right hand untouchables of the Andhra Pradesh were the most victims for a long time. They suffered and endured all insults from the upper castes. Being skillful weavers they were self employed for nearly nine months in a year, the remaining three months they took to agricultural labour and works. A Mala can marry as many as 18 times, without a wife he cannot participate in any affairs of the village.

The Missionaries who have reached by east-coast as early as A.D. 16th century, established schools both in English and vernacular and admitted the Scheduled Castes into the institution, provided free education and boarding as a mark of gratitude. The S.C. people embraced Christianity and those whoever converted began to feel high among themselves over the rest of the native untouchables. The newly converted untouchable Christian used to be called by fellow men as *Anyulu* or non-believers. The converts never accept any fruits/sweets or any other offerings from the sacrifices made by the caste Hindus or fellow untouchables. They began to educate their children and used to send to the church for Sunday prayers with a copy of vernacular Bible and a book of kearthans. More and more people embraced Christianity for two reasons, the first reason is that they are treated by caste Hindus very lowly and they were not allowed to enter the temple or not allowed to take the profession they like, secondly there was no such a discrimination if they embrass Christianity, moreover wheat, sugar, bread, biscuits, clothing, milk powder, etc., are given to them free of cost by the missionaries. Thus Christianity could attract many untouchables into their fold.

12. Resistance from the Dasaries

While Brahmins and other upper caste people embraced Christianity, there was no resistance from any corner of their community. It is very interesting to note that the Mala Dasaris, the priests of the right hand untouchables, gave a stubborn resistance for the Christian conversions. Fathers, priests and catakiests came to the Mala settlements to preach about Christianity and tried to baptise them. The Dasaries objected it and faught against the propagation of Christianity among the untouchables. There were many incidents in Andhra which culminated in the murder of Christian fathers thus we see the resistance for religious conversions from the priests of the Malas.

13. The Paleru-Upper Caste Relationship

It is well known fact that the Malas live on the outskirts of the village in clusters of tiny cone-shaped and square-shaped thatched houses known as *Harijanawada* or *Malawada*. These *wadas* which look like tiny hamlets are almost disconnected from the main village. It means that they are not living with the other castes. These *wadas* have their own wells, pumpsets and temples for worship. They are not allowed to draw water from public wells in the villages. Similarly they are not permitted to enter into the main temples for worship along with other Hindu castes. In these aspects, they are not treated civilly as self-respecting members of the community on par with the caste Hindus. This shows that Scheduled Castes are always kept at a distance signifying their low social status. They are still considered as outcastes or those outside the pale of the caste Hindu society as polluting communities. This would show the practice of untouchability. People belonging to the higher castes like Brahmins, the Vaishyas and the Shudras do not accept cooked food or water from these people. Although the people of the higher castes invite them for certain ceremonial dinners they are served separately, that is, in the courtyards. They are not allowed to sit or move along with the higher caste people. Instead they sit on the ground and eat. The higher caste people, as the ryots or owners of the agricultural land of the village, do however visit the *wadas* and bless the members of the Malas on ceremonial and social occasions. Even at these meetings, the caste people never accept food or water from them. They accept only betal leaves and nuts at the time of performing ritual ceremonies. Even the Brahmins who assist the members of the Scheduled Caste people in performing marriage or any rituals accept only rice, pulse and money as *dakshina*. It is learnt from a majority of the respondents that their marriage processions are not allowed to pass through the main streets of the villages. Social distance is maintained. But the caste Hindus are inter-dependent and they however maintain cordial relations with the Scheduled Castes for the sake of peace and harmony in the village. Especially for agricultural operations most of the Scheduled Castes are needed by the upper caste villagers. Any slight rupture or quarrel will disengage them from carrying out the operations in the farms. It is for this reason, the upper caste people restrain themselves in their attitudes. In spite of this fact, quarrels and minor scuffles are now and then witnessed between them. While on the other hand the Scheduled Castes help the villagers during the times of marriage, birth, and death ceremonies by drum-beating and playing other roles. In this way, we see that the people belonging to higher caste members and Scheduled Caste members are inter-dependent and accommodate themselves in an atmosphere of peaceful co-existence.

8

Struggle for Economic Freedom and Social Justice

1. Peasants and Communists in Coastal Andhra

During the late 1920s a strong peasant movement arose in the coastal Andhra districts which by the 1930s became the centre of the regional politics. This region of Madrasi presidency saw a tumultuous combination of a strong market-oriented peasant cultivation and the highest prevalence of the zamindari system in the face of the buffetings of the depression and the apparent prosperity of the war years. In caste terms, the peasant movement was based primarily on the Kammas, who found themselves politically confronting a Brahman controlled Congress and the landlords (often Velamas and Reddis) dominating the Justice Party. Some of the Kammas associated themselves with N.G. Ranga and latter struggled for dominance in the Congress, while the more radical youth took part in the formation of a communist party unit. Both sections fought it out in the late 1930's for control of the peasant movement and competed to win over and organise agricultural labourers and Dalits.

The organised peasant movement dated from 1923 when Ranga, a Kamma of Guntur district, returned from England and formed a local Ryot Association after the 1920-21 upsurge in the region. The organisation marked time during the dull decade of the 1920s but in 1928, the same year as Bardoli, put the cause of anti revenue movements on the political map. The Andhra Provincial Ryots Association was founded at Guntur. It had a moderate programmes of rural reconstruction, scientific agriculture, cooperation and organization on the immediate economic issues. But within a year a vigorous agitation against the Government proposed increase in revenue rates gave it a radical impetus, and by the second conference at Vijayawada, Ranga was putting forward the slogan of Kisan Raj or Ryot Raj (peasant rule). From 1930, demands were made for moratoriums on debt and the rent arrears. About the same time, a Zamindari Ryots Association (of tenants) formed in 1926 was taken over by new leadership associated with Ranga and took a radical turn including a big struggle against the huge Venkatgiri Zamindari in Nellore district in 1931. The demand for abolition of Zamindari began to be voiced.

Ranga was jailed during the agitations and after his release in 1934-35 he began to move into the Congress, while organizing both peasants and Dalits. He founded the peasants institute for training cadres at Nidubrolu in his home district of Guntur and began to tour the district with the slogan of 'Kisan raj'. During the same period a Harijan Seva Dal was formed with the active support of his wife and both toured in Guntur and Krishna districts, launching a temple entry campaign in the village of Govada. Associated in this Harijan work were other notable social reformers such as Unnava Lakshminarayana, author of *Malapalle* and Guduru Ramchandra Rao, the Krishna district reformer who had inaugurated the first Adi-Andhra Conference in 1917. The General Secretary of the Andhra branch of the Harijan Sevak Sangh; M. Bapineedu of the West Godavari District was also a colleague of N.G. Ranga.

Along with Ranga a few others began pushing for an all-India peasant organization. This was at first opposed by the Bihar movement, but it gained the support of Congress Socialist Party which was formed in January 1936 at Meerut by a group of young Congress leftists who, like Ranga were concerned to carve out for themselves a unique identity and base within the Congress fold. Thus an All India Kisan Congress, with Ranga and Jayaprakash Narayan as joint convenors, and Swami Sahajanand presiding, was formed during the 1936 Lucknow session of the Indian National Congress. It had two main points of action; a demand for abolition of all systems of landlordship, and a demand for abolition of land revenue (to be placed by graded income tax). A process of distancing from the Congress began with a change of name to 'All India Kisan Sabha' and though the second session in Maharastra in December 1936, with Ranga presiding again coincided with the INC session, it was the last one to do so.

When CPI organisation was initiated in Andhra in 1934, a struggle for dominance began in the Kisansabha and the Congress Socialist Party. The period between 1938 and 1942 saw intense factionalism among communists and non-communists in Kisan Sabha. Ranga, a leader of the Anti-communists faction, was a focus of this and in the fourth session of the sabha at Gaya in 1939 his presidential address was not accepted, while a strong political resolution reflected the left ideology of the time in stressing agrarian revolution as central to the worker-peasant alliance, and the unity of the people against imperialism through the Congress. Ranga visualised a democratic state of the Indian people, leading ultimately to the realization of *Kisan-Mazdur Raj*. Intense factional struggles were going on in the Andhra Ryots Association also, and the communists succeeded in winning over a large percentage of the cadre coming out of Ranga's Peasant Institute.

Hitler's invasion of the Soviet Union in June 1941 led the Indian communists to offer support to the British regime in 'People's War' against fascism; there was little programmatic difference between the communists and their 'Ranga-ite' or socialist rivals. Much of what went on seems to be a war of slogans: Ranga initially talked about *Kisan Raj*, the communists pushed *Mazdur raj* and in response Ranga adopted *Kisan-Mazdur Raj*. But if the communists were making this a point of difference it was a bit puzzling, since Lenin himself had declared the Russian revolution to be the 'democratic dictatorship of the proletariat and the peasantry'. While claiming to possess a 'scientific' ideology, the CPI appeared to suffer from good deal of ideological confusion as it stubbornly resisted bringing the peasantry into the slogan.

What *Mazdur Raj* or the 'dictatorship of the proletariat' in fact signified was a communist determination to keep control of mass organizations. The consequences of this were decisive when in 1942 a central Kisan Council meeting attacked the biggest mass independence struggle, the Quit India movement, as acts of mob violence, sabotage, distruction etc., which create conditions of anarchy and disruption which are being taken advantage of by the fifth columm agents for their nefarious ends and appealed to *Kisans* and the people to turn aside from the path of sabotage and terrorist and destructive activities. Within a year not only had Ranga quit the Kisan Sabha but such other major independent peasant leaders as Indulal Yagnik and Swami Sahajanand had also become inactive. Hard mass organizing work won the communists control of the Sabha in Andhra and many other areas nationally and in coastal Andhra they used the opportunity provided by the lifting of the British repressive machinery from 1943-44 to broaden their base impressively.

The Andhra communists were unique in India in being drawn from the main non-Brahman castes. Of their regional leadership, P. Sundarayya, Ravi Narayana Reddy and Badam Yella Reddy were all Reddis (the latter two from Hyderabad state), while Basava Punnaiah, C. Rajeswar Rao, C. Vasudeva Rao and N. Prasad Rao were Kammas. Their origin has been criticized as leading to a *kulak* oriented party with a tendency to compromise with rich peasant interests.

The rich Kamma *Kulaks* formed the class base of the Andhra communist party and provided the party with funds and workers. The leading communists of the Andhra delta were well-to-do peasants and came either from the Kamma or the Reddy caste of peasant proprietors. It was therefore to the interests of the rich peasants who dominated the party that all other subordinate agrarian classes, such as the small holders and tenants and share croppers (poor peasants), quite as much as the landless labourers formed an alliance and launched a combined effort against the handful of rich absentee landlords.

The approach rises many questions. First, it is unclear whether 'agrarian classes' can be so clearly demarcated, doing so has been most often a matter of dogma rather than empirical analysis. Second, characterizing caste-groups such as the Kammas and Reddis as peasant proprietors' also reflects a questionable absorption of caste into class, both groups, included a large range, form poor peasants (and even labourers in the case of some of the coastal Kammas) to landlords, most of the communist leaders did not in fact come technically from landlord and not even 'rich peasant' families. If this class/caste origin conditioned their approach, even a more severe question could be raised about the Brahman origins of Indian communists in other states and it leaves the question of how they could, if they did, continue to dominate a movement even when it recruited so many of a lower class/caste origins.

More important is the question of whose interests were objectively served at the time. While it was certainly in the interest of the rich peasants to form an 'alliance of all agrarian classes', it was equally in the interests of the landless and poor peasants. In fact the *Kulak* dominated leadership of the Andhra peasant movement did more to organize agriculture labourers than any other class in the country. With the foundation of the Agricultural Labour Union in Coastal Andhra it grew to a membership of 60,000 in 1945-46 compared to the figures of 5,000 to 15,000 in other regions. Local wage struggle began to be organized and many of these were quite militant. A study focussing on the West Godavari area shows a very militant line in the 1938-39 period, climaxing in a 15 day strike of 10,000 labourers in 13 villages, met with heavy state repression and the jailing and killing of leaders. It was partly because of this that after the revival of the Union in 1943 a strike for wages focused against the single biggest landlord in the village Hargopal, reporting on the study, considers this a retreat from militancy but it is equally arguable that the more moderate movement of the later period was more effectively in meeting the interests of the labourers. There certainly were limitations in agricultural labour organization and perhaps even more in confronting the problem faced as members of 'untouchable' castes, but it is hard to argue that these were due mainly to an alliance strategy.

There was also no clear difference between the communists (whether from 'Kulaks' or of other castes) and the non-communists on this issue. While Ranga is characterized as a typical 'rich peasant' leader, still his efforts to draw agricultural labourers and Dalits into an alliance during the 1930s and 1940s were not so different from those of the communists. As he wrote:

> The peasants institute has been advocating, from its very inception, a harmonious comradeship between the peasants and workers on the land, based upon a mutually, settled relationship between the prices of agricultural products and wages, both to be made dependants on decent and rising living standards of both peasants and workers. The Andhra Kisans have long ago realised the need for a common front to be put up by both the landed and landless Kisans.

Even stronger language about the need for an alliance was used by the Bihar Leader Swami Sahajanand in 1938:

> Of late, some people have begun a tirade against the Kisan Sabha in the name of agricultural labourers. According to them, Kisans are exploiters. Their object is not so much to serve them as to flirt with Zamindars who are the common enemy of both Kisans and Khet Mazdurs. They should realize that the service of the Khet Mazdurs and friendship with Zamindars are contradictory. The Khet Mazdurs are after all landless Kisans. Those who had lands yesterday have none today and those who have them today will lose them tomorrow, and thus while possessed of lands, they are Kisans and deprived of

> them, we call them Khet Mazdurs. But the process is progressively going on and there can be no strict line of demorcation between these two sections of Kisans. Those who seek to draw one are the common enemies of both. This hard hitting speech referred not to Trotskyites or other 'left' critics but to the Congress-sponsored activities of Jagjivan Ram. During the 1930s Ranga, Sahajanand, the communists and Ambedkar all called for a alliance between peasants and agricultural labourers. Arguments that this was mistaken or represent simply rich peasant interests have the flavour of the academy about them.

Yet there is an interesting difference between the way Ranga and Sahajanand articulated the issue. While Sahajanand insisted on no strict line of demarcation and distinguished his groups solely in terms of land holding, Ranga spoke of two clearly distinct sections which had common interests in the framework of a commercialized economy. The 'Bihar tradition' of rural organizing up to the present has been for radicals to include agricultural labourers along with the peasants in *Kisan Sabhas* or *Kisan Samitis* and speak of them as 'landless peasants': While the 'Andhra tradition' was either to form separate agricultural labou.ers organization or to speak clearly of *Kisan-Mazdur* and *Ryot Coolie Sangams*. This difference, it can be argued, reflected differences in commercialization and differing caste links with agrarian structure in the two regions. In Bihar there seems to have been more caste overlap, where -as in coastal Andhra the line between the 'peasant' and agricultural labourer coincided with the caste difference between the Kammas and Madigas and Malas. Dalit militancy was intensifying the militancy of agricultural labourers including the resistance to any form of bondage; Ranga, for instance noted in one of his studies that:

> In spite of such abnormal rise in this wages fewer and fewer *panchamas* are anxious to become annual servants because their standard of comfort and their idea of self-respect have changed for the better in the last 50 years. It is curious how these *panchamas* prefer to live an Independent day labourer's life to that of an annual servant or Paleru.

However none of the main 'Peasant Organizers', including the communists, theoretically recognized this role of caste. The issues of demands for wasteland (forest lands, government owned lands, *Porambok* lands in Andhra) were never given a special place in *Kisan Sabha* programmes, never did the communists recognize the way in which Vethbegar was articulated in terms of caste and represented the traditional feudal form of caste exploitation of labour. Yet both issues were coming up everywhere in Dalit movement, and both issues were to become central in the Andhra Peasant revolt. The problem was that regardless of how much they recognized the importance of or took up issues of 'Social Oppression', the Left failed to deal with the economic articulation of caste.

2. Dalits in Coastal Andhra

Following two conferences in 1930, 'Adi-Andhra' organising had come to a standstill for five years. The next initiative was that of the Gandhians: Congress 'Harijan' organizing began with the formation of the Andhra branch of the *Harijan Seva Sangh* at Vijayawada in November 1932. Two caste Hindu reformers, K.Nageswara Rao of Krishna district and M.Bapineedu, were its President and General Secretary respectively. Two Dalits, Vemula Kurmayya (Krishna District) and Narlachetty Devendrudu (West Godavari) were joint secretaries. Both had been active during the 1920's; Devendrudu had been chairman of the reception committee of the third Adi-Andhra Conference and was later nominated to the Madras legislative council, while Kurmayya was chairman of the reception committee for the eighth conference at Vijayawada.

Then Ambedkar's announcement of conversion from Hinduism in 1935 sparked another round of activity. Younger Dalits became energized, such as Eali Vedappalli (1911-71) of East Godavari, who organised a round of Adi-Andhra conference in that district, and Geddada Brahmaiah (1912-50), who became secretary of an Adi-Andhra Sangam in 1935, organised a number of district conferences, between 1938-1940 and edited an *Adi-Andhra Patrika*. Another publication, *Jayabheri*, was started by the well-known writer, Kusumu Dharmanna (1898-1948) of Rajahmundry. This became a sort of mouth piece for the Ambedkarite group. Dharmanna also presided over many Adi-Andhra Conferences in his district and had made use of the Dalit overseas connections, travelling to Rangoon to collect money for his weekly. He later became inclined towards Islam and established connections with B.S. Venkatarao in Hyderabad. He was known as a powerful poet, writer and speaker, with one of his poems, *'Nalladorathanamu'* ('brown bureaucracy') becoming famous as a Dalit reply to a popular song, 'We don't' want to be ruled by white people, Dharmanna asserted, 'we don't want a country ruled by black lords'.

State level Adi-Andhra organizing was resumed. In 1935, the tenth conference was organized at Rajahmundry, inaugurated by M.C.Rajaiah and with one of the older generation leaders, Kusuma Venkata Ramaiah (who had earlier been associated with the Ramachandra Rao Sevashram) presiding. This was evidently anti Ambedkarite in tone and very little of any consequence came from it. The eleventh conference was held in 1936 and then the twelfth and final conference at Tallarevu in East Godavari in 1938 saw a confrontation between the young radicals and more established organizers. The organizers in a period of reformist stress on temple entry, wanted a resolution for this, but the youth, led by Pamu Ram Murthy of East Godavari district, opposed it as a concession to Hinduism. Bhagyareddy, the invitee president of the conference supported this opposition in one of his last public acts. The final resolution included demands for reserved seat for untouchables from the panchayat level to the legislative councils, enforcing sanctions against those opposing the presence of untouchable children in schools; job reservations; formation of labour cooperatives and credit banks, and the demand for forests/ waste lands for Dalits. No mention was made of the agricultural wage issues coming up at that time.

But this was the last of the 'Adi-Andhra' conference. The largest section of Dalit leadership was getting absorbed into the Congress with its 'Harijan' terminology and its reiteration of a Hindu identity. The few who opposed this strongly such as Kusuma Dharmanna were discredited by their pro-Muslim stance. In many ways this reformist 'Hinduization' can be traced to the writings of Boyi Bhimanna, the young Dalit writer of East Godavari district who was described by some of the Congress Dalits as their guiding spirit.

Coastal Andhra presents an independent Dalit movement in the 1920s in a situation where agricultural commercialization laid the basis for a widespread rural movement, but without the urban industrial centre as found in Nagpur.

The districts of coastal Andhra including the erstwhile Srikakulam, Vizagapattnam, Godavari, Krishna, Guntur and Nellore along with the ceded districts of the Rayalaseema were included in Madras presidency during colonial rule. These were disperate regions, the backwardness of dry and sometimes drought-stricken Rayalseema contrasting with the economic energy that made the coastal region one of the most dynamic centres of development in the presidency. It was primarily in the latter that a Dalit movement emerged.

Major irrigation schemes on the Krishna and Godavari rivers launched during the nineteenth century laid the basis for intensive cultivation of rice and other cash crops for a growing market by the end of the 1940's, for example, over 52 per cent of the rice produced in West Godavari district was marketed, generating fast growing market towns such as Vijayawada, Eluru and Kakinada. The area though formally under ryotwari tenure, had a considerable degree of zamindari holdings and though the earliest industrial entrepreneurs were drawn primarily from large landlord families, merchants came from the traditional trading castes such as Vysyas or Komatis and Marwaris. At the same time, the development of agricultural enterprise provided the base for the assertion of a substantial peasant interest, mainly based among the Kammas. Commercialization meant uneveness, economic traumas and even degree of polarization during economic crises. It also eroded traditional caste and Jajmani ties which had bound the Dalit labourers and aided in the development of mobile labour force with opportunities for some of the Malas and Madigas to move ahead. Mala migration to Burma from the late nineteenth century onwards was also a factor responsible for the slow advance.

In these economic circumstances a considerable amount of social change, cultural ferment and political turmoil occurred. Christian missionaries, concentrating in the coastal districts, converted a good many untouchables (Malas and Madigas) and provided educational opportunities for many more. Hindu social reformers followed. Coastal Andhra was a site of one of the most radical elity-based reform movements outside of Bengal. Veeresalingam Pantulu was the nineteenth century pioneer, beginning with a bold widow remarriage movement and taking up issues such a dowry, prostitution, corruption of officials, and untouchability. He established the Brahma Samaj in Andhra and it was through this that the most important caste Hindu sponsorship of Dalit advance took place. Early issues included not only education but acquisition of land, for instance a Government of Madras Bill on Education 1895 called the '**Magna Carta** of *Panchama* education', provided for schools and hostels and given *Poramboke* (waste lands) for institutional sites. By the early twentieth century the Brahmo Samaj and other reformers were establishing *ashrams* for training untouchable cadre including a

Sevashram at Gudivada (Krishna district), started in 1912 by Sir Guduru Ramachandra Rao which called the most well-known exuntouchable activists on the time to work in all Telugu-speaking districts. Among those many were to be active later during the 1920's including Sundra Venkaiah, Kusuma Venkataramaiah, Kusuma Dharmanna and others.

The Congress was dominated by a Brahman elite till the 1930's. However, beginning with 1917 an emerging non-Brahman movement in Madras Presidency challenged this dominance, putting forth a radical rejection of Brahman dominance, and laid the basis for many of the themes influencing dalit movements, including a 'non-Aryan' or 'Dravidian' identity. But the Justice Party, the political wing of the movement, was in contrast to Maharashtra more elitist, with an Andhra leadership consisting primarily of Zamindars and larger land holders, giving little scope for the participation of middle peasant Kammas and Kapus (beginning to identify themselves on 'Reddis' in caste association). Though the Tamil non-Brahman movement became radicalized under the leadership of Periyar in the middle 1920's, taking up working class and anti-landlord issues and asserting both atheism and a radical perspective on women,s oppression, this had little impact in the Telugu speaking areas. Instead, in coastal Andhra, the peasant Kammas and Kapu-Reddis asserted themselves organizationally in the 1920s through N.G.Ranga peasant associations and the communist movement. Even before this, however, Dalits in coastal Andhra were asserting their organizational autonomy.

But, the contact they were doing so had powerful, integrative-Hinduistic pulls. Coastal Andhra also provided the base for an emerging regional-nationalist consciousness. Demands for a separate Andhra province began to be heard during the early twentieth century after the Bengal agitation against partition and the Swadeshi movement. Many nationalists organized the Andhra Mahasabha, which held annual conference from 1913 and also established a separate Andhra circle within the Congress organization from 1918. But this emerging Telugu consciousness remained strikingly Hinduistic. It had a reformist tinge with Veeresalingam, considered to be its fore runner as a founder of modern mass-oriented literature, with the Andhra Mahasabha in Hyderabad state associated with anti-untouchability efforts, widow remarriage and opposition to *vethbegar*. Yet in spite of this linkage to problems of the Dalits, Dalits themselves did not participate in the formation of the 'Telugu Consciousness', and it evolved first of all a Hindu consciousness. Partly this was due to the need to reject the synthetic 'Deccani' Hindu-Muslim culture that many in Hyderabad state were proclaiming. Nevertheless, it firmly identified early rulers such as the Satavahanas, Chalukyas, and Kakatiyas as Hindu, in spite of considerable Jain and Buddhist influences. Indian Unity also became symbolized as a Hindu unity and as Hargopal notes, an early twentieth century Telugu poem described India as a beautiful cow, the Hindus as its calves, and the whiteman as the exploiter making the cow by forcibly closing the mouths of the calves.

The Hinduistic and integrationist tendency can be seen clearly in the two famous coastal Andhra caste Hindu novels written about Dalits, i.e,. Malapalli or Mala village by Unnava Lakshmi Narayana and Harijana Nayakudu by Sri N.G.Ranga.

At a number of places in Andhra, Tamil Nadu, Karnataka, Kerala, Bihar, Maharashtra and Uttar Pradesh, Harijan agricultural labourers participated in the land grab movements of the late sixties; they also launched struggles demanding higher wages. In fact Harijan agricultural labourers and share croppers launched struggles even during the British period (Henningham, 1981).[1]

In 1961 there occured several incidents between the agricultural labour and the landlords regarding the payment of wages. Agricultural labourers, mostly coming from Scheduled Caste communities, used to migrate from one place to another place in search of work. The crop pattern of the Godavari district is placed on the irrigation timing. The irrigation of Godavari and Krishna district is a very important phenomena. First water is released after the summer in East Godavari district, ploughing starts first in the East Godavari district and all agricultural operation like seed bed preparation, sowing of seeds, transplantation etc., are completed in the East Godavari district. Agricultural operations start a little later in West Godavari district and still later in the Krishna, Guntur, Prakasam districts etc. As the agricultural operation in all the areas are not done at a time, the demand for agricultural labour is not very high. It is elastic, as such labour has no bargaining power, they themselves would migrate to the place where work starts. The landlords could bargain the labour to the lowest point whereas the labour could not demand for higher wages, as there is no demand for the agricultural labourer. Native coolies would never allow other agricultural labour coming from farer places with the fear that their wages will be reduced and due to uncleanly atmosphere caused by the newcomers would spread diseases like cholara, disrrbea, malaria and other contagious diseases. Free migration of agricultural labour also made the local agricultural labour not only weak but also discomfortable and therefore they stopped the entry of labour into the area who raise the wages. This was not liked by the local landlords who preferred the labourer coming from other places who are ready to do the work at the lower rate; thus there occurred many dommies, ryots or beatings with stick, iron rods etc., petty instruments, leading to the breaking of heads and killing of people. In 1981 a big dommie took place at Tundurru communist village in the Narsapur Taluq of West Godavari district.[2] This incident has a series of repurcussion in several villages in West Godavari district and many other places outside the district where the influence of communist party leaders was there. Communists always infused into the rithu coolie and other workers that land belongs to those who till it but not who own it. Wage earners were very much influenced by the most hopeful slogan "Dunne Vadide Bhommi". The land belongs to those who till it, *Krishna Patrika* a powerful journal published in Telugu from Machilipatnam, the headquarters of Krishna district of Andhra Pradesh and also Jameen Raitu, the most powerful publication published from Nellore, the most powerful political centre of Andhra Pradesh, brought to light all the information pertaining to struggle for social justice and economic upliftment raised by the raith coolies of different parts of Andhra Pradesh.

The following incidents happened in the West Godavari district would through much light on the atrocities committed by the upper caste landlords over the farm servants and agriculture labour and also the struggle of the sufferers in achieving social justice. The struggle for social justice is not a passing episode in the long suffering of the farm servants on the one hand and the agriculture labourers on the other, but it was a genuine struggle for freedom from bondage and right to bargain for justified wages. The role of the government in solving the problems of the quasi permanent farm labourer and the unorganised agricultural labour was ultimately guided by various incidents that took place in connection with the paleru's and the agricultural coolies.

3. Peasant Movement in Coastal Andhra

As India is predominantly an agrarian country 70 per cent of its population still depends upon agriculture for its livelihood. They are differentiated in terms of relationship regarding the ownership of land, viz., supervisory, agriculturists, owner-cultivators, share croppers, tenants and landless labourers. In local parlance they are known as Kisans or Kheduls and farm labour *ritu coolies*.[3]

An agricultural labourer in contemporary India is generally no longer laid down to the same master as was the case during colonial and pre-colonial periods in pre-capitalistic agriculture.[4]

3.1 Doddipatla Village Agricultural Labour—Landlord Confrontation

Doddipatla a rural village with 90 per cent of Scheduled Caste population with a cluster of hamlets around enjoyed the status of a semi-urban village on account of its proximity to Palakollu, a wealthier and prosperous urban centre, in Narsapur Mandal of West Godavari district. Many Vysyas, few Brahmins and a few Kapus have their lands in the village of Doddipatla and its contiguous regions. Doddipatla being geographically bordered by the river Godavari on the East. Communists used to cross the river Godavari and harbour in the Doddipatla village whenever there was a police raiding on them. Being a stronghold of communists the people of Doddipatla were influenced by the ideology of communism. As a result, the agriculture labour or Ryot coolies organised into strong unions and could demand higher wages and also stipulate hours of work from the landlords. The landlords who were also businessmen were living at Palakollu, Junnur, Digamarru and Narsapur, the urban centres of Narsapur. The agricultural labour, being strong on account of their unions could support the communist party and the leaders organised a protest against the landlords by not attending to the agricultural work.[5]

3.2 Raithu Cooli Struggle at Agartipalem

Agartipalem a highly educated Scheduled Caste dominant village in the Narsapur Mandal of West Godavari district was a leading star in many aspects. All the residents of the Palem were educated in one way or the other and many top most administrative officers, police officers, Doctors, Engineers, academicians came from this village. The early British educational institutions like vernacular schools, churches etc., brought new life into the lifes of these untouchables. They have no fear in attacking or fighting against atrocities. English education made them bold and fearless, even during the pre-independent India this village is considered to be the Kerala of Andhra Pradesh. The struggle between agriculture labour and the landlords was so high in the village that for a couple of years the landlords of Agartipalem and contiguous villages could not harvest their crops due to the resistance given by the Scheduled Caste agricultural labour. The Scheduled Caste agriculture labour of Agartipalem formed into a strong powerful village united organisation of agricultural labour to demand higher wages. When the landlords refused to raise the wages and also refused to employ labour of the village and tried to procure labour from outside, the villagers gave strong resistance to the entry of the outside labour. They were beaten with sticks and driven outside the village borders. As a result, all the standing crops withered and fell on the ground and could not be harvested. The landlords could not harvest their crops the coolies trampled the crops with their cattle and collected whatever paddy they could grab in the night; granaries of the landlords were broke open and the grain stolen by the unemployed agricultural labour at many places. Large heaps of hay (*Gaddivamu*) preserved for the cattle were burnt to ashes, cattle were stolen and were eaten by the Scheduled Caste people of Agartipalem. Police cases were filed and many of them were taken to police station - petty fines and imprisonments were pronounced on them. The people in the village continued their struggle against their landlords. As they have no work they have depended upon mostly fish, snails, fresh water muscles, lotus roots and their fruits (*Molla*). The subsequent year also lands were not ploughed and they became barren. All fertile fields were filled with weeds. Most of the wealthy cattle/healthy cattle were sold in the market of Palakollu to the butchers as there was no hay and fodder and other greens to the cattle. Most of the landlords preferred to leave the village to urban centres. As the end of the second year, government however intervened into the unsolved affairs of Agartipalem, some assistance was provided by supply of free rice, wheat, milk powder, clothing through the Christian missionaries, apart from this the sympathisers of the agricultural labour agitation collected some *chanda* or contributions and gave it to the leaders of the movement which was redistributed to the needy and poor. Several articles and appeals to solve the Agartipalem coolie-landlord issues were published in *Jameen Raithu*, *Krishna Patrika* and other newspapers. Sympathy was however mounting on the side of the coolies fighting for their rights. As a result, the revenue Tahsildar deputed by the Collector of West Godavari called for a meeting of coolies of the village and neighbouring villages to come to an understanding of the conflict.

The Raithu-coolie conflict started at Agartipalem village spread like wild fire into the neighbouring and distant villages; communist villages like Koderu, Ballipadu, Veeravasaram, Doddipatla etc., started organising processions in support of the cause of Agartipalem raitu-coolie conflict. A favourable under standing was established between the agricultural labour and the landlord.

3.3 Temporary break of Palerus/farm Labour Servants

As gulf between farm labour and the landlord increased and the palerus were not allowed to attend the duties of the landlords. If anybody by pressure or fear of landlords wrath secretly, attends, such members and their families were completely communicated from the mainstream of the social life in the village. For fear of excommunication, paleru families employed earlier straightaway refused to serve the landlords.

3.4 Entry of Backward Caste People as Paleru

Traditionally Scheduled Castes farm servants enjoyed the posts of Paleru but on account the incidence taken back simultaneously in some parts of Andhra Pradesh a new section of farm servants entered as there was a lot of demand for them. People belonging to Kapu, Gowda, Idiga communities and Chetti Balija opted for the traditional farm servant posts. This brought a tremendous change in the traditional employment pattern in the villages. Every village in Andhra Pradesh is endowed with its traditional techno-crafts, viz., carpenter, blacksmith, stone cutter, masons, potters known as the five great artisans (panchanamuvaru), apart from these barber, washerman, basket maker and weaver supplemented their rest of the requirements in the village, a washerman and weaver were always attached to wealthy families who could provide them continuous work. The entry of new caste of Palerus into the service of landlord created Palerus above Palerus or servants above servants. Palerus belonging to Kapu, Idiga, Gowda and other Sudra communities enjoyed superior social status over the Scheduled Caste palerus, they straight away entered into various parts of the landlords households while the farm servants of Scheduled Caste were not allowed to enter into the bungalow of the landlords. Thus with the entry of sudra farm servants, the Paleru of Scheduled Caste communities were driven to their original caste position.

3.5 Influence of Christian Missionaries

Ever since the coming of British into India, coastal tracts of Andhra Pradesh enjoyed the services of the British both evangelical and educational, people belonging to Scheduled Caste communities were taken on first priority into the churches and schools. Western education and teaching of Bible made Scheduled Caste people some sort of self-reliant in many respects. Christianity made them to live clean and neat and put them into regular religious way of life. It also knit them together in the feeling of Christianity. Now after conversion into Christianity they have only one god unlike many other petty gods like village *deities* whom they used to worship.

Secondly western education made them bold and clear in their ideas; histories of France, Germany, Europe and Russia made them revolutionary people who hither to believed in tradition, theory of Karma etc. Moreover they used to question such things once they are educated.

3.6 Influence of Dr. Ambedkar on Coastal Andhra

In the early 'thirties, Ambedkar concluded that the only way of improving the status of the untouchables was to renounce the Hindu religion. He appealed to his caste brothers, you have nothing to lose, except your religion (Keer 1954 : 273)[6]. In the early 'fifties' he found that Buddhism was appropriate as an alternative religion for the untouchables. It was their only salvation. He preferred Buddhism primarily because it is an indigenous religion of equality, a religion which was anti-caste and anti-Brahman (Lynch 1972; Kamble 1979).

Teaching and writings of Dr.Ambedkar, the great Maharashtrian social reformer, reached Andhra and he became their saviour. He was considered as the living Christ of the downtrodden. The life, history, the struggle for education and the insults he received from the caste Hindus while on service became the Messiah of Scheduled Caste. People in Andhra Pradesh, particularly those in coastal Andhra Pradesh, received the message of Dr. Ambedkar and preached to the nook and corner of every village. Every Scheduled Caste family in the coastal Andhra treated Dr.Ambedkar as their savior. He was considered as the living Christ of the downtrodden. The life history, the struggle for education and insults he received from the caste Hindus while on service became stories which were narrated as stories like Ramayana, Mahabharata among the Scheduled Caste people in the nook and corner of Andhra Pradesh.

The influence of the life story of Dr. Ambedkar was remarkable on the lifes of Scheduled Caste youth of Coastal Andhra. With the background of western education, with the discipline provided by Christian church, the ideas put by Dr. Ambedkar paved the way for emancipation of Scheduled Caste people, the ideas of Dr. Ambedkar as an architect of Indian constitution became very popular, his speeches and writings were translated into vernacular to make it known to the common man.

In Mogalturu, Doddipatla, Penumantra and Bhimavaram which are communist places, the ryots took inspiration from communist party that the land belongs to the people who plough it, i.e. 'Dunnewadi De Bhoomi'.

Communists in Andhra Pradesh organised Raitu Cooli Sangh, agricultural labour organisation and educated the coolies to fight for their rights to raise the wages and conditions of working hours; fight for better wages and less working hours were the demands. Hartals and stopping labour coming into the new areas became the order of the day. Agricultural labour used to borrow during slack seasons against the future agriculture.

3.7 Upraise of Raithu-Coolie Unions at Viravasaram, West Godavari District, Andhra Pradesh

Viravasaram etymologically means the residence of Heroe's situated 14 kms from Narsapur and 8 kms from Bhimavaram - it is on the Nidadavolu-Narsapur broad-gauge railway line favourably connected with the network of roads surrounded by canals and tanks. Being provided with fertile lands, it has provided sustenance for many a people through agriculture labour the Raith-coolies and compressed people belonging to Scheduled Castes, Gowda, Idiga, Sale and other minor communities. The Raith coolies of Viravasaram formed themselves into strong labour unions and could demand higher wages because of the influence of the communist party and its slogans and principles; thus Viravasaram occupied a very important position and was recognised as one of the strong holds of agricultural labour agitations, possessions and protests.

Being equipped with party discipline they could organise meetings very frequently to discuss about their issues and suggest ways and means for their problems to Viravasaram flashed into news July 29th 1970. When Raith coolies organised at Veeravasaram a strong protest by barricading the entry of agriculture labour through all roads connected with Bhimavaram, Palakollu, Narsapur and Nidadavolu. These agriculture labour who have finished their work in the East Godavari district, after summer first irrigation canals are released first in the East Godavari district, next in the West Godavari district and next in the Krishna district as such all the agricultural operations will be completed in the East Godavari district. As a result, ryots and dommies took place for a fortnight. Police could not control the ryots. Ultimately CRP was brought to Viravasaram and in the firing that took place two civilians and six Raith coolies were killed. The Government intervened into this affair with the help of District Collector associated with the labour conciliation officers and local MLAs. The issue was settled and labour from outside Godavari district could move to any place in search of work as the agriculture labour used to move to other places like Krishna, Guntur, Prakasam and Nellore district.

The long protest incident at Veeravasaram has a very deep impression on the peasant labour not only in West Godavari district but also on the contiguous districts in the east coast of coastal regions of Andhra Pradesh. The spirit of agitation is mainly due to the propaganda made by the Communist Party of India either raising a problem or solving it particularly with peasant workers was always started by the communists in the Godavari district.

3.8 Suicide Problem

Andhra Pradesh has several novelties in its life style the farmers (peasants of Andhra) have been accustomed for a new method to express their resentment towards the state policy - they have selected a method or suicide some times total suicide of the entire family whenever the crop failed or pesticides and manures used by them found to be fake and seeds sown of an inferior variety. Now a days we find many suicide cases of peasants. Government due to the pressure brought up by the opposition leaders in the State assembly and central Parliament began to pay an exgratia of Rs.1 lakh per head, brought to light, thus the series of suicide committed by peasants has become one of the unsolved problem connected with agricultural operations. Now a days, it has become very common to commit suicide. The impact of this system ultimately reflected very strongly in the minds of the common man and a very poor picture is depicted of the peasant in the society. Local, National and state newspapers contain innumerable incidents of suicide cases. Letters to the Editor and Editorials in the papers have criticised vehemently of the suicide method followed by the peasants. Money for suicide/suidice for money by the peasants could not gather any sympathy from the public.

3.9 Social Interaction

Society has a wonderful character. It attracts the opposite and distracts similar groups. In the present context of the region under study there are two groups of entities, the first one the landlord/owners group, socially superior, economically wealthy and culturally advanced. The second group is landless economically poor socially and culturally backward, highly vulnerable and a great pray for victimisation it always depended upon the land owners class. As untouchables and socially lower, they enjoy no status, no privileges when compared to their fellow land owning class.

This disparity however has two aspects, the first one being the water tight compartmentalization of vertical division, i.e., the upper caste who have been the land owning class could be placed above the landless. Even though the Scheduled Caste people have lands yet they could not enjoy the same status enjoyed by the landless Hindus. The second part of the situation is that there is a lot of attraction between these two opposite sections. There is a close relationship internally prevalent among these two groups, the landlord group and the paleru group. It has been noticed through the survey that illegal contacts prevail in such situations, i.e., the landlord Paleru relation. It is understood that such sexual relations are common occurrence. In many cases the Paleru's wife provides hospitality to the landlord, if she is very young she is in touch with landlords son, brother-in-law etc. Young and energetic palerus always spend their long hours in the premises of landlords cattle pen and household. Illegal contacts either with the landlords wife, daughters, sometimes young widow's of the house etc., maintain such sexual contacts with palerus. Whatever be the extent of affair things go well with a murmur/wishper but never cried aloud or made known to the public.

3.10 Illicit Relations made Public

Sometimes such secret and illegal sexual contacts are made public whenever a victim has a competition of lovers. If there are two landlords who are interested in the same girl she has to make it known to the village that she is exclusive keep of particular 'x'. By this there after no man would show any interest/interfere with her affairs, she is branded openly as the '*Munda*' or the keep of one particular wealthy man, he maintains her by providing all amenities, though not wedded legally she enjoys some status in the society as the keep of a wealthy respectable gentleman.

3.11 Murder and Arson

Not all illegal sexual contracts are digested by the people. Sometimes some where a murder, arson and poisoning etc., may take place. Cases pertaining to landlords family are not brought to light, they were not reported in the police station or not published in the newspapers, the suspected persons were caught red handed, killed with spheres and their bodies kept into heeps of hay, dumped in gunny bags and thrown into water some time burn to ashes etc. Very often the palerus are shown as hanging himself by committing suicide to a tree and cross bars of the cattle pen and sometimes consuming endrine, a powerful pesticide or rat poison.

3.12 Incident at Vempa Village

Vempa is a rich village situated near the seashore on the east coast of Narsapur Mandal, West Godavari district. It has rich lands connected with network of lagoons populated with Gowda (Toddy toppers and illicit liquor makers), Kapus cultivator's community, Malas (Scheduled Caste) and Pallekaru (fishermen community). In 1979 a Mala paleru working with a Gowda family was found missing suddenly. When reported to police it is found in the enquiry and after a prolonged investigation of three months, the dead body of the young Mala paleru was removed from a nearby lagoon. The post-mortem report revealed that the body of the diseased contained 29 spear stabs. Further investigation revealed that the mala paleru was having illegal relation with the young widow sister of the Gowda landlord under whom the paleru was working. A case was registered in the local police station. However, this issue was side tracked and brought into the Panchayat of the village elders and the report made by the victims wife was withdrawn and a compensation of 1 acre land was given by the Gowda to the victims family by the village elder's.

3.13 Incident at Poolapalli Village

Poolapalli village is situated six kilometres south of Palakollu, a prosperous market city with week-end sandy for cattle. Dalaries/Brokers purchase cattle at cheaper rates and keep them at Poolapalli in large sheds and keep them grazing and feeding to make them fat to fetch higher price. Such cattle pens were looked after by the palerus. As the Dalaries move from place to place to purchase cattle at cheaper rates they have little time to spend with their families, it is very convenient for the ladies who are alone to maintain sexual relations with the palerus. It is found that when Paleru belonging to Mala community was found missing from the service of a Kapu Dalari the parents of the paleru were taken to police station and they were asked to bring their son who is said to have stolen the jewellery of Kapu's wife. The family members of paleru were beaten in the police station. When they confessed that nothing is known about their son a bond was executed for Rs.10,000 against gold supposed to have been stolen from the house of the Kapu. After one year, the heap of hay of the Kapu which was sold to some other fellow, as the Kapu wanted to migrate to some other place. The purchaser was removing the heap of hay on cart loads and it is found in the heap a dried up dead body of Mala paleru of the Kapu. It was reported in the police station and the Kapu and his wife were arrested for killing the Mala paleru for having illegal contacts with his wife.

3.14 Double Murder of Mala Paleru and a Kapu Widow at Kavitum Village

Some 16 Kilometres north of Palakollu town of West Godavari, two dead bodies tied together to heavy stones, floating on the canal in a decomposed conditions have been noticed by the police on 16-10-1979 after *panchanama*. The bodies have been identified by the people who gathered there, the male body as Mala paleru and the female body as a young widow sister of one Kshatriya landlord of Kavitum village. The paleru Venkanna was working in the farm of the landlord from the age of 10 years, past 15 years he was with the family, every year one bag of paddy was added to his salary, he was considered as part of the Kshatriya family, good food was given to him. He enjoyed better treatment in comparison to other families. Landlords' younger sister was married to a nearby family. Her husband died in the next year and she came as widow to her brother's house and began to stay. Her closeness with the paleru led to illegal contact and got pregnant. On enquiry of the elders of the family it was revealed after a great torture, the paleru was responsible for her pregnancy. The young widow and the paleru were killed and their bodies are tied to heavy stones and thrown into canal. After a couple of days as the body swolen began to float and were collected at Kavitum locks where they were identified. Though the bodies are identified their killers are not identified therefore no case would be registered for taking action. It became a lorestory episode leading to murder and a wishper among the people.

3.15 Severed Head of a Mala Paleru kept on the top of toddy tree at Sammaladivi

Sammaladivi a seacoast village famous for cashewnut, toddy and casarina trees, fisherman and Gowdas are the dominant communities in the village, a few Malas and a few Visyas also live there. The Visyas being moneylenders finance for toddy and jaggery industry. Malas work as agriculture labour and palerus also on annual and biannual contract. A Mala was working in the agriculture farm of a Gowda who was having jaggery and toddy industry. The Gowda was also having a few toddy makers and their service, very often used to move to nearby town for taking orders of jaggery baskets. One day in the early morning, crows were making alarming sound in a distant place. Around the palm tree all the crows in the village gathered there and the scene, naturally attracted the people who went there. It is learnt that a human head was kept at the top of the toddy tree, when it was reported to the police, the head was brought down and identified as that of the paleru of Gowda. Police investigation proved that the Gowda who suspected the integrity of his wife with the paleru got him beheaded with the help of one of his toddy makers who kept the head of the paleru, at the top of the toddy tree. The Gowda being very rich manipulated the murder of his farm servant and pretended innocence of the incident. The mala paleru murders could not be investigated in the absence of evidence however, a case was registered.

3.16 Incidents not Brought to Light

Illegal incidents happened in rich families are never reported for the fear of social defame. Only rape and other atrocities committed on the families of palerus and other Scheduled Caste people are reported, published for want of political advantage, much *hangama* and window decoration are attached to such incidents. Politicians of different parties take up such cases to fight against the ruling government, much more harm is done to the victims than what she is given an exgratia by the government. Thus victimisation in the case of these people is open. The foregoing incidents related to atrocities against women would show the plight of women category under review.

References

1. Ghanshyam Shah, *Social Movements in India - A Review of the Literature*, 1990, p.112.

2. Locally slogans raised as *Dunnevadide Bhoomi* or the land belongs to those who till it. This was very much supported by the communists for this suited their communism. Many coolies prefer to take land on lease for cultivation and continued for paying the rent for many years and never vocated it with the hope that land would become their own as credited by communists.

3. Thanks to the influence of western scholarship, kisan is often translated as 'peasant' in the academic literature published in English. The term peasant is ambiguous and used differently by different authors or variously by the same author in different studies. On the one hand, it is used for those agriculturists who are homogenious with small holding operated mainly by family labour and on other hand it includes all those who depend on land including landless labour as well as supervisory agriculturists. To club together agriculture labour and peasantry raises some problems.

4. Eric Wolf emphasised in 1955 that ownership of land was critical criteria for defining 'peasants'. Peasants are defined as population that existentially involved in cultivation and make autonomous decisions regarding the process of cultivation.

5. Traditionally, there is no stipulated hours of work for agriculture labour in Godavari districts, village agricultural labourers have to reach the work spot as early as 5 a.m. and work upto 2 p.m. with a small break to take their lunch or *Chaddi Annamu* brought in large single box.

6. Keer, D. 1954 : 273, *Dr. Ambedkar Life and Mission*, Bombay, Lynch, 1972; Kamble, 1979.

7. Kamble, J.R. 1979. *Rise and Awakening of Depressed Classes in India*. Delhi, National.

9
Summary and Conclusion

Geographically the West Godavari District in Andhra Pradesh occupies a very important place by virtue of its part played in the sphere of agriculture. Being fertile and fed with a network of convenient canal irrigation, drawing its source from river Godavari, it has been rightly labelled as the granary of Andhra Pradesh. Agriculture is the main occupation of the people.

Being agriculturally advanced the district is endowed with 16.15% of Scheduled Caste population who attend as farm labour of the district. The district being rich in agricultural activities, attracted agriculture labour from the contiguous districts such as Vijayanagaram, Srikakulam, Visakhapatnam. On the north, Krishna, Guntur, Prakasam and Nellore from the south.

A quasi permanent tenure of employment of farm labour is prevalent in Andhra Pradesh, vernacularly known as paleru, also known by different names such as Kamathagadu, Kattubanisa and paleru. Paleru is the popular word current in West Godavari district. Extensive land has been brought under plough due to favourable irrigation facility and agriculture has become the main occupation of the people in the district.

The institution of *Paleru* was a decent one in the beginning. It meant a co-plougher. Due to the entry of Scheduled Caste people as *Palerus*, it gathered some inferior status. People began to look at it as almost a synonym for a slave. *Palerus* who were socially backward, economically poor became permanent farm servants by taking indiscriminate loans from the landlords. In order to repay the amount borrowed for higher rates of interest, all the members of the family, one way or other, were involved in the farm labour.

As they were indebted to the landlords in many respects, the Palerus began to feel that their landlords were their protectors, guardians, godfathers and well wishers of their families. The palerus voted for the landlords' candidate during elections for political elections fought unto the last against the enemies of their landlords, even at the cost of loosing their own relatives favour. Freedom of any sort was unknown to the paleru.

Their children could not be sent to schools or any other work with the fact that they may incur the displeasure of their landlords.

In the service of their landlords the paleru and their families spent their lives and rendered faithful thankless service for many a generation.

Economically the Scheduled Caste palerus could not grow above the grass-root levels politically. They have been faithful servants. They suffered all sorts of social discrimination deprived of social justice. The number of atrocities committed on these people, their women and children would show that how much of social injustice was done to them.

A good number of atrocities committed on these farm-servants, would show that they could not report or revolt against the high-caste wealthy and influential landlords. Social justice was not achieved by law courts, but very often through riots and duels.

Atrocities and crimes committed on these people were compensated by payment of money. High caste people began to believe that any atrocity committed on the farm-servants and their dependents can be settled by payment of money as compensation.

Palerus began to take shelter under the hood of the cobra, their farm landlord.

Missionary education, through Christian gospel, made these people to fight for their rights and question the baseless authority exercised by the upper castes on them. Christian priests and village school masters also played an important role in educating the untouchable lot.

The degree of untouchability through social discrimination and economic and political exploitation was so high as long as the Scheduled Castes followed Hinduism. Therefore in Southern India many people belonging to Scheduled Caste communities converted themselves into Christianity. Conversion into Christianity means a new way of living. Many farm-servants stopped employing their children as palerus. Free boarding and educational institutions started and efficiently run by different Christian missionaries in the Godavari Delta admitted many children of the Scheduled Castes palerus.

New employment opportunities in the Arabian-Gulf countries for skilled and unskilled labour for the people of Godavari Districts was great a blessing. About 60% of the Scheduled Castefamilies went to the Gulf countries either as skilled, semi-skilled or unskilled labourers. They have earned enough money, brought gold and electronic goods which have a resale value. The lucrative employment in the Gulf made the Scheduled Castes population of the West Godavari rich and influential. Many Scheduled Caste people gave preference to be employed as domestic servant in the household of an Arab Shaik than to be a Paleru at his native place.

Gulf employment for the Scheduled Castes people of Godavari gave a death blow to traditional institution of Paleru. In the domestic front, the development of acquaculture in the form of fish, prawn and crab-ponds, most of the paddy growing fields were converted into ponds. The management and maintenance of acres of tanks does not require that much of labour as required for the agricultural operations of the same area. Very few men can attend to the management of thousands of acres of fish ponds. Thus palerus required for agriculture farms were replaced by acquaculture technicians. This was another death -blow for the traditional paleru system in the West Godavari District.

1. The Scheduled Caste palerus of West Godavari were socially oppressed, economically poor, culturally and educationally backward. The present study reviews the achievements and pit-falls of the Scheduled Caste population in general and Scheduled Caste palerus in particular during past 30 years.
2. The Scheduled Caste paleru families completely depended on everything, they have no knowledge of the beneficial and welfare schemes provided to them by the state and central governments because of their illiteracy. If at all they know anything of some help, it was the Christian Missionaries who used to give rice, milk powder, clothing and free boarding and education to their children for embracing Christianity.
3. The palerus and their family members never exercised their adult franchise at their own choice. In fact, they have no knowledge of free will or freedom as they are accustomed to lead the life of servitude and segregation.
4. The palerus never dared to report the atrocities committed on them by their landlords or their relatives.

5. They stick on to the age-old type of employment without changing their traditional way of tenure employment. They could not improve their standard of living because of traditional way of employment which secured no extra income. Their entire economy was fixed by the loans and customary perks and *mamuls* given by their landlords.
6. The Missionary activities in the West Godavari district in fact gave new life to the farm-labour by providing free education and vocational training to the children of the palerus. The missionaries also educated them in the fields of law, liberty, civil rights etc. The moral education given by the Christian fathers, brought many changes in the families of the paleru. Most of the Scheduled Caste men stopped drinking, gambling and involving in criminal activities.
7. It is the opinion by consensus that social justice was tendered with concern by the missionaries and the church but never through the class/caste ridden. Hindu society - the recipient class of farm labourers never forgot to acknowledge their obligation to the church. Arab dollars, fragrance and crockery, perhaps, can never subdue the intimate attachment with the classless, mentally and physically free society offered by the missionaries. Their commitment to Christianity lingers even to this day.
8. The advent of aquaculture resulted in the reduction of cultivable land. Large tracts of land to the tune of 75 per cent was converted into fish and prawn ponds. As a result, demand for agriculture labour and farm contract labour decreased tremendously.
9. Employment opportunities in the Gulf countries gave a golden opportunity for the Scheduled Caste people of the West Godavari to develop economically, politically and socially. They have improved their lot through the Gulf money acquired through employment. They have brought gold and costly equipment from the Gulf countries and became rich very soon.
10. The West Godavari district is frequently affected by floods, cyclones and inundation caused by breaches. As a result, people hitherto lived in thatched and mud-walled houses began to construct pucca concrete buildings with the money acquired through the Gulf employment.
11. Most of the Scheduled Caste people who had been to the Gulf for employment acquired lands, coconut gardens and also fish ponds. Acquaculture made them more wealthier than before.

12. The role of the State and Central Government in the economic and political development of the Scheduled Caste in the West Godavari is very much nominal. Many of the Scheduled Caste families never care for the welfare schemes extended by the social welfare department. Many wealthy scheduled caste families who have converted into Christianity feel it low to accept the help from the Government. They prefer to call themselves as Christians than Scheduled Caste people.
13. With the educational development brought about by the missionaries, economic soundness achieved through the Gulf employment and acquaculture, the Scheduled Caste people could bring into disuse the shameful and indecent institution known at Paleru system and fought in a organised way for achieving social justice.
14. Today the term paleru means a shameful one. No one would prefer to be called as Paleru any more, even though once one happened to be a paleru to a landlord. By slip of a tongue if anybody addressed somebody as paleru, then there would be a duel. No Scheduled Caste man would accept the term paleru in use or usage.
15. The institution of paleru once prestigious to a Scheduled Castes man, which gave him continuous employment, security to the entire family finally fell into disuse within a period of three decades. It is evident by this that an old and mean or filthy institution or practice will not be annihilated by law or government.

It is only a sound economic condition backed by a free choice of vocation alone can wipe off an unwanted custom, practice or even tradition. As long as they were illiterate and poor, they would not fight against the atrocities committed on them and fight for their rights.

Technical Glossary

Ayyagaru

In Telugu language *Ayyagaru* is the master, the elderly man and the superior. Low class people always address the caste Hindu males as *Ayyagaru*. *Ayyagaru* also means respectable father. It is very disgusting to note that even a small boy of the caste Hindu community is addressed by an elderly man of a low caste man as *Ayyagaru* or my master.

Anyulu

Literally means others in Telugu language those who do not follow Christianity. Being allien faith followed by many people in the area. Christians who are allien to India feel that they are the original people and the natives who follow Hinduism are allien.

Battem

Battem is a Arabic word who's original form is *Batta* which means allowance given by the employer to meet the raise in the cost of living. *Batta* was become *Battem* in Telugu language. It is associated with another word *Jeetam* which means salary. The paddy and other articles of food maintainance of life given to farm servants.

Chiguru

Literally means twig. It is an end product of country liquor made out of Toddy juice. It is double distilled liquor is prepared from toddy and the liquor is distilled again to obtain a fine variety of liquor called *Chiguru*. It is consumed by very rich and aristocratic people in Andhra. It is not sold for public. It is prepared for families to serve exclusively to costly guests.

Chanda

It is a free contribution towards the performance of any social religious and cultural functions; given by residents of a locality. It is not returned back. It has become a customary contribution. People come openly to collect *Chanda* sometimes by employing force etc.

Dakala

It is an Arabic word mixed Into Telugu usage. *Dakala* means to join. It is used to denote a system of agricultural labour who attend to the work of a particular farmlord. *Dakala* system is not a permanent way of employing farm labourers. They are more than coolies and less than *Palerus*. However, they feel themselves superior to daily wage earners.

Dommee

It is sudden riot, between two rival groups. In Andhra, *Dommees* occurred very frequently among agriculture labour one group of one area and another agriculture labour of outside the area. Whenever the local labour refused to work or the farmlords neglected the local labour and brought outside labourers to their fields. The local labourers used to obstruct the entry of outside coolies these used to occur Dommees wherein several innocent people used to dies. Sticks, spears and lathis are generally used by these participants.

Gaade* (Or) *Puri

Paddy is stored in an instrument called *Gaade*. Split bamboos are woven into a role of the required size and two lids on the top and the other at the bottom are arranged. Mudpase mixed with cow-dung and turmeric powder is parted both on the interior and exterior of the *Gaade* which is placed on a high pedestal. The *Gaade* is filled with grain and preserved from rats and other insects which eat away and spoil the grain.

Puri is made out of hay thread. Hay is twisted into long road and that is woven like a *Gaade* to store grain in it. The interior of the *Puri* is pasted with cow-dung turmeric etc., to prevent bacteria and preserve the grain for future.

Katnam

It is Telugu word used in different contexts to denote different meanings. By all means, it is connected with the payment of money only. It is a usuary payment of bridegrooms gift. Sometimes it denotes the customary small payments or presentations given to a low class servant including the farm-servant. House barber washerman and the cobbler are given certain gifts as *Katnam*.

Kallu

It is a natural juice derived from toddy and date palm trees. In the forest regions Kallu is also obtained from a tree called "Jeeluga". It is a seasonal drink and more over the poor mans beer.

Munda

It is a Telugu word which means an un-wedded spouse. Most of the farmlords maintain a second woman or even a third woman to maintain his status. Rich farm-owners of coastal Andhra Pradesh feel it is a high social status, if they maintain more than one woman. The woman maintained by the farm owner also feel superior to the rest of the common wedded woman. Such woman is called openly as the *Munda* of a landlord.

Mamoolu

It is an Arabic word mixed with the local Telugu language. It denotes a customary payment. There is no legal sanction for this payment. Dasarah season Mamoolu or payment is made by householders known as Dasara-mamoolu. For example, Rowdy mamoolu, police mamoolu are some of the customary payments in vague.

Nemani

It is a type of agriculture labour employment. It is not a fixed or permanent one but executed without a break. All the agricultural family members in the village attend to the agricultural operations of the Munsiff Karanam and Jamindar. They accept no payment but attend to the Lunch or supper hosted by the Karanam / Munsiff / Jamindar, whose work they have attended.

Panchangam

It is the epimary through which annual seasons, crop-produce, calamities, constaltations bad or good are calculated. Every Indian for that matter if he is theist completely depends upon the epimary for anything and everything.

Peeta

It is a small stool. In the present context of the paleru furniture, *Peeta* is referred to as an item of household furniture. The Scheduled Caste Palerus had no furniture. The only one they had was a low stool known as Peeta.

Sakunam* (or) *Omen

People believe in good and bad things and attribute to God and devil respectively. In order to know in advance the happenings of future people go for *Sakunam* to the fortune tellers or soothsayers.

Voli* (or) *Bride Price

According to the custom prevalent in ancient times, a wife is brought through marriage by purchase. Some amount is paid to the parent of the bride before marriage. This payment would entitle the husband as superior and gives the right of ownership over the girl, he marries.

Vatana

It is a type of custom of attending to agriculture labour. Some people regularly attend to a farm even though they are offered high wages by some other farmlord. *Vatana* system raises the status of the worker. He feels more than a *Coolee*. It provides a regular supply of workers to a landlord.

Bibliography

Books

Adrian C. Mayer, *Land and Society in Malabar,* Oxford, Oxford University Press, 1952.

Andre Gunder Frank, *Capitalism and Underdevelopment in Latin America; Historical Studies of Chile and Brazil,* New York, Monthly Review Press, 1967.

Atchi Reddy, M. 'Labour Relations in Andhra Pradesh Agriculture, 1881-1981', *Indian Journal of Labour Economics,* XXVI: 3, October 1983.

Atchi Reddy, M. *Tenancy Report 1985*, Chapters 3, 11, 15, 16 and 18.

Atchi Reddy, M. 'Agrarian Structure of Nellore: Tenants and Tenancy, 1800-1980', *Social Scientist*, No.166, March 1987.

Atchi Reddy, M. 'Labour Relations in Andhra Pradesh Agriculture 1881-1981'.

Atchi Reddy, M,. "Cooperative joint farming in Nellore District: A Measure of Equity" *Indian Jr. of Agl. Economics,* XLI, Conference Number.

Baden Powell, B.H. *A Manual of Land Revenue System and Land Tenure in British India*, 1982.

Baden Powell, B.H. *Land Revenue and Tenure in British India,* London, 1894.

Bagal, J.C. *History of the Indian Association, 1876-1951.*

Baker, C.J. *The Politics of South India, 1920-37*, 1976.

Banerjee, H. Agrarian Society of The Punjab, 1848-1901, 1976 (unpublished Ph.D. Thesis.

Barrier, N.G. "The Punjab Disturbances of 1907", The Punjab; Past and Present, October 1974.

Blyn, G. Agricultural Trends in India, 1891-1947, 1967.

Bowani Pathak, 'Character of the Indian Bourgeoisie', *Liberation,* No. 2, December 1967.

Brown, J. *Gandhi's Rise to Power*, 1915-22, 1972.

Chaudhuri, B. Agrarian Relations in Bengal, in N. Sinha, ed. *History of Bengal.*

Chaudhuri, B. Peasant Movements in Bengal, 1850-1900, *Nineteenth Century Studies*, 1973.

Chaudhuri, S.B. *Civil Disturbances During the British Rule in India, 1765-1857*, 1955.

Chaudhuri, The Process of Depeasantization in Bengal and Bihar, *Indian Historical Review*, July 1975.

Choudhury, S. *Peasants' and Workers' Movement in India 1905-27,* 1926.

Conrad Wood. The Moplah Rebellions Between 1800-02 and 1921-22, *Economic and Social History Review*, January-March 1976.

Dagfinn Sivertsen, *When Caste Barriers Fall,* London, Allen and Unwin, 1963.

Daniel and Alice Thorner, *Land and Labour in India,* New York, Asia Publishing House, 1962.

Darling, M. The Punjab Peasant in Prosperity and Debt, 1928.

Datta, K. *History of the Freedom Movement in Bihar*, Vol.1 and 2.

Datta, K. *The Santal Insurrection of 1855-57*, 1940.

Desai, M. *The Story of Bardoli*, 1929.

Dhanagare, and G.C. Shah. Traditional Society and Political Mobilization: The experience of Bardoli Satyagraha, 1920-1928, *Contribution to Indian Sociology*, new series 8, 1974.

Dutt, R.C. "An Apology for the Pabna Rioters", *Bengal Magazine,* September 1873.

Elliot, C.M. Caste and Faction Among the Dominant Castes: The Reddis and Kammas of Andhra, Kothari.

Fuchs, S. *Rebellious Prophets*, 1965.

Gene D. Overstreet and Marshall Windmiller, *Communism in India,* Berkeley and Los Angels, University of California Press, 1959.

Gopal, S. *Jawaharlal Nehru: A Biography*, Vol. I.

Gopalan, A.K. *Kerala, Past and Present,* London, Lawrence & Wishart, 1959.

Guha, R. "Neel Darpan: The Image of a Peasant Revolt in a Libeal Mirror", *The Journal of Peasant Studies,* October 1974.

Hobsbawm, E. *Primitive Rebels*, 1974.

Joshi, P.C. 'Unmasked Parties and Politics', March, 1940.

Karat, P. The Peasant Movement in Malabar, 1934-40, *Social Scientist*, September, 1976.

Kathleen Gough, 'Caste in a Tanjore Village', in Edmund R. Leach (ed.), *Aspects of Caste in South India, Ceylon and Pakistan,* Cambridge, the University Press, 1962.

Kesava Iyenger, S. *Economic Investigations in the Hyderabad State,* Hyderabad, 1932.

Khusro, A.M. *Economic and Social Effects of Jagirdari Abolition and Land Reforms in Hyderabad*, Osmania University Press, Hyderabad, 1958.

Kling, B. *The Blue Mutiny: Indigo Disturbances in Bengal, 1859-60*, 1966.

Kripa Shankar: *Concealed Tenancy and its Implications for equity and Economic Growth*, Concept Publishing House, New Delhi, 1980.

Krishnamurthy, J. 'Agricultural Labour Force in India: A Note', *Indian Economic and Social History Review,* IX.

Mao Tse-tung, 'How to Analyse the Oasses in the Rural Areas', *Selected Works,* New York, International Publishers, 1954.

Menon, A.S. *Kerala District Gazeteers,* Trivandrum, Government Press, 1962.

Mishra, G. *Agrarian Problems of a Permanently Settled District of Bihar* : Champaran, 1976.

Misra, B.B. *Select Documents on Mahatma Gandhi's Movement in Champaran*, 1963.

Moore, B. *Social Origins of Dictatorship and Democracy*, 1967.

Mulle, R.E. *Mapila Muslims of Kerala*, 1976.

Murthy, C.S. Influence of Socio-Economic Status on Contractual terms of Tenancy" , *Economic and Political Weekly*, XXII, 39, 26 March 1987.

Namboodiripad, E.M.S. *Kerala Yesterday, Today and Tomorrow,* Calcutta, National Book Agency, 1967.

Nicholson, F.A. *Report Regarding the Possibility of Introducing Land and Agricultural Banks into the Madras Presidency*, Vol. I, Madras, 1985.

Nilmani Mukharji. *The Ryotwari System in Madras,* Calcutta, 1982.

Palit, C. *Tensions in Bengal Rural Society, 1830-1860,* 1975.

Panikkar, K.N. *Peasant Revolts in Malabar.*

Philips, C.H. *The Evolution of India and Pakistan*, 1858-1947.

Radhakrishnan, P. Peasant Struggles and Land Reforms in Malabar, *Economic and Political Weekly*, December 13, 1980.

Ranadive, B.T. 'Struggle for People's Democracy and Socialism-Some Questions of Strategy and Tactics', *Communist, II,* June-July, 1949.

Ranga, N.G. and Swami Sahajanand Saraswati, *History of Kisan Movement*, All India Kisan Publications, Madras.

Ray Choudhury, N. *Tribal Uprisings in the Second Half of the Nineteenth Century*, 1978 (unpublished Ph.D. Thesis).

Reddy, P.C. *A.P. Land Reforms Act, 1973: A Handbook*, Prabhat Publications, Nellore, 1975.

Saradamoni, K. *Emergence of a Slave Caste*, 1980.

Sarkar, T. The First Phase of Civil Disobedience in Bengal, 1930-31, *Indian Historical Review*, July 1977.

Sarveswara Rao, B. *The Economic and Social Effects of Zamindari Abolition in Andhra*, Government of India Press, Delhi, 1963.

Sathianathan, W.R.S. *Report on Agricultural Indebtedness in the Presidency of Madras*, 1935.

Sayana, V.V. *Land Sales, Land Values and Land Transfers*, S. Chand and Company, Delhi, 1952.

Sayana, V.V. *Sharing and Fixed Tenancy Systems*, the Business Week Press, Madras, 1949.

Sen Gupta, K.K. *Pabna Disturbances and The Politics of Rent, 1873-85*, 1974

Sen, S. Agrarian Relations in India, 1793-1947, 1979, Ch.3.

Sen, S. and Narain, D. Impact of Price Movements on Areas Under Selected Crops, 1900-1939, 1965.

Siddiqi, M.H. *Agrarian Unrest in North India, 1918-22*, 1978.

Singh. *The Dust Storm And The Hanging Mist*, 1966.

Subba Rao, D.V. et al.: "Degradation of Agro-Eco-system – An Exploratory study on Cotton Farming", *Indian Jr. of Agl. Economics,* 1987.

Sundara Raja Iyengar. *Land Tenures in the Madras Presidency*, Madras, 1918.

Sundarayya, P. *Telangana People's Struggle and its Lessons*, Calcutta, 1972.

Suresh Rambhai. *Vinoba and his Mission*, Wardha, 1954.

Thomas W. Shea. 'The Land Tenure Structure in Malabar and its Influence on Capital Formation in Agriculture', unpublished Ph.D. thesis, University of California Press, 1965.

Thorner, Alice and Daniel. *The Working Force in India* 1881-1951, Bombay, 1960.

Whitcombe, E. *Agrarian Conditions in Northern India, 1860-1900*, 1971.

Williams, R. *India in 1920-21*, 1922.

Committees

Agrarian Reforms Committee (1949) of Hyderabad.

Royal Commission on Agriculture in India, 1927, Vol. III. Evidence taken in the Madras Presidency.

Acts / Ordinances

Hyderabad Tenancy and Agricultural Lands Act, 1950.

Hyderabad Land Revenue Amendment Act, 1952.

Hyderabad Prevention of Victims Ordinance, 1952.

Reports

Agricultural Census of Andhra Pradesh 1970-71, 1975-76, 1980-81, Bureau of Economics and Statistics, Government of Andhra Pradesh.

General Administration Report, Patna Division, 1875-76.

Planning Commission, Government of India: *Implementation of Land Reforms,* Delhi, 1966.

Planning Commission, Govt. of India: *The First Five Year Plan,* New Delhi, 1951, Chapters I and II.

Report of Land Revenue Commission, 1940.

Report of the Andhra Land Reforms Committee, Kurnool, 1955, p. 6.

Report of the Congress Agrarian Reforms Committee, New Delhi, 1949

Report of the Deccan Riots Commission, 1875, Vol. I.

Report of the Special Officer on Land Tenures in the Ryotwari Area of the Madras Province, Govt. of Madras, 1951, Chapter VI, Para 2.

Report of the Zamindari Committee, 1937, Madras 1939

Report on the Political Situation in Bengal (confidential), January to September, 1936.

Reports of the Land Reform Committees of various States compiled during the 1950s.

Season and Crop Report of Andhra Pradesh 1956-57, Bureau of Economics and statistics, Govt. of Andhra Pradesh, Hyderabad, 1959.

Settlement Report, Midnapore, 1911-17.

Gazettes

Gazette of India, 18 January, 1902.

Madras District Gazetteers, Tanjore, Madras, the Government Press, 1906.

Tripura District Gazetteer, 1975.

Index

M

V

W

Z